TWAYNE'S WORLD AUTHORS SERIES

A Survey of the World's Literature

CHINA

William Schultz, University of Arizona

EDITOR

Wen I-to

TWAS 580

Wen I-to

WEN I-TO

By KAI-YU HSU

San Francisco State University

TWAYNE PUBLISHERS

A DIVISION OF G. K. HALL & CO., BOSTON

895.1
W467K
1980

Library of Congress Cataloging in Publication Data

Hsu, Kai-yu, 1922–
Wen I-to.

(Twayne's world authors series; TWAS 580: China)
Bibliography: p. 224–37
Includes index.
1. Wen, I-to, 1899–1946—Biography.   2. Poets,
Chinese—Biography.
PL2823.E5Z69   895'.1'15   [B]   79–22385
ISBN 0–8057–6422–4

Contents

About the Author

Kai-yu Hsu started his writing career in China in the 1940s. Between his baccalaureate (literature, Tsing Hua University, 1944) and his Ph.D in modern Chinese literature and thought (Stanford, 1959), he served in the China-Burma-India Theater as a soldier, was on diplomatic assignments in Washington, D. C. and Europe, worked as a journalist in San Francisco's Chinatown, and free-lanced. Since 1959 he has been professor of Chinese, Comparative Literature, and Humanities, and has chaired the Foreign Language Department and World Literature Department for several terms at San Francisco State University. He started Chinese studies programs at San Francisco State, and was the first to organize Chinese language instruction for secondary schools in the western States and Hawaii. He founded the Chinese Language Teachers Association of America.

Among his major publications are: *Twentieth Century Chinese Poetry* (Doubleday, 1963; Cornell, 1970), referred to by critics as a modern classic; *Chou En-lai: China's Gray Eminence* (Doubleday, 1968), which remains the only authoritative work on the late premier of China, and has been published in six major languages of the world; *Asian-American Authors* (Houghton-Mifflin, 1972), the very first book on the subject ever published; and the *Chinese Literary Scene* (Random House and Penguin, 1975). The last mentioned was the result of Hsu's six-month revisit to his homeland after thirty years of absence.

Currently he has just completed three books, all scheduled for publication before the end of 1979: *Literature of the People's Republic of China* (Indiana University Press), *Ch'i Pai-shih's Painting* (Taipei: The Art Book Co.), and *Wen I-to: Biography of a Modern Chinese Poet* (Boston: Twayne).

Preface

When T'ang Sui confronted the first emperor of China, the tyrant Ch'in Shih-huang-ti (d. 210 B.C.), with a dagger, he declared that although an educated intellectual's anger is evidenced in only two slain bodies and a blood stain five feet long, yet the whole universe wears white in mourning. Something of a deeprooted tradition is reflected in this well-remembered story: A *shih* (a cultivated and morally upright gentleman) must be capable of acting in accord with his moral convictions even to the extent of taking the law into his own hands.

When Wen I-to lay in a pool of blood, perhaps not quite five feet long, on that fateful day in 1946, there was no dagger in his hand, but the world was shocked, and many, from Peking to Washington to London, were grief-stricken. Was Wen I-to— a cultivated poet, artist, scholar, and finally political crusader— consciously living up to that same ancient Chinese tradition?

To trace the beginning, the growth, and the end product of Wen's cultural and intellectual life may very well show that he was the very embodiment of the T'ang Sui tradition, and that the grief felt on this untimely death has caused enduring repercussions throughout the world.[1]

In many ways—less melodramatic perhaps—this is not a story of just one man, but of a whole generation of Chinese intellectuals whose footprints criss-cross the pages of modern Chinese history.

KAI-YU HSU

Tiburon, California

Acknowledgments

Twenty years is a long time, yet not long enough to see much change in the follies of man. In 1958 I wrote to Peking Library for some simple and basic information about Wen I-to; they ignored my request. Today in 1978, I still cannot obtain any word about Wen from the People's Republic of China other than what has appeared in the official press in recent months, mostly sanitized hagiography. My polite, noninsistent inquiries while in Peking in 1973 produced a near disaster. I never succeeded in my effort to read Wen's one hundred-seventy-one handwritten manuscripts and personal papers locked up in the national library there.[1]

This explains why it has taken me twenty years to revise my doctoral dissertation. My debt to the dead, and to some still living, must be paid. I want to thank my many scholarly friends Takeuchi Minoru, Kushuhara Toshiyo (of Kyoto), Norair Taschian, Edith Yang (San Francisco State University, for Russian and Japanese sources), Yü-ming Shaw (Notre Dame University); and libraries here and overseas (chiefly Hoover, Canberra, Chicago. Harvard-Yenching, University of California at Berkeley, Library of Congress, Kyoto, London, and Leiden); and Wen's brother (Wen Chia-szu, my teacher of French poetry with whom I was reunited in 1973), Wen's accessible friends (Liang Shih-ch'iu, Ku I-ch'iao, Wang Chi-chen, and others); and the National Endowment for the Humanities and the Social Science Research Council for grants to buy time and travel. All inadequacies in this book are, of course, mine, but any merit in its organization and presentation must be credited to Professor William Schultz for his patient editing. I would like to quote more from Wen's widow and from his old friend Liang Shih-ch'iu, but her severe illness in 1973 and his wish to reserve certain privacy for Wen must be respected.

So here's to my happy memory of the three years in Kunming, listening to your lectures, talking with you about your poetry studies and my immature exercises called verse, working with you on oral interpretation at the interpreter's training institute where you saw me off to the army—that's the last time I saw you—and, above all, just to you as a memorable human being, my beloved teacher:

You gave life to dead water,
But the alive will again die;
Where now is your name written—
On water or in sky?

When the past summons the present,
By a red candle yours'll be read;
The water you stirred will be—
Anything but dead.

Chronology

1899   November 24, born in Hsi-shui, Hupeh province.

1904   Begins study of Chinese classics at home with hired tutor.

1909   Attends grade school in Wuchang, the provincial capital.

1911   Returns home to avoid the outbreak of the Republican revolution in Wuchang.

1912   Enters the Tsing Hua School in Peking.

1916   Starts publishing essays and poems in school journals.

1922   Completes ten years of study at Tsing Hua, graduation delayed a year due to participation in student strike. February, marries Kao Hsiao-chen. July 16, sails for the U. S. September, starts classes at the Art Institute of Chicago; continues to publish essays and poems in China.

1923   September, starts classes at Colorado College, Colorado Springs; continues to major in art. September, first collection of poems, the *Red Candle*, published.

1924   Summer, enrolls in the Art Students' League of New York.

1925   Involved in group promoting cultural nationalism; writes articles on literature; stages plays. June, returns to China. Fall, starts teaching at Peking School of Fine Arts.

1926   Involved in political-literary journals; key contributor to the "Poetry Journal" of the *Peking Morning News*. Fall, brief stay at the Academy of Political Science, Wu-sung, Shanghai, as dean of students.

1927   Spring, brief service in the political department of the government at Wuhan; returns to teaching at Wu-sung. Summer, plans the literary monthly *Crescent*; brief employment at the Assessor's Office, municipal government of Nanking. Fall, starts teaching English literature at the No. 4 Sun Yat-sen University.

1928   Anthology *Dead Water* published. Poems and essays published in the *Crescent*. Fall, heads up the Chinese literature department, Wuhan University; starts publishing studies on ancient Chinese literature.

1929   April, resigns from the editorial board of the *Crescent*.

1930   Spring, resigns from Wuhan University. Fall, becomes head of the Chinese literature department and dean of the college of arts, Tsingtao University.

1931   January, last poem "Miracle" published.

1932   Fall, returns to teach Chinese literature at Tsing Hua University.

1933   Fall, starts the *Hsüeh-wen* monthly; concentrates on research in the Chinese classics.

1936   Summer, visits the oracle bone excavation site at Anyang, Honan province.

1937   July 19, leaves Peiping for hometown, Hsi-shui, after Japanese occupation of Peiping. Late fall, teaches at the temporary campus of the university-in-exile, outside of Changsha, Hunan province.

1938   February 19, starts long walk with over two hundred students from Hunan to Yunnan, arriving in Kunming on April 28. May, starts teaching at the National Southwest Associate University, first at Meng-tzu, then in Kunming.

1939   Summer, involved in staging plays. Fall, starts sabbatical leave to study the *Book of Changes* and Chinese myths.

1941   August, in charge of the Chinese literature section of the Tsing Hua Research Institute.

1942   *Annotated Ch'u-tz'u* published. Studies and edits new poetry.

1943   November, publishes essay praising the new poet, T'ien Chien; more essays on the relationship between culture, literature, and society.

1944   Speeches and essays on current events and the war situation. Starts seal-carving to supplement income. End of summer, joins the Democratic League; edits the *Democratic Weekly* for the League. December 25, joins a student demonstration against civil war for the first time. Continues to publish results of research on classical studies.

1945   Active in political forums. August 10, shaves off beard upon Japanese surrender. Dec. 1, police attack on university campus, killing four students and wounding over twenty.

1946 More emotional political speeches. May, the university starts moving back to Peiping. July 11, the last batch of university students leaves Kunming; Democratic League leader Li Kung-p'u assassinated. July 15, killed in ambush near his residence.

Prologue

The eucalyptus trees of Kunming, the mile-high capital of Yunnan province, greet the perpetual cool breeze with songs whose moods change from morning to night, but not much from winter to spring. They are cheery at daybreak, nervy by noon, but—it was five o'clock in the afternoon that day, July 15, 1946—a bit disquietingly melancholic toward dusk.

On Fu-yung-tao, a short but rather wide terrace near the Northwestern corner of the old city, the stone pavement glistened under a setting sun. No one was there to be seen; only a scrawny stray mut sniffed against the wall where peddlers of breakfast snacks had long cleared away their booths for the day. It looked up furtively at the sound of muffled footsteps, tensed, and instantly darted into a side alley and disappeared.

Several men in short jackets walked up the incline, eyeing the alleyways left and right, and exchanging silent glances. They circled back down the incline and split into two groups before disappearing into two separate alleys. Almost immediately a young man of nineteen came up from Hsi-ts'ang-p'o (West Granary Slope); he caught a glimpse of the disappearing men, paused a moment in his walk, and then quickened his steps toward a house at the upper corner of the terrace. The young man was Wen Li-ho, Wen I-to's eldest son, and a sign on the house said "The Democratic Weekly."

Along with many young college students, along with the other six members of the Wen family and the families of Wen's close friends, Wen Li-ho had been worried about his father's safety. Rumors about secret orders from the Kuomintang and other Rightist forces to silence Wen I-to, fed by the assassination of Li Kung-p'u a leader of the Democratic League only four days before, had been keeping the young Li-ho awake for nights. His seriously ill mother had bid him never to let his father out of his sight, and that afternoon, after accompanying his father to the Democratic Weekly office for a press conference,

Li-ho had plied the two hundred-fifty yard pavement between the office and their apartment in the University Faculty housing compound on West Granary Slope. He was nervous, thinking that now the last batch of the Lienta students and faculty, his father's admirers and supporters, had left for North China, and he fumbled in his pocket to feel the most recent anonymous warning letter he had received. Something told him that the shadows receding in the alleys did not bode well, but he kept reassuring himself that his father's national reputation probably would be enough to deter the assassins. He went home, and back to the journal's office again. It was close to five o'clock now and one of his father's associates had just stepped out, then finally his father emerged.

Fatigue did not cover up the flush of excitement and emotional strain on Wen I-to's face. He smiled at his son and the two walked down the slope toward home. Feeling somewhat relieved that another day had drawn to its close in peace, Li-ho even paused to buy an evening paper and glanced at the headlines as they walked. Just one more turn and their home would be in sight, some ten to twelve paces away, but it happened. From what seemed to Li-ho to be all directions sounded pistol reports. His father dropped to the ground and he half-rushed and half-fell over him. The next thing he knew he had rolled off his father and the pain in his leg and chest was choking him and blinding his vision. He vaguely saw his father, face already blackened and distorted, in a pool of blood, and a short distance away those short-jacketed men stood in a row, the muzzles of their guns still spitting fire. . . .[1]

Wen I-to died a hero's death when his shouted challenges to the Rightist secret agents, voiced only a few hours before, were still reverberating in the air above Kunming. What had given him the vision, the strength that steeled him in his last days? Was it a romantic poet's longing for death, or a fanatic cultural chauvinist's bravado, or a committed revolutionary's calculated move to shock the world with his blood? Did his life leave anything indelible in Chinese history?

Many threads in the development of the man and his ideas which are traceable help explain his sense of drama and poetry, his fascination with color, and his absorption in ancient myths that probe the secrets of life. Less than three months before his death, Wen I-to adapted the "Nine Songs" of the *Songs of the South (Ch'u Tz'u)* into a liturgical opera, a solemn song and dance piece, which opened with a scene of grandeur:

Prelude[2]

(Eveningtide. Drumbeats sound from faraway, closing in from all
   directions, getting closer every second.)
(On the backdrop is a giant aura—like an aurora—lighting up the
   entire sky.)
(Incense smoke wafts about, weaving through the air.)
(Shamans, male and female, along with wild birds, animals and marine
   life under their control, stand in respectful attendance.)
(The King of Ch'u, wearing a jade-handled sword on his left, and a
   jade ring on his right, enters, walking in cadence to the soft
   but solemn music.)
(His entourage takes up positions behind the monarch, all below
   the altar.)
(From the right side of the altar, a song rises in the midst of the
   chorus led by His Lordship Ch'ü Yüan.)

A Male voice (singing solo):

The day is auspicious and the hour, blessed,
   let all be prepared to please the Lord of Lords on High;
My hand on the long sword with jade handle,
   I listen to the gems and gold ringing, ling-lang, ling-lang . . .
(The king advances three steps to perform the rites. . . .)

One can see the colors and smell the scents that Wen I-to deployed through his reconstruction of an ancient song sequence, and one could be readily led to associate their origin with Wen's study of Fra Angelico and, more importantly, his over thirty years' readings in classical Chinese poetry. However, one rarely calls to mind another scene that provided an early seed for Wen's poetic imagination. It happened about thirty years before, when Wen I-to was beginning to read, under his father's tutelage, the *Songs of the South* without much comprehending them:[3]

The waves on Wang-t'ien Lake lapped at the shore; their rhythm, constant, unexciting, almost hypnotic on such a warm summer day. But a short distance away, the rhythm of cymbals and drums promised more action; about half of Hsia-pa-ho Village's women and children were there, filling the ground in front of the village temple. Inside the temple, the shrine was perfumed with incense and abundantly decorated with flowers (paper and real) and buntings of all colors. But the statue of the village's guardian goddess was missing; she had been invited, with a similar ceremony, by the neighboring village to bless its spring festival. Now it was time for her to be welcomed back to her own sacred abode.

From down the road along the lake shore came notes of two so-na, that fippled trumpet-flute which dominates Chinese folk music nationally, but particularly in the middle reaches of the Yangtze River. A few children skipped ahead, chattering, and from time to time turning back to look at the pair of censer carriers who held their smouldering pots on long sticks; behind them came a pair of faithfuls, young muscular men stripped to the waist, each with two small, lighted oil lamps hooked into their chests—they were repaying the goddess for the favor she had done them; behind them walked several pairs of tribute bearers carrying decorated baskets filled with offerings, edible and nonedible; in their midst walked the priest in a flowing, yellow, Taoist robe, his hair held in a knot on top of his head with a donut-shaped skull cap. He alone stepped in cadence to the music; while the rest of the procession just scurried along. He had to be solemn, even majestic, for he was the chief steward ushering back the Goddess from the neighboring village. His mumble was drowned in the sustained, shrill notes of the so-na and the children's ceaseless chatter. The Goddess herself sat in a sedan chair, lacquered, sequined, and festooned all over, providing for the one within the kind of privacy and secrecy which befitted the mystery of her looks, identity and origin.

The procession neared the Hsia-pa-ho village temple. A child in the relatively hushed waiting crowd suddenly recognized one of the penitent faithfuls and yelled out his nickname. A murmur of echoes rose as others also began to recognize different persons in the procession, and greetings were exchanged that threatened to halt the column's advance. But the two penitent faithfuls tried to hold a blank face, ignoring the taunts and inquiries. "Hi! Second Family Fortune, your oil is spilling!" They ignored it. "Shun-wa's daddy, don't those hooks hurt you?" They also ignored it.

Wen I-to was there, standing next to his cousin, a strong youth who looked twice as tall as he. Wen I-to wore a blue long gown he had inherited from his elder brother, and a pair of half-new, homemade black slippers. He didn't follow the crowd to yell; he only wished that the three windows on the sedan chair were more than peepholes, for he had been told that the Goddess was actually the very pretty teenage daughter of Widow Wang on the northern side of the village. Others had told I-to that she was none other than the pockmarked wife of the caretaker of the temple—"you could see her every morning emptying dishwater behind the temple," they had said. Still others insisted on saying that the Goddess, the statue one could see on the shrine altar on days when she was not invited away, was the mummified virgin who had devoted herself to the Buddha some four hundred years before and had died in crystalline purity. They had argued, and the argument was kept lively right there among the spectators that day, but they all had agreed that whosoever the Goddess might be, her power, or black magic, was awesome, and they bore a long line of witnesses to prove the point.

Wen I-to tried to edge up to the sedan chair; the crowd was too much for him, and his cousin, ever protective of him, kept him from getting lost in that maelstrom of humanity. The whirlpool of people, with the sedan chair in the center, surged toward the temple door. Shouts were heard to close the door as soon as the sedan got inside; some eager hands and legs were caught in the door and cries of pain punctured the music. Half of the band went in but the other half was left outside, yet the music went on. For a while even the priest was helplessly locked out. I-to's cousin hurried home with him to get away from the chaos.

At home I-to doodled on paper trying to sketch the Goddess and her entourage. He first modeled her after his aunt whose clever scissors had cut many paper figures for his amusement, superimposed his Goddess on a favorite illustration found in one of his story books, then added colors and costumes and headgear. Finaly he went back, alone, to the village temple to catch a glimpse of the statue. There in the semi-darkness of the interior of the shrine, he thought he saw not the Goddess herself, but her frightening apparition. . . .

CHAPTER 1

Childhood and Early Education (1899-1912)

HSIA-pa-ho Village is a small but rich "fish and rice" village located at the confluence of the Pa and the Yangtze rivers outside the Hsi-shui county seat in Hupeh province.[1] The Pa River is not large enough to cause much commercialization of the village; life there has for centuries been characterized by a seldom interrupted agricultural rhythm, liberally punctuated with time-honored seasonal fêtes and folk rituals. Many of these village activities, especially those related to myths and legends, have retained a strong local color in that their styles and features have been continued in the tradition of the ancient state of Ch'u (3rd c. B.C.), only the names of most of the ancient characters involved have been replaced by more recent local heroes and heroines.

It has been a peaceful village; there have been five upheavals since the mid-seventeenth century, but disorder did not seem to have seriously affected the dwellers. Yet the village's proximity to the Yangtze River has prevented it from being isolated; in summer when the water is high junks can reach either Hankow upriver or Kiukiang downriver within a day. These conditions plus the unfailing yield of the fertile soil make the area prosperous, with many families of means. It was here, in an old house facing a small lake (Wang-t'ien Lake) and surrounded by pines, that Wen I-to was born on Nov. 24, 1899.[2]

The Wen family, according to one oral tradition, could be traced back to the Sung Dynasty statesman Wen Tien-hsiang (1236–1282), who fought for his country and finally died a patriot's death at the hands of the invading Mongols.[3] His descendants fled from Kiangsi to Hupeh, settled at Hsi-shui and changed their surname from *wen* ("culture") to the homony-

mous *wen* ("hear") of Wen I-to. For many generations the
Wen clan was known in Eastern Hupeh for its wealth, its extensive landholdings, and its members employed in government
service.[4] During the nineteenth century, at least six members
of the Wen clan passed the imperial examinations and had
successful careers.[5]

Wen I-to's father, a little too late to pursue further the same
course of advancement, only obtained the first degree of *hsiu-
ts'ai*. He was a man of lean physique but abundant energy,
regulating his own life and the life of his family in a puritanical spirit. Determined to personally commence the education
of his five sons in the strict Confucian tradition, he insisted that
they adhere to a rigid schedule of study. He himself set an
example of sternness and austerity, living simply, smiling rarely,
and almost never leaving his library. Even after he passed the
age of seventy, he continued to apply the same strictness in
training his grandsons who had, in addition to their school les-
sons, to complete the assignments he gave them every day. He
explained the *Four Books* and the *Five Classics* to the children
and required them to memorize them. How strictly he controlled
his children was illustrated in his interception of Wen I-to's
letters to his wife when I-to was studying in America.[6] In the
father's eyes, it was highly improper for a man of Confucian
ethics to write sentimental letters to any woman, including
his own wife. With all his attention to the welfare of his sons,
however, the senior Wen spent no time teaching his daughters
and granddaughters, whose education, he believed, was properly
his wife's concern. Such discrimination later caused I-to much
unhappiness when he repeatedly requested his father to provide
for the girls' education.[7]

Wen I-to's mother was kind, hardworking, and almost exces-
sively fond of cleanliness.[8] She acquiesced in her husband's
severe discipline of the children. At times the amount of study
required of her sons worried her, but her mild protests were
ineffective.[9] Wen's memory of his mother, although pleasant,
retained nothing significant. There is nothing in his intellectual
development that marks clearly the influence of his mother. As
far as can be ascertained, the only thing he did specially for her
was a letter written in red ink on pink stationery addressed to

her on Mother's Day in 1923, when he was a homesick student in America.[10]

At first Wen apparently submitted to his father's will: he was well-versed in the classics and extremely studious, and showed signs of literary promise. His eldest brother wrote in reminiscence that once while the young boy was absorbed in his reading in the garden, a centipede crawled up on his trousers. Unable to arouse him from his absorption, some one brushed the insect away, whereupon he expressed indignation at being disturbed.[11] On his own wedding day, when the ceremony was already underway in the main parlor, Wen was missing. His elder brother searched all over the house and finally found him in a quiet corner reading his favorite classics. Long years of such concentrated study weakened his eyes but perfected his command of the literary language; he willingly exchanged many hours of play for praise from the elders, "*shao-nien lao-ch'eng*" ("though young, mature"). It isolated him from his brothers and cousins, and made him an occasional target of their brotherly ridicule, but endeared him particularly to his father.

Young Wen I-to preferred poetry to the *Four Books*, the *Book of History*, and other classical works on ethics and philosophy, which caused his father some concern. Chinese tradition called for a man of lofty ideals to internalize the moral and social values embodied in such books, but Wen registered his defiance and turned to the belletristic tradition. He learned by heart the entire *Book of Poetry*, many T'ang poems and related commentaries, and practiced writing poems in the same style. In what little time he had after reading and writing, he practiced calligraphy—a habit which he later kept up even under the most difficult circumstances.[12] His early, unusually strong inclination toward art was observed by his aunt, who had to satisfy him by teaching him extremely intricate scissor-cutting.[13] He made his own designs to decorate his room, anticipating the interior decoration of his famous studio in Peking twenty years later. He learned seal-carving, which stimulated his interest in ancient script. His artistic bent was partly encouraged by the traditional concept that calligraphy, painting and seal-carving were "elegant pastimes" which contribute to a person's refinement, but within him there developed early a conflict between the verbal and the nonverbal which competed for his time and attention. At the present stage of his development, however, the family tradition weighed heavily in favor of literature, and T'ang poetry offered him much comfort. There are enough T'ang poets who painted pictures with words; as Su Tung-p'o (1037–1101), himself a most distinguished calligrapher, painter, and poet, once said, "Tu Fu's poems are figureless paintings, Han Kan's paintings are wordless poems."[14] T'ang poetry temporarily resolved the conflict for him.

While continuing his studies with his father, Wen I-to also had other teachers. At the age of six, he was sent to a nearby school run by an oldfashioned scholar who instructed him in the regular Chinese texts, including the *Erh-ya* (an ancient Chinese lexicon) and the *Four Books*. The next year his father hired a tutor, Wang Mei-fu, to teach him at home. Wang had attended a modernized school; he added history, ethics, and a bit of natural science to Wen's curriculum. This was Wen's first exposure to the new ideas then germinating in China. When he was eleven, his father sent him to a modern primary school at Wuchang, where every day after school he received additional instruction from his uncle, a scholar with serious interests in modern knowledge. Wen I-to studied English, arithmetic, and the writings of Liang Ch'i-ch'ao (1873–1928). Although it is not clear how much of Liang's thought was absorbed by Wen's youthful mind, judging by his later writings, it seems quite certain that Wen was impressed by Liang's eloquent prose style as well as his political criticism and ideas concerning Westernization. These impressions were to be deepened later at the Tsing Hua School where he continued to study Liang's works.

Wen I-to's schooling at Wuchang was interrupted two years later when the Revolution of 1911 swept over central China. To the regret of his father, there were no more imperial examinations as avenues for advancement. Fortunately, a special examination was announced to select able youths for study abroad after a period of preparation at the Tsing Hua School, the predecessor of the Tsing Hua University.[15] Filled with the new hope of making his son a *yang chuang-yüan* (foreign-trained, first-class scholar-official), the father entered his son in the preliminary examinations in Wuhan. But Wen's knowledge of English and sciences was almost nil. With trepidation he attempted the various parts of the test; the result in most cases was disastrous. However, he passed the Chinese part, writing in the style of Liang Ch'i-ch'ao with such distinction that he was accepted as an alternate. On the way to Peking for the final examination, he crammed in the subjects which he had failed. The strenuous effort, along with the withdrawal of one competitor, finally earned him admission as one of the only two successful candidates from his home province. The family rejoiced with mixed feelings about the prospect of his going far away to Peking for eight years, then still farther away to America for five long years. Admiration in the home village expressed itself in many ways, culminating in the action of Mr. Kao, a distant relative and old friend of the senior Wen, who betrothed his daughter Hsiao-chen to this young man of great promise.[16]

CHAPTER 2

Life at Tsing Hua School (1912-1922)

Nine years at Tsing Hua,
looking back—
at an expanse of desert in autumn night,
a lone firefly
gleams and then glows as one gazes,
though all around it, only chill and darkness,
    confused and unfathomable.
Late in spring now, when the red fades but the green
    has gained full sway:
Here I come to Lotus Pond—
The weight of quiet presses on the water
that has no wrinkle at all—
a stretch of dead silence!
Suddenly the spirit of quietude withdraws,
shattering the mirror,
and everyone heaves a sigh of relief.
Look! The flame of the sun's smile—its rays of gold,
seeping through the foliage to sprinkle on my brow;
Now by the sun-god I'm crowned
the king of the universe!

Wen I-to, "Looking Back"[1]
Spring, 1921

WITH what outlook and emotions did Wen I-to embark on his schooling in Peking? He had been to school in Wuchang, but that was only a day's journey from home, and there he had remained under the immediate supervision of an older relative. He was overjoyed by, and his family heaped praise on him for his success in the entrance examinations to Tsing Hua, but he couldn't quite forget his cramming, unsuccessfully, for the English language test. The examiners had marked him down in English, a subject he knew he would have to make up. Thus in the fall of 1912, it was with mixed feelings that he began his ten years of study at the American endowed Tsing Hua School.[2]

During his stay at Tsing Hua, he accepted many new ideas and reexamined old beliefs. Nothing happened to disturb the well-regulated life of his Hupeh family, or to strain his relationship with it. He spent only two months every year with his parents; the rest of the time he stayed in school. Always an avid reader, he applied himself to a rapidly widening range of books, and had more than a full share of the rich, varied, extracurricular activities encouraged at the new school—except athletics. The stimulating new life nurtured his prolific writing, which marked his intellectual growth in two stages, with the May Fourth Movement of 1919 constituting the critical turn.

I   The Tsing Hua Environment

The Tsing Hua School, as Wen first saw it, was a unique educational experiment in modern China.[3] Founded in 1908 with Boxer Indemnity funds to train Chinese youth for their country's modernization, it offered a program roughly parallel to that of the American high school aimed at three aspects of a youth's development: his mind, his body, and his moral sense.[4] The campus was located at the site of a former Manchu palace, about nine miles northwest of downtown Peking. Such a distance insured a great measure of isolation in those days of poor transportation. When Wen enrolled, the buildings and grounds were already quite well developed, and further improvements were made during the years of his stay. The architecture recalled the splendor of Chinese palaces. The students liked to associate the creeks and bridges with the Grand View Garden of the novel *Dream of the Red Chamber*. The willows against the red lacquered columns were suggestive of the pictures painted in late T'ang and Sung poetry. In 1912, the school was still entirely free, tuition, room, board, and all. Most of the students came from rather well-to-do families; they received generous pocket money which was entrusted to the school controller to prevent misuse.[5] Many students, but not Wen I-to, brought along personal servants to augment those hired by the school.[6] This was in keeping with the pre-Republican tradition that each candidate preparing for his imperial examinations must have—even when his family could ill afford it—a personal page to attend to daily menial chores. When a student found the food not to his taste, he was permitted to replace it by ordering other dishes at his own expense. Such practices were a source of friction between the richer and the poorer students, and fostered a revival of some of the old, decadent habits of the traditional literati—alcohol, sex, and other forms of irresponsible hedonism. Wen and his close friends criticized the trend in their school paper. The school tried to maintain a healthy atmosphere by scheduling ample physical exercise and a wide range of supervised extracurricular activities. To change the students' attitude toward manual labor, the school mobilized them to repair roads and later added boy-scouting and military drill.

The faculty consisted of Chinese and Western teachers. The former instructed almost exclusively in classical Chinese literature and history, while the latter taught Western literature and the sciences, and directed extracurricular activities. Student self-government was encouraged, with each class having its own organization. Drama, music, speech and debate (in both Chinese and English), science, and literary clubs were promoted. With the personal blessing of the president (principal), the number of officially registered clubs reached twenty-three by November, 1916.[7] The speech and debate groups, in which Wen soon assumed a leading role, were the most active, with at least one meeting per week. Wen helped choose the debate topics, mostly concerning the political and social problems of China, but he did not completely ignore world affairs and other less controversial issues.[8]

There were frequent "ethical lectures" given by faculty members and outside scholars. Most of these lectures concerned famous men of the past. The Sung philosopher Lu Chiu-yüan (Lu Hsiang-shan 1139-1192,), the loyal Han dynasty statesman Su Wu (d. 60 A.D.), the loyal Ming statesman Shih K'o-fa (d. 1645), as well as Columbus received equal attention. Liang Ch'i-ch'ao was invited to lecture on methods of study and the purpose of life. Lin Shu (1852-1924), the great translator of Western fiction, discoursed on good faith as a key to moral behavior, which he had observed in Western novels and identified with the Confucian teaching of *hsin* ("faithfulness"). Ts'ai Yüan-p'ei (1868-1940), who had resigned from the Ministry of Education to assume the presidency of Peking University, resolved for the Tsing Hua students the conflict between humanitarianism and patriotism. Ts'ai warned them not to swallow Western culture uncritically, lest they become Westerners—a theme that Wen took to heart and returned to again and again in later years. The noted Confucian scholar Ch'en Huan-chang (1880-1933) lauded the Confucian Society organized by some students to defend Confucianism against Western "cultural aggression,"[9] as did a member of the Peking Parliament, Wang Ching-fang.[10] There were also special serial lectures that featured visiting Western scholars, such as John Dewey and Robert M. McElroy to talk on Pragmatism and Western political thought.[11] The Tsing Hua curriculum was a rich fare which generously feasted Wen I-to's hungry, formative mind.

II *Youthful Excitement with Drama and Poetry*

Wen concentrated on English because it was opening to him a wide and wonderful world of Western literature. He worked diligently to improve his proficiency in the language, including writing letters in English to his schoolmate, Wang Chi-chen, during summer vacations.[12] The physical sciences were just a duty to him. But in Chinese literature he rode in comfort and glory. For him, schoolwork was anything but onerous, which allowed him ample time for all extracurricular activities— all except the soccer field, which he dodged at great risk because physical education was required for graduation. But he and several other schoolboys like him, all having come from gentry families where manual labor was regarded as menial, devised a scheme which allowed them to sneak away from all meetings except the final examination, when one of them nearly drowned in the swimming pool.[13]

Other than his notoriety in shunning physical education classes, Wen's multifaceted talents earned him a fine reputation and put him in great demand. When the school wanted to establish a primary school for the neighboring village, the pres-

ident summoned Wen to draft a charter in his elegant composition; other student groups and clubs sought him out to
draw and paint illustrations, posters, yearbook covers and
souvenir banners for them, and they gave him an award for
his art.[14] In student government, he served on the executive
committee for his class; he headed the speech club, the debate
team, and organized a literary society and a drama society. He
busied himself with so many things that, at times, he wondered
aloud about their validity. As he wrote in his diary, still in his
elegant classical Chinese style, "These past months I have been
busy doing everything except serious study. What good will
these activities do me? . . . I must concentrate on literature
and art, biding my time. Someday I will accomplish something
great."[15] But popularity and success were heady wine, which
he could hardly resist, and he continued to rehearse plays, sometimes for months at a stretch, sacrificing sleep and skipping
meals. Then he would heave a long sigh and remind himself,
"It's fortunate that my effort was not in vain. The play was a
success. I'm glad I can return to my books from now on."[16]
He did return to his books in classical Chinese and nineteenth-
century English poetry. Because his literature classes did not
focus exclusively on poetry, he pledged himself in 1919 to a
self-study program, a two-year in-depth reading of poetry from
the Ch'ing Dynasty back to pre-Ch'in works.[17] His reading was
meticulous, and by 1922 he had reached only the late T'ang
and Sung. Thus he was still reciting the poetry of Li Shang-yin
(the "ninth century Baroque Chinese poet," 813-858) and
Lu Yu (a model "patriot" general-statesman-poet, 1125–1210)
while packing his bags to go abroad.[18]

He started writing for the school publication, the *Tsing Hua
Weekly*, quite early and co-edited it during the years 1915–1917.
During these three years, the *Weekly* showed certain clear
shifts of emphasis. Moral exhortations gradually gave way to
discussions of specific problems facing China.[19] These articles
reflect a growing sense of national pride and a more sophisticated interest in Western ideas.[20] Explorations of the thought
of Bacon, Carlyle, and Martin Luther replaced tales of the life
of Napoleon, Nelson, Benjamin Franklin, and Daniel Webster.
Similar shifts in topic were also reflected in Wen's contributions.

His first articles were only literary comments and reflections, his reading notes on classical Chinese works. They reflect an admiration for the patriots Su Wu (d. 60 A.D.) and Li Ling (d. 74 A.D.) a rather romantic attachment to Li Po (701–762), and his interpretation of Chuang Chou (4th cent. B.C.), the Taoist philosopher's love for his wife, but nothing of present day concerns. Later he began to write on timely subjects and revealed his basic attitudes toward a wide range of problems. Only occasionally did his puritanical upbringing result in his urging moral education, and as late as 1921 he still expressed dismay at the suspension of the ethical lecture series on campus. He regretted the emphasis on pure scholarship to the neglect of cultivating the students' moral sense.[21]

III *Still a Worshipper of Antiquity*

The ancient Chinese classics (*Book of Rites, Book of Poetry, Book of Music*, and *Spring and Autumn Annals*) contained "universal principles unchangeable till the end of time," so declared Wen I-to in 1916. He urged a revival of their study because,

if we expound the true teachings of the ancient sages so that the entire world will know that our sages stressed actual practice, as against empty talk, then our culture will not diminish. Furthermore, if we develop modern learning in our own language to enable those without the knowledge of foreign languages to penetrate its essence, not only will modern learning thrive in our land, but also the Westerners will one day come to China to learn. Would not this be splendid?[22]

He argued that the sages' teachings constituted the national essence of China, which argument he adopted from Liang Ch'i-ch'ao. Wen also saw a direct link between culture and literature, and compared the decline in Chinese literature after the Sung dynasty with the waning of Hellenic culture, thus reflecting the influence of the T'ang dynasty classicist Han Yü (768–824) and Thomas Carlyle. The modern Chinese reformers, in Wen's view, were at fault because they upheld Western culture and slighted the ancient learning of China; as a result the courses in Chinese literature at Tsing Hua had become "no more than a ritual." He admitted that "writing one poem cannot repel an enemy attack and composing one piece of prose cannot dismiss poverty,"—this from the Han dynasty statesman Pan Ch'ao (32–102) and again Han Yü—thus indicating Wen's persistent inclination toward action. But he still believed in the value of devoting oneself to the creation of immortal words, as he wrote, one year later, in an open letter addressed to his friends, "If one could expound the sages' teachings, leaving immortal words to posterity, it would be much better than dying and rotting away together with the grass and plants."[23] The letter was couched in the elegant, classical *p'ien-wen* style of four- and six-syllable lines.

Wen, however, did not advocate a complete return to classical literature as it had been studied in the late imperial period. He said, "the surviving savants of the imperial dynasty have retired to keep company with deer and antelopes, while frustrated old Confucian scholars have been running around like mad."[24] They were incapable of bringing about the rejuvenation of Chinese culture which had to be accomplished, if China was to survive, by rediscovering the great ideas in the sages' teachings and actually practicing them! Wen was in sympathy with the scholars Ku Yen-wu (1613–1682), Wang Fu-chih (1619–1692), and Yen Yüan (1655–1704), with whose works he was very familiar.[25] It also indicated his acceptance of the activist attitude encouraged in the stories about Franklin, Nelson, and other Western heroes

IV Belief in Action—But With Restraint

Wen's belief in "actual practice" is further mirrored in another essay which he wrote six months later. "The Expanded Definition of the New *Chün-tzu* (Gentleman)" is an attack on the Confucian idea of personal perfection:

The *Commentary on the Book of Changes* says, "Without thought, without action, remaining completely immobile, one understands the universe through direct intuition." This I call the "old *chün-tzu*" who stresses inactivity. Inactivity upholds conservatism, with the defect of vainly talking about virtues and righteousness without practicing them. . . . The new *chün-tzu* stresses activity. The principle of activity is progress. . . . That the Western countries enjoy peace and prosperity is because they have more new *chün-tzu*.[26]

He criticized the self-styled *chün-tzu* who "look down upon menial work, misconstrue their scholarly strolls as the essence of the sages' teachings, refer to themselves as Confucians simply because they wear long gowns with wide sleeves, and regard their mumbling and chanting as learning." He agreed with Yüan Mei (1716–1797), who had said that "with fewer such scholars the world would be peaceful." There is no indication that he was on bad terms with the Confucian Society at Tsing Hua, which boasted an attendance record of almost the entire student body.[27] But his criticism of the old *chün-tzu* seemed to refer to many supporters of the Society who "ran around like mad" urging the government to adopt Confucianism as China's official state religion. They apparently believed that China needed a religious faith in order to achieve prosperity as Western society had, but Wen only defended the rational and universal value of Chinese traditions. He stressed "action" to save China's declining fortunes, but he accused the modern Chinese of unprincipled action and of bringing chaos to their country.[28]

Some of his schoolmates went even farther than he in advocating activism and cultural chauvinism. They quoted Theodore Roosevelt's speech to prove how Chinese pacifistic attitudes had harmed their country, cited the "Hung-fan" chapter of the *Book of History* to show that ancient Chinese sages had anticipated Aristotle's scientific speculations, and admonished their fellow students not to accept everything Western merely because it was new.[29] They all shared a sentimental attachment to classical Chinese literature and traditions, but Wen suggested removal of the encrustations—the hundreds of years of misinterpretation—in order to bare the true essence of China's cultural heritage. They all agreed on the need for action and practical knowledge, but Wen stressed the importance of moral sense as the guiding light.[30] Up to May 4, 1919, Wen remained quite moderate in his views and said nothing particularly critical of the Western influence in his school, which steadily increased as the ideas of Darwin, Spencer, Kant, Hegel, and Marx became subjects of daily conversation on campus. The only thing he staunchly defended was the merit of the classical language. He argued against critics of Yen Fu's translation of the *Evolution and Ethics* into *wen-yen* (classical language), opposed a proposal to adopt *pai-hua* (the vernacular) at the editorial conference of the *Tsing Hua Journal,* and continued to write prose, poetry, personal correspondence, as well as his diary in his cultivated *wen-yen.*[31] But the trend toward adopting *pai-hua* became evident, particularly after the May Fourth Movement, and it did not take Wen long to recognize the trend.

V   *The May Fourth Movement—a Desk Assignment*

The May Fourth Movement was brewing. For weeks the air over the campus was charged with tension, yet no unanimous course of action could be easily found. The politically oriented school administration, with its head appointed by the Ministry of Foreign Affairs rather than the Ministry of Education, had to echo the wishes of the bureaucratic authorities then in Peking. Most of the students, though aroused by the national humiliation for which they blamed the government, were mindful of the official injunction forbidding them to participate in politics.[32] Others were restive, but hesitated to jeopardize the enviable future careers promised by the government. On May 4, 1919, several thousand students in Peking marched on the government in protest against the Paris Peace Conference and China's conciliatory attitude toward Japan. At the critical moment when the Tsing Hua students were debating on what to do, Wen I-to swung them into action by copying the stirring patriotic verse of the Sung dynasty general Yüeh-Fei (1103–1141) on a huge piece of red paper and pasting it on the door of the mess-hall.[33] The next morning everybody at the school read it. A decision was reached that afternoon, and a delegation was elected. Tsing Hua pledged united action with the demonstrating groups in the city. Wen, with his literary skill and handsome calligraphy now badly needed in propaganda work, was elected secretary of the delegation. He represented Tsing Hua at the All-China Student Federation meetings in Peking, but most of the time he stayed in school to draft and copy propaganda leaflets. His role, however valuable it might have been to the movement at the time, caused him some regret because it kept him from marching at the head of the demonstrators and deprived him of that chance for heroic action.[34]

The incident ushered in a different atmosphere at Tsing Hua. Having observed that their voice was heard throughout the country, the students felt that they were politically of age. The mass demonstrations did away with their sense of isolation from the students in the city of Peking, and symbolically, from the outside world. Their organization improved as their leadership shifted from obedient, teachers' pets to capable elected hands and minds. At the height of their enthusiasm, the school administration bungled its effort to halt the demonstrations: on the evening of August 23, 1919, when the students were meeting on the current situation, the president ordered the electric wires cut to black out the meeting. When the angered assembly refused to disperse, the president summoned the local militia unit, a few miserably poor peasants dressed in tatters and carrying paper lanterns, to the scene to "suppress a student rebellion." The result was simply comic. The ineffective and unwise move only served to mark a total bankruptcy of the administration's prestige among the students, who henceforth identified it with the inept government of Peking.[35] Against both authorities the students' defiance mounted. Intellectually they were no longer satisfied with cliché ridden discussions of political theories. Therefore, when Wen I-to was appointed to the editorial committee of the *Tsing Hua Journal* in June 1919, for the first time in its four-year history the *Journal* printed lead articles that specifically commented on current events—the Paris Conference and the disarmament issue. An epigraph asking "Have you forgotten the May Seventh Incident?" appeared on the margin of every even-numbered page. May 7 was the day when concerted student demonstrations were held in many Chinese cities and Tokyo, and the students, arrested on May 4, were released from the Peking prison.

VI   *New Attitudes, New Conflicts*

The changed atmosphere on campus affected Wen. His patriotic sentiment was intensified, his attitude towards Western

influences at Tsing Hua embittered, and his faith in the validity
of Chinese traditions modified to the extent that he turned
away from the classical language. Now he could see the significance of the life of China's youth only in terms of their
potential contribution to the salvation of their country because
"the threat of foreign aggressors has become imminent."[36]
His soaring phrases about "expounding the ancient sages' ways
for posterity" gave way to a call to duty and pointed denuncia-
tions of the government. As he wrote in a eulogy dedicated to a
schoolmate, Hsu Yüeh-che, who died after clashing with the
police during a demonstration:

With the world full of evil, few in power are not wrong-doers. They
open door after door to bow in the robbers who divide up our territory. Everybody eyes the flagrant acts, but who dares to challenge
them? You pitied the cowards and stood up at the crossroads to
protest. When you were with us you had not been in good health.
Yet as you started on your fatal journey you never showed any sign
of regret. In the morning you left, and at night you failed to return.
. . . Remembering that our country's crisis is not over, what can we
offer to console your loyal soul? We can only swear to heaven that
although the Ch'u state may be reduced to only three families, it will
yet destroy the aggressor Ch'in.[37]

Wen's patriotic feelings, however, were accompanied by a
strong revulsion against war which he expressed eloquently in a
poem entiled "T'i teng hui" ["The lantern parade"].[38] The poem
was inspired by a student lantern parade in Peking to celebrate
the surrender of Germany. After declaring that it was fitting
for the Chinese to rejoice with the Allies over the conclusion of
the war, he reminded the reader of the continued civil war and
the suffering of the people. Thus, as he watched his schoolmates
celebrate,

> In the jingle of merry bells
> I hear the clanging of the war mounts' stirrups.
> In the gleaming lights among the darkened trees
> I see the shades of the dead hovering over a graveyard.
> . . . .
> As I sit here alone in deep reverie

My chagrined soul flees south.
It climbs over mountains of dead bodies
And wades through pools of putrid blood.
. . . .
The crops in the field are burned, all black.
Under them lies a farmer, long dead.
Hungry owls call, but cannot awaken him.
They feed on him and carry morsels to their nests.
. . . .
Ah, the beans weep in the pot for their own stalks
      are being burned to cook them.
Who can share this sorrow of mine?

Written in the traditional pentasyllabic *ku-shih* (ancient poetry)
style, the poem anticipated one of his well known *pai-hua* poems
("The Deserted Village") written eight years later.

VII *Criticism of American Culture*

A conflict was developing within Wen. On the one hand, as
he became more acquainted with them, he came to admire
contemporary Western literary criticism, aesthetic theories, and
the sciences. On the other hand, his patriotism and what he saw
at Tsing Hua steadily strengthened his opposition to certain
other aspects of Western culture. The Tsing Hua students had
become overconfident and developed a number of undesirable
traits. Discipline disappeared after the students twice succeeded
in turning the school president out of office and rejected a third
candidate before he even saw the campus.[39] Wen commented,

Since the drive to expel Mr. Chang, every day we hear the demand
for improvement of our Chinese courses. . . . Yet the very same
people ostensibly concerned with our training in Chinese behave
so abominably in the Chinese classes. They cheat, argue, completely
disregard classroom order. . . . These are the same people who uphold
honesty and integrity in the English classes. The moment they step
outside English class, they remove their masks worn only to deceive
the *yang-jen* [foreigners], and expose their true selves![40]

Elsewhere he bitterly criticized his schoolmates for treating
the school as a hotel where rich men's sons came to await their

turns to study abroad. He pointed out that the school administration had lost its control over the students whose own self-
government—something the school had tried to promote—had
also become totally ineffective. As a result the school had been
turned into a place for "tobacco, wine, sex, and decadent
music."[41] His disappointment with the school culminated in an
extremely intemperate attack on the "Americanized Tsing Hua"
in 1922, shortly before his departure for the United States.[42]
"On the basis of my own ten years of study, I conclude that
American culture is not worthy of our assimilation," Wen declared to his schoolmates. "It brags about its material, economic,
and practical success, but it is mediocre, shallow, vain, impul-
sive, and extravagant." He elaborated each point at length, saying that the mediocre individual of the American type aims
only at becoming "a very good fellow," and the typical American
crowd is ruled by "mob spirit." He praised Eastern civilization
as an ideal way of life, and quoted Wordsworth's apostrophe:

> Oh, raise us up, return to us again,
> And give us manners, virtue, freedom, and power![43]

It may have been mainly an outburst occasioned by a controversy in which he opposed the school administration. In the
summer of 1921, a delegation representing the faculties of eight
public schools in Peking called on the government to demand
their back pay. The delegation was met with abuse, whereupon the Peking students went on strike in protest. The Tsing
Hua student body, against the wishes of the school administration, voted to support their Peking friends. At that time Wen's
class had already completed the prescribed eight years of preparation and was about to take the final examination. Facing
severe penalties, many students submitted written apologies
and were pardoned. But Wen and others stood firm. The impasse
was settled with a compromise whereby the defiant students of
Wen's class were to stay at Tsing Hua for another year.[44]

The rebellious in Wen could surface, even explode, when he
embraced a strong cause, but the force of habit and the rational
in him held him in check and brought him back to moderation.
He denounced the extreme leftist influence among his school-

mates.[45] He maintained the same ambivalent stand when he later berated the communists in 1926, and when he urged his friends to be patient with the Kuomintang government in 1936.

VIII   *Deification of Poetry and Art*

The politically moderate Wen I-to was conservative about the classical Chinese language, opposing its abandonment by the *Tsing Hua Journal*, and continuing to use it himself to translate English literature *à la* Lin Shu. Then, in mid–1919, he had to admit defeat when he tried to translate Arnold's "Dover Beach."[46] He managed to imprison Arnold in the pentasyllabic classical Chinese verse form and to force the equivalency between Arnold's grief over the loss of the Christian faith and a Chinese traditionalist's regret over the loss of the "ancient Chinese way of life under the sage kings." Arnold's "turbid ebb and flow of human misery" became the Buddhist *k'u-hai* (sea of suffering) and, when Wen came to the apostrophe in the third stanza,

> Ah, love, let us be true
> To one another! . . . .

he gave up trying. The ideological and linguistic gap was too great, and out of desperation he turned to *pai-hua* a few months later. He started calling for a halt in the practice of writing poetry in the classical language.[47] He published his first *pai-hua* poem, "Hsi-an" ["The Western Shore"], in July, 1920, embodying the theme that light lies on the Western shore across the river of ignorance.[48] He saw the need for a person like him to dedicate himself to building a bridge across the river, however strenuous a task it might be, which symbolically spoke for his sense of mission to be accomplished partly by going to study in the West, in America. As has been observed by other scholars, including Yokoyama Eizo, it was an early expression of Wen's vision of a rejuvenated world culture to rise from a union of the East and the West, as he explained in his 1943 essay "The Historical Movement of Literature."[49] Clumsy archaism and trite expressions are found in the poem, but the relentless striving for poetic effect already shows great promise:[50]

> Boundless bitter fog pasted all over the sky
> Presses against the endless dead sleep which fills the river.
> . . . .
> As the wicked fog stares at the dead water,
> Everything is once again the same as ever before.

The poems he published in the subsequent twelve months exhibited an increasing command of *pai-hua*, resorting less and less to archaism.[51] A set of themes which later recurred often in his works was already developing: death as the ultimate proof of man's dedication to his ideal, passionate love for beauty, and the unfathomable mystery of nature. He also began to mold images that became the distinguishing hallmarks of his poetry: the chilly wind, the stagnant water, the cold moonlight, and the frozen snake. He had by then internalized much of British Romantic poetry. Keats, Shelley and company had already become his daily visitors, and some Victorian giants, e.g., Tennyson and Browning, had also captivated his imagination. The search for absolute beauty had led him from the uncarved, unpolished block of Taoist thought to the Western grotesque; Wen had begun to introduce the beautiful in what had been ugly or even repulsive to the mundane senses. He was bent on pursuing the striking, the unforgettable, the kinds of sense experiences that could produce in man a lasting, thoughtful response amounting to, possibly, a religious conversion.

After a year's experimentation, Wen came to certain conclusions about what the new poetry should be: Imagination and feeling constitute poetry's soul, when feeling is expressed in depth and with intensity, and imagery is derived from an ecstatic experience which Wen compared with the Taoist "spirit journey," achieved by an "uncluttered mind suddenly seeing itself."[52] He described poetic feeling as an aesthetic experience different from physical sensation, although he failed to characterize the nature of the difference.[53] Poetry, he said, could accommodate any subject except the trivial—he did not define triviality and judging by his emphasis on the serious and intense nature of poetry, he seemed to be talking about superficiality rather than triviality. He would not object to social criticism or psychological exploration in poetry, but he would not use the scientific or philosophical value of such subjects as a criterion for judging poetry. Music and the color of language are the body housing the soul of poetry; they should be cultivated because "a beautiful soul loses its charm if it is not joined to a beautiful form."[54] He sought the unusual and startling, so he urged learning from Tu Fu (712–770) who always "attempted the breath-taking" in poetry as did Keats;[55] he also sought the subtle and elegant, thus he loathed "the taste of our 'national treasure' music in the basement of our dormitory . . . oh, no, not that, don't you ever try the rhythm of those drums and gongs!"[56] He would not hesitate to make use of Western poetic stanza forms, but he advised the modern Chinese poet to study classical Chinese poetry seriously, because there was much one could learn from the skill and technique of the old masters. In this last respect, Wen seems to have anticipated the next half-century of development in modern Chinese poetry; as late as the mid-1970s poets like Kuo Mo-jo (1892–1978) and Tsang K'o-chia (1904–   ) continued to echo Wen's advice. The rest of his poetics was later much modified as time and his own response to the world around him changed: By 1940 he had replaced the subjective expression of a poet's own view of life with national needs and people's wishes, subtle chamber music with drumbeat, and refined aesthetic taste with primitive sensorial response. Only one thing he maintained, and that was his serious attitude toward poetry. He had said in the early 1920's that he would not write poetry unless something inside of him threatened to explode. This is why he stopped writing in 1930 until he exploded again in 1944.

As he began to formulate his poetic tenets he also clarified his basic ideas about art. To him, a world without art would be unlivable. He held that art cultivated the noble character and sentiment of mankind and built a bridge between the world of beauty and the world of imagination, between the banal and the sublime, between matter and mind.[57] He was drawn to the aesthetics of the pre-Raphaelite Rossetti (his sensual mysticism or mystical sensuality), to the impressionism of Keats who equated beauty, art and truth, and to the art theories of Marie-Jean

Guyau (1854–1888) and Leo Tolstoi. Guyau's moral philosophy, stressing the selfless in man and the function of art to help man participate in the universal life which compares well with Tao, appealed to Wen I-to; Tolstoi's noble idealism, putting art at the service of peace and humanity, touched the saintly sentiments in Wen I-to. Wen was further impressed by the literary criticism of Albert Mordell who made good use of Freud and some early lines of psychological perception in literature, and Wen also found support in the epistemology of Immanuel Kant for an understanding of how literature works on men. From this wide range of ideas he selected the basic ingredients of his developing thought. At the age of twenty-one he firmly believed in spiritual value and spiritual satisfaction, and accepted the creation of beauty as a noble ideal worthy of the greatest of men.

Thus he thought he had made an exhilarating discovery which led to his logical decision: Art was superior to science because the latter merely contributed to man's material well-being; he chose art as his major subject of study abroad. With a pious sense of self-dedication, he called on his schoolmates to go beyond securing factories and warships for China by aiming at the elevation of world culture and the education of mankind. The time was late 1921, when Social Darwinism, having fired the imagination of Chinese youth for two decades, suffered a reversal in China. Man's progress had so far been expressed in his material civilization, Wen paraphrased Liang Ch'i-ch'ao, "but the result was none other than a shocking bloody war!" Then, proclaiming his faith in the nobility of man, Wen refuted Darwin's idea that "struggle for existence" was the main force behind man's real progress.[58] Wen wanted his fellow men to reach for a higher plane of life, and he himself marched forward to set an example, quoting Browning:

> Ah, but a man's reach should exceed his grasp,
> Or what's a heaven for?[59]

IX *The Making of a Poetic Motif—the Red Candle*

All these thoughts and ideas went into his poetry during his last two years at Tsing Hua. It amply adorned the pages of school publications and later was collected, forming two-thirds of his 1923 anthology the *Red Candle*.[60] The poems had already adequately described the configuration of a poet's mind.

Guided by his concept of art, Wen's search for ideal beauty went on to tell the poet to sacrifice himself for his twin ideals —"Love and Beauty"—without recourse, without reserve:

> From the window pours soft lamplight—
> Inlaying two rows of yellow squares on the wall.
> A tangle of black snakes, two jujube trees' shadows,
> At the foot of the wall lie as they fall.
>
> Ah, that big star above, the moon's companion!
> Why do you hold these eyes of mine?
> But the bird of my heart at once stops its spring songs
> Because it's heard your music, silent but divine.
>
> As it listens it forgets itself,
> All it seeks is you out there.
> It has broken the bars of its prison,
> But suddenly you're gone to nowhere.
>
> A chilly gust around the house's corner heaves a sigh,
> Startling a lazy snake; it rolls over again and again.
> The moon turns a shocking white, perhaps angry now?
> But the gaping window seems to show a broad grin.
>
> The pitiable bird of my heart has come home now,
> Its voice hoarse, eyes blinded, and heart ashen gray;
> From its two wings drips blood, drop by drop—
> The price of love and the karma of Beauty.[61]

Wen dedicated a poem, "The Loyal Minister of Art," to Keats, in which he likened Keats to the most lustrous of the pearls that adorned the royal robe of the "king of art." Then, after addressing Keats as art's "loyal minister" and quoting the famous line, "Beauty is Truth, Truth Beauty," Wen concluded:

> You truly gave your life to Art.
> O, you, loyal and virtuous soul!
> Your name is not written on water,
> But cast on the precious tripod of the sagely sovereign.[62]

The poem yielded a hint of a partial solution of the conflict between Wen's rational self, with its goal of searching for truth, and his emotional self which strove for beauty. Keats gave him great comfort with the celebrated marriage between truth and beauty—the "prefigurative truth" of the youthful phase in Keats' intellectual development.[63] It was precisely this youthful dedication to an ideal that never ceased to appeal to Wen.

He went further than Keats by adding love to the equation. As we have seen in his earlier poem "Love and Beauty," he had already equated the search for Beauty with the lover's quest for his beloved. Wen's idea of love was a sublimated sentiment quite akin to the Platonic ideal. This was a time when the traditional bourgeois Chinese ambivalence, or even hypocrisy, toward sex was rectified by Dante with his Beatrice and Goethe with his Werther. Consequently, Wen did not object to sensuality in poetry, but he insisted that it must be first transformed into poetic feeling.[64] Fifteen years later, he applied the same yardstick to the sensual elements in the *Book of Poetry* and the *Songs of Ch'u.*

Such an attitude led Wen to cast his poems with a love theme in general terms, even when they seem to be addressed to a person, not an object personified. He had no strong attachment to any one individual, man or woman, during his Tsing Hua days, not even to his wife after their arranged marriage in February, 1922, which he refused to talk about before his friends upon his return to school that spring. His intense feeling for her developed much later.[65] The love poems he wrote in 1920–1922, therefore, had as their object a mixture of his ideal values—beauty and truth, and a poet's pursuit of them, as can be seen in the "Champion":

> O, my love, you are a champion;
> But let's play a game of chess.
> My aim is not to win,
> I only wish to lose to you—
> My body and soul,
> Both in their entirety.[66]

Carried to the extreme, the sense of self-dedication and sacrifice with which Wen was preoccupied led logically to a fascination with death, which is the theme of the following poem,

> O, my soul's soul!
> My life's life!
> All my failures and all my debts
> Now have to be claimed against you,
> But what can I ask of you?
> . . . .
> Death is the only thing I beg of you.
> And to you I offer my life, my supreme tribute.[67]

The object of the apostrophe is the same poetic object of worship as Wen identified in all his love poems of this period. The life of Li Po offered him a classic illustration which he used in his long poem, "The Death of Li Po," dramatizing the legend that the famous T'ang poet was drowned while trying to embrace the moon's reflection in a river.[68] The one hundred eighty-one-line poem reveals Wen's ideas about and attitude toward poetry quite fully. Its epigraphic quotation from Li Po's poem addressed to a poet friend Meng Hao-jan (689–740), praises Meng, "Being drunk with the moon you often attain saintly virtues. And being in love with flowers you prefer not to serve in the king's court." A second quotation from Li Po identifies Li himself with the "madman of Ch'u" who sang a song ridiculing Confucius for his futile, self-appointed task of righting the wrongs of the world.[69] Wen's own prefatory note explains that he was trying to "depict the character and personality of the T'ang poet," not rewriting history.

The poem starts with a description of Li Po, who, totally drunk, knocks the candles from the table in order to let the moon shine more brightly,

> Like a hungry lion discovering his prey
> He stares, frozen, at it with wide-open eyes,
> Then quietly and slowly lifts his front paws
> To strike, like a sudden thunderbolt . . .

The drunken Li Po addresses the moon pleading with her to come out, while claiming his own celestial lineage as a banished immortal fathered by a star. As the beautiful moon rises Li Po sees her as the fairy lady standing in attendance with a peacock fan behind the Jade Emperor in heaven, and beseeches her to allow him to be close to her. He refers to the enmity he has incurred with the T'ang emperor's favorite woman and bodyguard because of a poem he wrote, and to his involvement with a rebellious prince. His reminiscence leads him to,

> Gradually fan his heart that has nearly burned into ashes,
> And finally again turn to drinking to drown the fire of sorrow. . .

But the flames of sorrow, fed by wine, burn ever brighter, triggering his imagination to enter a world of celestial beauty. Now he takes wings and soars closer to the moon until her brilliance makes him realize his impure substance, and he feels rejection and banishment back down to earth. Then the reflection of the moon in the pond leads him to assume that she has fallen into water, and his attempt to rescue her ends in his own drowning,

> He struggles to leap upward, and lifting his head
> Once more he sees the full moon serenely glued to the sky.
> But he is exhausted, breathless; he wants to laugh,
> No sound comes. He only thinks, "I've rescued her back to heaven."

The lengthy notes Wen I-to attached to the poem demonstrated his erudition and his conscious effort to master an impressive array of historical and literary allusions to serve as his poetic images, of which the heart burning into ashes quite appropriately became the motif of his *Red Candle*.

Of the forty poems written in his Tsing Hua days and included in the *Red Candle*, no less than eleven treat beauty as an ideal which either appears as the poet's object of love, or the meaning of his life, or the *raison d'être* of the universe. Love itself is a dedication which takes its supreme form in death, and death itself is experienced either as an ecstasy (in "Death") or as a perpetual rest (in "Impression"). The image of burning repeats itself many times, as in "Trouble Started by a Game,"

"Incense Figure," and other poems. Art and poetry become the currency accepted by love ("Debt of Poetry"); music is fit material with which a palace of art can be built to shelter and comfort any and all souls ("Yellow Bird"). The poet's soul is lofty and pure ("The Soul of Red Lotus"), and unconquerable ("Snow"). Dream frees man from a world of bondage ("Rainy Night" and "Defeat"), whereas the world of reality threatens him. The poet pursues joy ("Beauty and Love") and finds joy in the growth of life ("Joy" and "Wish"), and he pleads for relief in behalf of all humanity when he is actually faced with a war-ravaged reality,

> O, My Lord! When you look at this much-abused world,
> Don't you ever shudder, O, My kind-hearted Lord![70]

The snake image, very possibly inspired by Coleridge, appears superimposed on bare-branch trees ("Impressions of An Early Summer Night" and "Beauty and Love"), nothing sinister, but rather suggestive of the sinewy movement of Chinese calligraphy ("The First Chapter of Spring"). Western images are used very rarely, such as the angel image in "Joy," but traditional images abound and are quite refreshingly and skilfully employed, e.g.,

> The string music sieved through the green window screen,
> Painting a picture of a Beauty sleeping in spring,
> The tender affection, the bashful languor,
> Like that, and like that, now far, now near. . . [71]

The picture of a sleeping beauty is very traditional, even overused, but as a metaphor for langorous music it is an original usage.

In these poems, Wen I-to's diligent and imaginative effort to approach the poetic from Western impressionistic models while relying upon native Chinese ingredients was successful enough to be an inspiration to his generation of Chinese poets, though his crowning success was yet to come. Chu Tzu-ch'ing (1898–1948) remarked that the appearance of these poems gave *pai-hua* poetry a new lease on life because earlier experiments with the spontaneous and the clever had just about exhausted themselves.[72] Where the other poets had failed in breaking into really new territories, Wen succeeded, and the vagueness of theme in some poems, the occasional slips into trite expressions, did not impair the overall lasting value of his contribution.[73]

CHAPTER 3

Study Abroad (1922-1925)
–from Palette to Poetry

That was the day when you lighted a red candle,
Searching for a way to live.
Singing sad songs you searched,
And the touched red candle shed tears——
tears blended with
warm blood.
—K'o Chung-p'ing, Yenan, 1946[1]

I Journey to America

IN the spring of 1922, Wen I-to went home to marry Kao Hsiao-chen. A plain but pleasant girl still with bound feet, she had the rare distinction of having been an honor student at the Hupeh Normal School. Wen had known about her, and seen her at a distance, but had never spoken to her before. The wedding ceremony was conventional except that, because of Wen's objection, the kowtow ritual was omitted. The bride and bridegroom only bowed three times to their parents.[2] The honeymoon was spent at the old house, which was shared by about thirty close relatives, during which time Wen worked on his study of *lü-shih* (regulated verse) and taught poetry to his wife and the younger members of the family.[3] Wen kept the same study, and the newlyweds' living quarters had a measure of privacy in the huge compound. His memory of that month, and the month of June of that year, always recalled to him the picture of "reading at night with a 'red sleeve' (a lady? wife?) to add incense to the burner on the desk," a picture of marital bliss often portrayed in classical Chinese poetry. His obsession with art and poetry always enabled him to see or create an extra

49

touch of interest in his environment. Now it was traditional
literati refinement, later in 1925 it manifested itself in the interior decoration of his study influenced by Van Gogh and Cézanne,
still later, in 1942, when wartime stringencies deprived him of
all the bourgeois amenities, it found expression in his way of
conducting classes at the National Southwest Associate University in Kunming.

On July 16, 1922, he sailed for America. In spite of his reservations about American automobile traffic which almost stopped
him from embarking, in spite of his occasional outbursts against
the materialistic American culture, he was sanguine about his
new venture, including the sea voyage.[4] His head was full of
words and rhymes; he had hoped to write much about his trip
as he had promised his friends of the Literary Society left
behind at Tsing Hua. Upon boarding the ship, a luxury liner,
the following lines by Kuo Mo-jo were ringing in his ears:

> Ah, the limitless sky and ocean!
> One floating bubble of quicksilver!
> Above, there are stars in clear waves;
> Below, surges liquid crystal.
> When all lives are asleep
> I alone, wearing a cloak of white peacock feathers,
> Gaze at the sky, on an ivory boat,
> Far, far away from the world.[5]

But life on the ship, comfortable though it was, failed to meet
his expectation. To him, the fellow passengers were vulgar,
sharing none of his poetic interests. There was too much noise,
too much gambling. "I can foresee that my life in Chicago will
be twice as uninspiring," he wrote to his friends at Tsing Hua.[6]
He tried to read, but unfortunately only a story about anti-
Chinese feeling in Japan absorbed him, making him wonder
how the Americans, a race much further removed from the
Chinese than Japanese, would behave.[7] The muse did not visit
him; he only managed to sketch a few caricatures of his fellow
passengers for the daily paper printed on board.

His brief stop in Japan was much more pleasant than that of
his schoolmates who had passed through there earlier.[8] The

May Seventh (1919) incident in Tokyo, involving over twenty Chinese student demonstrators who were arrested by the Japanese police, had been about forgotten. Japanese students even sent delegates to greet and guide Wen. He was immediately swept off his feet by the picturesque quality of the island country. "As to natural beauty," he said, "the mountains and trees of Japan are excellent. The kind of wind-swept cypresses we have at Tsing Hua grows everywhere here. With a tree like this, simply add another object, anything, a man, a rickshaw, or a hut, and you have an extremely refreshing composition." He was also full of praise for the costume, architecture, and other arts of Japan. The only thing that marred his pleasure in touring Japan was the guide who insisted on taking him to see the pride of Tokyo, which turned out to be a huge department store! "Japan is wonderful," he sighed, "but the Japanese people are finished if they are all like our guide Matsumoto."

II *Life in Chicago (August 1922–September 1923)*
Monroe, Sandburg, and Amy Lowell

Already full of misgiving, he arrived at the Art Institute of Chicago on August 7, 1922. He had a month to explore the city before starting school. Lo Lung-chi (1896–1965) and another friend shared a rented house with him.[9] They lived on bread, canned fish, and plain water, augmented with one restaurant meal a day. Wen was tithing his living allowance to finance the publication of his first poetic anthology—a standard practice among Chinese writers in those days. Fortunately, the museum was free and the movies were inexpensive; they modified his opinion of America. He did not repeat what he had said about the soulless and artless American movies at Tsing Hua, instead he conceded that "the level of aesthetic appreciation of the Americans is really higher than ours."[10] But he complained in the same letter that after only a week he had already had enough of Chicago. Leisure gave him a good opportunity to reflect on a wide range of questions, from his own future career to the future of Chinese literature, from his "uninspiring daily life" to death. It also accentuated his loneliness which he hoped would decrease as soon as school started.

The school started on September 25. His enthusiasm toward the art classes was high, but poetry made strong claims on his time. He wrote in March, 1923:

I was very absorbed in school and thought of illustrating my own poems. But the moment I stepped into my room, Byron, Shelley, Keats, Tennyson, Tu Fu, and Lu Yu were waiting for me on my bookcase, on my desk, and in my bed. And I itched to be with them again. Then the light of my reason would burn bright, compelling me to resume my systematic study of the six T'ang poets and philosophy. At other times letters from Shih Chao-ying and Lo Lung-chi would remind me of my other interests, and I would again want to promote this and reform that. . . .[11]

He was torn between his rational and emotional selves, between philosophy and poetry, between service to man and service to art, and between criticism and creation. The conflict, as we shall see, accompanied him throughout his life, and it was during those periods when he successfully resolved the conflict between his rational and emotional selves that his creativity blossomed in a variety of forms. Meanwhile he tried to study everything, including history,[12] in which he sought the key to the minds of the poets. His friends of the Literary Society at Tsing Hua kept him supplied with the latest publications in *pai-hua* literature, which he read critically.

Soon he came to know a few Americans in Chicago who were interested in poetry. Among them was a Mr. Winter[13] who taught French at the Art Institute. He was an American with a "China fever," a collector of Oriental *objets d'art* and a translator of Baudelaire. Unmarried, he lived alone with a huge Chinese cast-iron bell. When gnawed by loneliness at night, he would manage to move the bell close to his bed and strike it. Such idiosyncracies and a well-cultivated sensitivity for poetry drew Wen to him. At Winter's house they often stayed until the wee hours in the morning, talking about China and planning to collaborate in translating classical Chinese poetry. On the desk was a censer, from which issued Chinese, Japanese, and Indian incense to fill the room. Looking down on them from the wall was a painting by the American host, a portrait which Wen, without introduction, recognized at first glance as being of the legendary founder of Taoism, Lao Tzu. Through other friends also interested in poetry, Wen met Harriet Monroe, who founded the magazine *Poetry* in 1912, Carl Sandburg, and Amy Lowell. "I am really luckier than all other Chinese students who have come to Chicago," he wrote to his family in November, 1922. "They stayed by themselves, not knowing how to associate with the Americans. I am the only exception."[14] And he told in detail of his happy hours at the hospitable homes of his American friends.

His studies and his environment spurred him to write at a feverish pace. Hardly a week passed without his writing a lengthy letter to a friend about a new poem, a critical essay on a current publication, or a stanza of a *pai-hua* poem. His creative impulse was at its peak, and as new experiences and reading widened his intellectual horizons, the nebulous ideas of his Tsing Hua days appeared in sharper relief in his writings.

III *Wen the Romantic—Love, Beauty, and Death*

Daily Wen was drawn closer to the nineteenth-century English Romantic poets, and in his study of the Chinese poets he also moved toward those who resembled Keats, Byron, and Shelley. The themes of their poetry dominated Wen's mind: relentless striving for beauty as an ideal of life, search for truth as the principle of the universe, attraction to death as the ultimate self-dedication to one's goal, intense preoccupation with color, and worship of love. Separately and together these ideas contributed to the central conflict in his intellectual development.

The central motif in Wen I-to's world of poetic imagination now came into focus, and that was his *Red Candle* image, which he fashioned into a prefatory poem for the first collection of his creative works. In the burning candle he saw the truth that a poet must destroy himself in his self-chosen task, just as a candle must burn in order to emit light. Addressing the candle, he wrote:

> As you shed a drop of tear, you lose a bit of your heart.
> Though tears and disappointment are your fruit
> The creation of light is your cause.[15]

With the same metaphor he also sought to explain the eternal conflict between body and soul as he saw it. He regarded the body, with all its mundane desires, worries, and confusion, as the prison from which the soul seeks freedom. The soul, once released from bondage, finds its destiny in beauty. The confusion that shrouds the soul of the ordinary person is what a poet must attempt to dispel by burning himself into a shining light, for the light will penetrate the prison walls to rescue the benighted soul.[16] What he meant here by "soul" was partly inherited from the traditional Chinese concept of *hun*, the spirit, or something less tangible than body but not necessarily immortal, and partly from the concept of *ling*, intelligence or efficacy as a god is supposed to be intelligent and efficacious. Wen was influenced by the generally Western, though not always Christian, concept of soul—an immortal entity separable from man's physical existence. Thus when Wen spoke of soul, he referred to the noble intelligence and moral awareness of man that put him on a higher plane than beast.

Wen found the idea of total dedication to an ideal beauty, by a strange coincidence, in the works of two poets, Li Shangyin and Keats, who lived a thousand years and half a world apart. From Li he quoted the line, "Only when the candle is burned to ashes, its tear will dry,"[17] and used it as an epigraph for the *Red Candle*. In the quoted line, Li originally expressed the unending sorrow of parting with a loved one, but Wen borrowed it to express the poet's dedication to ideal beauty. Not long before, Wen had criticized Li as "an abnormal product of his time" with a "poisoned mind,"[18] because some of Li's lines, without too much stretching of the imagination, contained sexual symbols. Li has been regarded by many critics as the leader of a new school of late T'ang poetry that rebelled against the realism and social consciousness championed by Tu Fu and Po Chü-i (772–846).[19] Like his immediate predecessor Li Ho (Li Ch'ang-chi, 790–816), Li Shang-yin stressed personal feeling and indicated his belief that literature should be independent of life. As one critic has pointed out about Li, literature was not a tool for the betterment of society or human destiny, but its highest attainment was beauty, and art (*i-shu*) had no other value than its beauty (*mei*).[20] It was with such

convictions in mind, according to this critic, that Li strove
for the beauty of music and lyrical quality in his works. Wen
admired Li's attitude toward poetry, but when Wen looked
around and faced social problems, he reproached Li's lack of a
sense of social responsibility. Here again, Wen was torn between poetry and reality.

He frequently associated Li with Keats because of their
common attitude toward the same ideal and the common characteristics of their works—intense feeling and dazzling beauty.[21]
And as the red candle burns out like the burning out of life,
the idea of death also seemed to appeal to Wen with a morbid
fascination quite apart from any philosophical significance. As
he wrote to Liang Shih-ch'iu on May 15, 1923, telling of the
suicide of a Chinese student named Sun over his failure at
school: "This man knew the futility of life and had the resolution to die. He really ended his life. If one wants to die, die.
My hat off, my hat off . . . I want to say for the thousandth time,
my hat off."[22] Wen was not given to brooding. There may be
loud lamentation, but never fatalism, in his poetry with tragic
themes. In this instance the end of Sun's life impressed Wen not
with its tragedy, but rather its gusto. More often, however, death
raised a number of fundamental questions in his mind. When
another Chinese student died in an automobile accident in
Colorado in September, 1922, he wrote a friend: "This news
makes me think of bigger questions—the meaning of life and
death—the great puzzle of the universe. The last several days
I have been very absentminded. They say I am losing my mind.
But isn't he too senseless who cannot lose his mind over these
big questions?" And his own answer at the moment was a poem,
"Death:"[23]

> O, my soul's soul!
> My life's life!
> All my failures, all my debts
> Now have to be claimed against you,
> But what can I ask of you?
>
> Let me be drowned in the deep blue of your eyes.
> Let me be burnt in the furnace of your heart.
> Let me die intoxicated in the elixir of your music.
> Let me die of suffocation in the fragrance of your breath.

Or may I die ashamed in front of your dignity,
Or frozen in your unfeeling chill,
Or crushed between your merciless teeth,
Or stung by your relentless poison-sword.

For I shall breathe my last in happiness
If my happiness is what you decree;
Otherwise I shall depart in endless agony
If my agony be your desire.

Death is the only thing I beg of you,
And to you I offer my life, my supreme tribute.

There is still another aspect of death that absorbed him—
death in ecstasy. To die at the moment of supreme joy, which
could thus be arrested for eternity, was a triumph. Just as
Browning made a moment into eternity by prolonging "The
Last Ride" forever, or as Keats captured his "joy forever" on
the Grecian Urn, or as Arnold let Empedocles fling himself into
the crater of Etna only to hear the song of Callicles rising up
toward the sky,[24] so Wen said he would like to end his own
life at the very moment he succeeded in perfecting "The Sheath
of My Sword,"[25] a thing of fantastic beauty. The sheath is an
imaginary work of art wrought to perfection. With all the
jewels Wen had collected from the sea and the colors and
forms he had seen in dreams he shaped and carved a Chinese
Taoist god, a Buddhist god, a Venus, a singing minstrel . . . all
on the sheath:

I shall sketch a portrait of the T'ai-i deity,
      fair-complexioned with a flowing beard,
reclining in the petal of a pink lotus blossom
which floats in white clouds made of ivory.
I shall use black jade and gold threads
to fashion an incense burner, cloisonné in thunder whorls;
with the wafts of smoke rising above it carved only of
      transluscent opal.
An exquisite figure ascends vaguely from where the smoke disperses;
could it be a Venus with all her charms revealed . . . ?
This piece of rose jade should match her skin color very well.
. . . .
Then I shall use agate to carve a statue of the Buddha,
three-headed, six-armed,
riding on an elephant of oolite stone,

with coral flames issuing from his mouth,
and silver threads twining into a serpent to gird his waist,
and an amber halo over his head.
Another figure, a blind minstrel, I shall add,
strumming on a single-stringed ancient zither,
    sitting on a bamboo raft.
(This must be as finely wrought as Wang Shu-yüan's scene of
  the "Song of the Red Cliff" carved out of a single peach stone.)
Let emeralds, lazurites and amethysts
pile at random into a sweep of angry waves;
trimmed with fine filigree
to suggest the glittering sprays.
A firmament of black gold above it all,
lighted by a single star—a diamond.
. . . .

Wen labors hard through this one hundred ninety-one-line
long poem, day and night, and adds his music to his work of art,

    Spring grass greens, and the green ascends my front steps,
    as I work together with the season of spring;
    when crickets start singing their autumnal tunes,
    I, too, hum my songs, while continuing my work.
    I work, singing my songs all the while:
    The notes of my music
    all flow forth from my finger tips.
    I shall work the songs into layers of lace,
    showing coiled dragons, paired phoenixes,
        heavenly horses and unicorns,
    and sacred mushrooms, white lotus blooms, Buddha's
        swastikas and double-victory patterns,
    with ancient Han-dynasty friezes of all colors
    framing them, on the outer-most ring.

    If a few corners still lack decoration,
    butterflies should fill them just right:
    A tortoise-shell carved Liang Shan-po,
    an imperial-seal jade carved Chu Ying-t'ai,
    green jade, red carnelian, white agate, blue crystal . . .
    shaped into butterflies of all hues.
    Then my great task is done!

The finished work, featuring a galaxy of legendary figures including Liang Shan-po and Chu Ying-t'ai, two immortal lovers, is a "palace of art" in which to keep his sword asleep in peace, and Wen himself is ready to die drunk with its dazzling beauty.

The high degree of sensitivity to color which Wen's poems exhibit is not surprising in view of his continuously cultivated interest in painting. Keats' "Ode to Autumn" became Wen's favorite because of the immediacy of physical sensations it suggests: the rich purple of the ripe grapes and the tantalizing flavor they give upon breaking on "the palate fine." Among the early twentieth-century Western poets, it was also those with an intense color-consciousness that found Wen's favor. It was John Gould Fletcher who, Wen gratefully acknowledged, "awakened the sense of color"[26] in him, and inspired him to write the poem "Autumn Forest" which he described as a study of color suggested by a view in Chicago's Jackson Park:[27]

Water in the creek
As purple as ripe grapes
Rolls out golden carp's scales
Layer upon layer

Several scissor-shaped maple leaves
like crimson swallows
Whirling and turning, rising and dipping
On the water.

Thick and fat like bears' paws,
Those dark brown leaves
Scattered on the green.
Busy, timid squirrels
Scurry out and in among the leaves,
Gathering food for the approaching winter.

Chestnut tree leaves, now of age
Complained to the western wind all night long,
Finally win their freedom.
With a deep blush on their dry faces,
They giggle and bid farewell to the ancient branches.

White pigeons, multi-colored pigeons,
Red-eyed silver gray pigeons,
Raven-like black pigeons,

With a golden sheen of purple and green on their backs—
So many of them, tired of flying,
Assemble beneath the steps.
Their beaks buried in their wings,
Quietly they take their afternoon nap.

Crystalline air, like pure water, fills the world;
Three or four pert children
(In orange, yellow, and black sweaters)
Dart through the lilac bushes,
Like goldfish cavorting among the seaweeds.

Aren't they a forest of masts on the Huang-p'u River?
Those countless ascetic poplars
Stand piercing the slate-blue sky in stony silence.
That aspen poses like a gallant youth,
Draped in a gold-embroidered cape.
Resting one hand on his hip,
He gazes at the jade-green pool,
Admiring his own reflection.

As they lean on the zig-zag crystal balustrades,
The morning sunbeams smile at the world.
From their smile flows liquid gold—
Yellow gold on the oaks,
Red gold on the oaks,
White gold on the barks of the pines.

Ah, these are no longer trees,
But tinted clouds—
Of amber, of agate,
Fanned by sensitive winds and kindled by the sun.
These are no longer trees,
But exquisite, bejeweled clouds.

Ah, these are no longer trees,
But a palace in the Forbidden City—
Yellow-glazed tiles,
Green-glazed tiles;
Story upon story, pavilion on pavilion—
The silvery songs of the birds
Imitate the chimes under the flying eaves.
These are no longer trees,
But an imperial capital in full regal splendor.

You, majestic, festooned autumn trees!
Neither brocades of Lord Ling-yang,

Nor carpets from Turkey,
Nor the rose window of Notre Dame,
Nor the frescoes of angels by Fra Angelico,
Can rival your colors and brilliance.

You, majestically garbed autumn trees!
I envy your romantic world,
Your bohemian life,
And your colors.

I'll ask T'ien Sun to weave me an embroidered robe[28]
So that I may wear your colors;
Or press you from grapes, oranges, and kaoliang
So that I may drink your colors!
And from Puccini's *La Bohème*,
And from the seven-jeweled censer of Po-shan,
I will listen to your colors,
And inhale your colors.

Ah, how I long to lead a life of colors,
As dazzling as these autumn trees!

The juxtaposition and parallelism of Chinese and Western images, a hallmark of Wen's earlier poetry, are in full evidence here. The poem also shows his penchant for erudition nurtured by long years of exposure to traditional Chinese poetry. Lord Ling-yang, a legendary immortal, and T'ien Sun, another name for the Weaving Goddess in heaven, are paraded to suggest the etherealness of the colors. The incense burner of Po-shan, some ancient versions of which dating back to the Han dynasty can be seen in the Palace Museums of Peking and Taipei, features a cover in the form of a sacred mountain fashioned out of gold and bronze inlaid with jewels.

In a slightly different vein, he philosophized on colors and compared life to a piece of uninteresting white paper at the beginning; but this piece of paper, in due time, acquired various colors as life acquired feeling, motion, hope, and disappointment; and Wen confessed:

From that time on,
I adore my life
because I love its colors.[29]

Most of the sixty-two poems included in the *Red Candle* make lavish use of color words. In many cases the effect achieved is remarkably impressive.

IV *Wen the Homesick Patriot—the Sun, the East, and the Motherland*

Beneath the profuse colors of Wen's poems in this period, there is a nationalistic refrain composed of a nostalgia for his homeland and a dislike of America. Loneliness began to grip him the moment he boarded the ship for America. A star he saw over the Pacific reminded him of the homeland that he had left behind, and he began to feel that he had been "banished beyond the reach of affection."[30] Soon after he arrived in Chicago he wrote to his friends, "Without leaving the country you cannot know the taste of homesickness . . . I will copy two poems to show you how I have been feeling lately." In the poems he copied are the following lines:

> Oh, the sunshine that pierces and hurts my heart
> Has again driven away a traveler's home-coming dream,
> And given him another twelve hours' longing pain.[31]

"The Lone Swan" is the subtitle under which the above poem and others in a similar vein appear in the *Red Candle*. The lone swan, in his imagery, is an unfortunate, lonely and lost soul, who has gone astray from his fellow travelers. He felt that he was an "Exiled Prisoner," and in "Late Autumn" he wished to "curl up like a cat in front of the fireplace" to dream of his country, home, alma mater, old acquaintances, and the bygone days, the thought of which he could no longer bear.[32]

Homesickness led him to over-idealize his country and prejudiced him against anything nonChinese. In his "Sunshine Rhymes" he turned away from the fascinating colors of Chicago's Jackson Park:

> Oh, Sun, you have risen over the building,
> Haven't you just arrived from our East?
> Is everything well in my homeland—everything?
> . . . .

> Oh, Sun, this is not my river, not my mountain.
> Here, the wind and cloud carry strange colors,
> Here, mournful are the songs the birds sing.

In "Remembering Chrysanthemum" he presented a kaleidoscopic collection of chrysanthemums of all sizes and colors before he addressed them:

> Oh, the grand harvest of Nature's beauty!
> Masterpieces of autumn in our motherland.
> Oh! the flowers of the East, the flowers of the learned!
> Isn't T'ao Ch'ien, the poetic soul of the East,
> Your very own soul in another incarnation?
> Isn't the Double-ninth Festival in our fatherland, the day
> We drink on a hilltop, an auspicious day of your birth?

> You resemble not the roses here, those blooms of carnal desire;
> The trivial violets can compare with you even less.
> You are flowers with a history, with an established way of life.
> Oh, you famed blossoms of Chinese heritage, 4,000 years old![33]
> . . . .

Thus, to our young Chinese poet in America, his homeland became the crystallization of beauty. Furthermore, the beauty of his motherland, her noble culture and glorious history, were at present under the threat of ugly, aggressive, foreign (though modern) influences. In "A Lament under the Great Wall," a one hundred sixty-eight-line poem written in February, 1923, he saw the Great Wall as a tombstone perpetually marking a deceased soul of China—the China of peace, grace, beauty—of yesteryear.

> But today's enemy is
> Natural disaster? man-made holocaust? black magic or evil winds?
> Oh, monsters with copper muscles and iron bones,
>   spitting fire and fume,
> Oh, it is just about putting out our sun and our moon,
> And about to destroy our world—our entire world.

> Oh, from now on where do we find towering pavilions with
>   pearl curtains half raised?
> Where burners shaped like sleeping ducks spit incense,

and wine flows from dragon-head spigots?
Where the peace is insured through songs, and order
    through the dances?
From now on where do we find stone lanterns and red braziers
    adorning a Taoist retreat?
Where a tree spreads its lush shade in a courtyard
    overflowing with red sunshine—
And a boy prepares tea, burning a bundle of dried vines?

Where is there any more plum blossoms in winter outside the window,
    and slanting bamboo trees,
And inside, a quiet one plucking alone a string instrument
    made of aged *wu-t'ung* wood?
And where is there a farmer, a hoe on his shoulder,
    treading the rays of a setting sun,
His song reverberating on this side of the mountain,
    as he disappears on the other side?
And where is there a fishing boat tied under a spreading willow tree,
And an old fisherman who lingers under light wind and fine rain,
    not hurrying home?

Then, having idolized the image of traditional China, Wen de-
clares his resentment against the intrusion of Western material
progress:

    From now on only numerous smoke stacks,
    Like so many poisonous serpents, their heads poised,
        waiting on the horizon;
    Like so many devils, startled, frightened,
    Raising their giant arms high, pleading for mercy from Heaven.
    From now on the streets with their thousands of staring eyes,
    Only skeletons salute skeletons, and they chase along,
        one after another.

Thus, the poet under the Great Wall cannot help but cry,

Crying for the inevitable passage of youth anywhere under the sky;
Crying for the end of all banquets since time immemorial;
Crying for the permanent disappearance, like vanishing clouds,
Of the majestic and shining beauty of our China.[34]
. . . .

In "I Am Chinese," he enumerated the stunning features of

China's land and history to support his assertion about his racial and national identity, for which,

> The soul flame in my heart burns
> Leaping higher and higher;
> I tremble as I burn for my motherland.[35]

Wen read with elation John Gould Fletcher's poem, "Chinese Poet Among Barbarians,"[36] but he reacted with intense indignation to the antiOriental feeling in the United States. In January, 1923, he wrote to his family:

The experiences of a Chinese young man, who has a mind of his own, in America defy description. Wait till the end of the year after next, when I come home to spend the New Year with you around the fire. Then I will tell you in detail . . . I am not a man without a country. We have a history and a culture of five thousand years. In what are we inferior to the Americans? Should we say that because we cannot manufacture guns and cannons for massacring people, we are not as brilliant and superior as they are? . . . . After my return I would rather advocate friendship and alliance between China and Japan against the Americans than advocating friendship between China and the United States against Japan.[37]

At this time, he read Kuo Mo-jo's "Wei Yang," a short story depicting the author's difficult life in Japan, and grieved over the lot of his contemporaries and momentarily wished for "escape from reality to poetry."[38] He wrote to his brother to defend Chinese fine arts, particularly those of the T'ang and Sung period.[39] In his letters to his family, he also expressed increasing concern with the unrest in his homeland, and his conviction that China's future lay with the farmers whom the Chinese intellectual must try to educate. He had begun to see the importance of educators in China.[40]

V Wen the Rebel—Family Pressure and Red Beads

In contrast to his nationalistic spirit, his rebellious spirit is less noticeable in his early writings. Before he left China, he was an obedient son at home, not even objecting to the marriage arranged by his parents, as many of his contemporaries did at the time. To be sure, he was involved in the May Fourth Movement demonstration against the government, and participated in the strike against the school administration at Tsing Hua, but generally he was not defiant of traditions or authority. After his marriage, however, he began to feel the pressure exerted by his father increasing, not so much on himself as on his wife. The father's interception of Wen's letters to his wife was bitterly resented. He suffered immeasurably and only the fear of a worse rift in the family prevented him from open rebellion. In December, 1922, his first daughter was born. His father withheld the news from him for a long time, and even then only casually mentioned it in a letter.[41] Wen took this to be a clear indication of his father's discrimination against girls; for if his child had been a son, he was sure his father would have immediately heralded the news with elation. He now worried over the welfare of his wife and daughter whose position in the old family was anything but enviable. The Wen family was not poor, but according to tradition every married son should earn his keep and contribute to the family treasury. Since Wen, still a government-subsidized art student at twenty-three, could neither send money home nor soon embark on a lucrative career, his own wife and daughter became a burden to his relatives. Such a thought depressed him and angered him, as he wrote in his "Red Beads" in the winter of that year:

> We are companions
> First whipped together,
> Then whipped apart.
> Oh, you, almighty whip!
> Should I sing praises
> Or curses
> Of You?

> We, the weak, are but sacrificial fish and meat,
> Once valued by the supplicants
> Who put us in ritual vessels,
> Placed before the shrine of "tradition."
> How proud we were supposed to be!

> We are a pair of red candles
> Lighting up the festive banquet for the celebrants.

We each stand at one far corner of the table,
Quietly letting our lives burn away,
To add gaiety to their gathering.
When they finish their revelry,
Our life will have been burnt up also.
. . . .
Sour, sweet, bitter, and biting,
Are the beads, though all
Red in color.
Give the biting ones to tradition,
Let it taste them first![42]

The forty-two-stanza poem was dedicated to his wife with much tenderness, as revealed in stanza No. 14:

I am sending these poems to you;
It matters not if you cannot read them all.
Just rest your fingertips on these words . . .
The throbbing you feel will pulsate
In unison with your own heart.[43]

But she never saw the poem until long after its publication. The resentment made Wen an enemy of those old traditions that denied the basic rights of man.

VI Wen the Literary Crusader

His experiences in America intensified the clash between Wen the homesick patriot and Wen the Romantic poet; the former he identified with his rational self and the latter his poetic self. Without being aware of it he was seeking justification for his pursuit of art and poetry, and he found it in a self-cultivated sense of mission. "I feel that I have a mission in Chinese literature," he wrote to the members of the Tsing Hua Literary Society in September, 1923, "and to carry it out I am anxious to found a magazine."[44] In subsequent months he laid out elaborate plans for the endeavor with the ultimate purpose of promoting a new literary movement in China which he called "literature for beauty." His belief was that the artistic and literary quality of modern Chinese writings must be elevated, regardless of genre and subject matter. He took violent exception to Hu Shih's plea for "popularizing" *pai-hua* poetry, and resented Hu's meddling in literary criticism.[45] Still clinging to Ts'ai Yüan-p'ei's theory of aesthetic education and Pope's definition of a critic,[46] he began to wonder about the validity of his studying Western painting in preparing for a career as a creative artist. He wrote in February, 1923:

> I have gradually come to realize that I should not become a Western artist, no matter how much talent I possess. I am now studying Western painting to be an art critic. . . . I hope to be an evangelist for art, rather than a creative artist.[47]

And a month later he wrote again:

> My concept of the word "literature" is a faith, a vision, and an ideal— not just a means of giving vent to my personal feelings. . . . I want "consciously" to render some service to mankind.[48]

Determined to lead a literary crusade, he built his criteria of literary criticism on the tenets he had worked out at Tsing Hua. Toward the end of 1922 he outlined his views on rhyme, language, Westernization, and imagery in modern Chinese poetry. He believed that the Chinese language offered an unusually rich range of rhymes of which the Chinese poets ought to avail themselves. "Rhyming helps to develop rhythm and to perfect the art of poetry; not using it would be like starving in front of a royal banquet. Nothing is more foolish than that!"[49] He cited his own poem, "Sunshine Rhymes," to prove his theory, saying that he felt no strain at all in using the same end rhyme throughout all of its twelve stanzas.[50] Most of the poems in the *Red Candle* show a conscious exercise of rhyming, though not completely successful in every instance. Chu Hsiang (1904–1933), the shortlived poetic talent, later Wen's close associate upon his return to China, detected some faulty rhymes in Wen's proud work "The Death of Li Po," and others.[51] In some cases the problem occurred due to Wen's Hupeh province accent which differed considerably from standard Mandarin.

While accepting *pai-hua* as a promising poetic medium, he

criticized the indiscriminate use of colloquialism in poetry. The first task, he suggested, was to develop a poetic *pai-hua* by distilling the poetic and musical elements from the ordinary language. Then the poet would be able to, as he must, go beyond the "natural rhythm" advocated by Hu Shih. "If we don't admit that new poetry with refined rhymes adapted from classical poetry is beautiful," he said, "then we have only two choices: be content with bad poetry, or write poetry in a foreign language."[52] The adaptation he had in mind meant critical selection from China's literary heritage, not inept borrowing of old expressions of which many are dead and can no longer be used today.[53]

Deeply convinced of the value of Chinese culture and the greatness of Chinese literature, he opposed the tendency to Westernize Chinese poetry but accepted a judicious adoption of "Europeanized sentence structures" when it aided the creation of complex imagery. His view was that simplicity is different from childishness, and the latter is not a virtue in poetry; in this he agreed with Fu Szu-nien (1896–1950), who accused the Chinese writers of the early 1920's of "manifesting sterility of thought" when they said they were trying to write simply.[54] Wen felt that it was desirable to learn from Western poets the art of creating complex imagery, but to borrow directly whole sets of images, as Kuo Mo-jo did in his *Goddess*, would be divorcing Chinese poetry from its proper cultural context, which Wen called "local color."[55] Kuo's multiple references to Venus, Apollo, Cupid . . . even Christ were most objectionable to Wen, who wondered if the poet was not a Westerner speaking the Chinese language. He admonished Kuo to learn to appreciate the intrinsic value of Chinese culture—its quietude and refinement—and not to be overwhelmed by the crude slogans of the Westerners. The *Red Candle* abounds in demonstrations of Wen's tenet. The loyal minister image used in his praise of Keats is followed by a direct quotation from the third-century stateman Chu-ko Liang, "Your minister (*ch'en*) will exert and exhaust himself [to serve you] until he dies!" It immediately brings to the mind of a Chinese reader the vivid picture of a traditional Chinese sovereign-minister relationship which Wen equated with the art-artist relationship. In "The Sheath" he used a long sequence of Chinese images, including the historically celebrated lovers Liang Shan-po and Chu Ying-t'ai, the most famous archer in Chinese history—the Han dynasty general Li Kuang, the Taoist god T'ai-i, and the T'ang poet Li Po. One of the most skilfully employed metaphors is the "candle wick" in his "Red Candle." "Burned wick," or "wick burned into ashes," pronounced *hui-hsin* in Chinese, also means "to be disappointed." Thus the lines,

As you shed a drop of tear, you lose a bit of your heart.
Though tears and disappointment (a consumed heart) are your fruit,
The creation of light is your cause.

are at once appropriate and suggestive.

But Wen was not committed to cultural chauvinism. He allowed his dedication to art to transcend national boundaries when he defended the use of "local color" not for its own sake, but to enrich the art of all mankind. His motto was that a full-color oil painting is much richer than a one-color pencil sketch, and that art thrives in "unity in variety," not monotony. His world had been opened wide to the variety of Western poetry and painting, with ample attractive models for him to imitate and emulate. The choice of Tennyson's "Palace of Art" as the prologue to "The Sheath" was not accidental. Wen acknowledged openly the sources of his nonChinese images.[56]

In general, he preferred the critical criteria of the Art-for-Art's-Sake school. In actual application, however, he found it difficult to be consistent. His "cultural context" or "local color" theory is from Taine, whose idea he skillfully paraphrased in November, 1922:

Poetry, like any other form of art, is an embroidery with time as its warp and space its woof. . .because it is born from life, and life is no more than the footprints of time and space.[57]

Shortly afterwards he made use of this criterion to comment on a modern anthology, and concluded that it was good poetry because it reflected the "spirit of the time—the twentieth century," which he described as "motion, rebellion, science, cosmopoli-

tanism, and the unconquerable optimism of youth."[58] Yet, in
February, 1923, as he argued for "pure art," he had to admit
that "to appreciate art one must sever oneself from reality." He
had to stand against the Art-for-Life's-Sake school, or the real-
ists who insisted on using art to interpret and comment on life.[59]
Thus the more zealously he defended his position, the more
conscious he became of the gap between his attitude toward
art and the harsh reality that faced every Chinese. He continued to find some comfort in the thought that his belief in
pure art was not selfish, that his determination to promote a
literary movement in this spirit would rejuvenate Chinese literature and culture, and that his self-chosen role of art critic would
educate the Chinese and uplift the level of Chinese aesthetic
appreciation. But he was not completely happy with his own
rationalization.[60]

VII   *At Colorado Springs (September 1923–September 1924)—
Cézanne and Matisse*

What made him most unhappy in Chicago, in spite of his
feverish study and writing and social activities, was still loneliness. He wanted to go to Boston where a few of his Tsing Hua
friends had congregated, but a letter from his best friend, Liang
Shih-ch'iu (1902–   ) helped him decide to move to Colorado.
"My life in the past year has been very miserable," he wrote in
reply, "there is nobody around to talk to except a girl classmate
with whom I occasionally exchanged a few casual remarks on
literature. I have had enough, and from now on I must hang on
to one of you."[61] In late summer 1923, he transferred to Colorado
College.

He and Liang Shih-ch'iu, a literature major, lived in the same
rooming house and boarded with the landlady.[62] They almost
never saw the landlord, a compositor working night shifts at a
newspaper plant. The landlady and her three daughters, whom
the two Chinese students had to face at every meal, were very
uninteresting. The two women roomers occupying the floor
above them were even more ordinary. With these ladies Wen
and Liang had nothing in common. Lack of congenial company
and finances caused them to move to Hagerman Hall[63] on cam-

pus, which operated no dining service. To save money they often lived on a loaf of bread and a pot of tea or coffee which they prepared on an alcohol burner in their room. Gradually they expanded their "home-cooking" menu a bit to include fried eggs. The absentminded poet did not always have luck with the burner; at least once he knocked it over and the curtains nearly caught fire. In panic Wen burned his hands and lost a good portion of his rich black hair and bushy eyebrows.

There were altogether nine Chinese students at the college, and they organized a club.[64] The campus atmosphere at Colorado Springs being much less cosmopolitan then, they kept very much to themselves and had little association with their American schoolmates. Even Wen who had had much social contact with the Americans in Chicago spent his off-hours entirely with Liang.

Wen was the only Chinese student majoring in art at that time. His talent and personality were quickly recognized and appreciated by his teachers, the Leaming sisters, who were the only art professors there. The small size of the art class made possible good teacher-student contact. Once Professor Susan F. Leaming observed to Liang Shih-ch'iu, "Mr. Wen is really a rare artist. You don't have to look at his work, he himself is a work of art. Look at the lines on his face, the smile on his lips, there is perfect rhythm about him."[65] His hair, a windswept loose bush, covered his neck. The black rims of his eyeglasses had given way to white metal. A black necktie and a paint-stained studio smock completed his rather Bohemian getup that soon became a familiar campus sight. He had stopped pencil and charcoal sketch practices, painting now exclusively in oil. He was everready for his brush and easel, and never wanting to be caught out of his battle dress, so he wore his smock everywhere. His painting, however, was just the opposite of his living habits. It was "meticulous and very beautiful," and yet he seemed to be doing it so effortlessly; "he had a feeling of rhythm of line and color that was so natural and easy."[66] Professor Leaming was so impressed with his work that she encouraged him to submit an entry to an annual exhibit at New York. Whereupon he locked himself in his room for a month working on his entry, refusing to be interrupted even for dinner.

A sense of urgency impelled Wen to learn fast and accomplish

something—an urgency generated by his conviction that the
Americans had gone way ahead of the Chinese in their aesthetic
cultivation, therefore he must catch up with them—and by his
intense dislike of living among those Americans who looked
down upon the Chinese as a race.[67] He applied himself to the
canvas with a feverish intensity which translated itself into
powerful pure colors and sinewy forms—the latter very much
aided by his background in and mastery of Chinese calligraphy.
The art courses introduced him, if not in great depth, at least
systematically to the evolution of the great Western traditions.
Fra Angelico's brilliant, well-defined hues attracted him, though
he preferred to transpose those colors onto nature and thus
found the Impressionists around the turn of the twentieth century
much more suitable for his palette.[68] Cézanne he adored, the
Pointillist Signac he imitated, and he even did portraits à la
Matisse and Derain at their Fauvist height; one of them shocked
the model, his friend Liang Shih-ch'iu, who argued with him
because he turned away from the Chinese landscape painting
tradition and preferred Chinese floral painting—the type represented by Ch'en Shih-tseng (1876–1923)—for the dash and energy of its calligraphic brushstroke.[69] Yet Wen would not follow
Ch'en Shih-tseng; for that Wen would rather find satisfaction
in Chinese calligraphy itself, which he did. It was the man, the
artist, and the unrestrained assertion of his individuality through
the Impressionist's and the Fauvist's canvas that arrested Wen's
attention.

Liang Shih-ch'iu said that thanks to Wen's failure to win
more than one recognition in that all-important year's end ex-
hibition in New York, the world gained a fine poet and scholar;
others, however, regretted it, bemoaning the loss of a potential
painter of genius.

Wen and Liang were required to take a make-up course in
mathematics. Liang did, but Wen refused, saying that he would
rather not graduate than waste his time on something he did
not like. There were two courses in Liang's program, one in
modern poetry which dealt with about twenty late nineteenth-
century and early twentieth-century poets, and one in Tennyson
and Browning. Although these courses were not a part of his
curriculum, Wen went to the classes with Liang and studied

seriously on his own. He liked particularly Kipling for his rhythm, and Hardy and Housman for the strength and depth of their feeling, so quietly expressed and yet so disquieting. Both he and Liang were primarily absorbed in these poets who dominated their off-class discussions. It was during these discussions and with Liang's encouragement that Wen's interest in literature, particularly poetry, gradually overpowered his interest in painting, finally leading to a decisive change in career.

His stay of a year at Colorado Springs was rather uneventful. However, a few episodes occurred to bring the patriot in him to the foreground. One of his Chinese schoolmates there was denied service by a barber; one graduation ceremony Wen witnessed embarrassed the Chinese students because American girl graduates refused to march in pairs with them in the procession; and a quarrel of poems in the campus paper.[70] The last started with an anonymous poem entitled "Chinee" in the campus publication, *The Colorado College Tiger*, on March 25, 1924, which asked what lay behind the masklike faces of the Chinese students.[71] In a tone half-serious and half-jesting, the author wanted to know if the thoughts of his Chinese schoolmates were of "cunning, of vice, or of wisdom only," and if they preferred their own Oriental "embroidered satins" to American tweeds. To this both Liang and Wen replied with a poem. Liang's was a short one, comparing the bewildered author of the "Chinee" with one who adored the beauty of the corals on the king's crown, and yet wondered about what they looked like at the "bottom of the far off Pacific." He told the questioner that the corals were as red as the "petrified blood of Christ." Wen wrote six stanzas of blank verse to challenge the questioner to "sit down and sip a cup of tea" with him. But,

> You who would not set your thoughts afloat. . .
> You who are so busy and impatient
> Will not discover my meaning.

So Wen chose to be silent, and he said,

> In silence I shall bear you
> . . .a jade tea-cup

Transluscent and thin,
Green as the dim light in a bamboo grove;
I shall bear you an embroidered gown
Charged with strange, sumptuous designs—
Harlequin in lozenges,
Bats and butterflies,
Golden-bearded, saintly dragons
Braided into irridescent threads of dream;
I shall bear you sprays
Of peach-blossoms, plum-blossoms, pear-blossoms. . . .[72]

Through the gifts that the Orient had to offer rather than his own words which the questioner could not understand, Wen believed that the Chinese would be appreciated, perhaps not in the way they should be appreciated but at least appreciated. A note of sarcasm was woven into these lines; Wen implied that his country and culture were above and beyond the understanding of an American who could call him a "Chinee." The reply gained the Chinese students considerable prestige on the campus, and thereafter he heard no more slighting expressions.

Some shifts in Wen's view of poetry were reflected in the essays he wrote at Colorado Springs. His essay on Tagore, written in late 1923, attributed little value to profundity of thought in poetry, if it failed to communicate directly and forcefully with the reader.[73] To him, literature is the expression of real life, and even metaphysical poetry fails as poetry if it relates an intellectual experience that can hardly be shared with everybody. Wen criticized Tagore for his "failure to grasp reality." The Indian poet might have felt the beauty of "soul," said Wen, but he failed to convey the beauty of "senses." As to the form of poetry, Wen compared lyrical poetry with painting and stressed the importance of form. He agreed with Walter Pater who saw the most perfect union of form and content in lyrical poetry. Wen's theory of form seemed to be based on the tenets of Impressionism expounded by Shaftesbury, Akenside, through Keats down to Swinburne: Man has a natural propensity toward form—a manifestation of his innate aesthetic sense which is linked to his innate affection for virtue. One notices here how the traditional Chinese sense of the affinity between the beautiful and the moral worked in Wen's mind.

In developing further his theory of poetic form, Wen in Colorado remained the same as the Wen in Chicago. But his new view on the relationship between literature and life which yielded the formula "literature of life" moved much closer to the "literature for life" school of thought which he had condemned only several months before. With his essay on Tagore, he bade farewell to his earlier attitude that art must be appreciated in spite of, rather than in connection with, reality.

VIII *In New York City (September 1924–May 1925)—Dramatics and Politics*

Wen left Colorado in the summer of 1924 with an excellent academic record but without receiving any degree.[74] The nonconformist in him caused him to seek learning in substance and to resist any set curriculum toward a diploma, and his move to find a more challenging intellectual life in New York was anything but a thoughtless decision.[75] Noting Wen's fondness for incense burning, featured prominently in the *Red Candle*, its rich imagery involving the irresistible waft of smoke forever rising in graceful patterns—sublimating itself and its worshipful companion—toward the ethereal blue, Liang gave a precious censer to Wen and waved goodbye, while he himself set out for Boston. Wen enrolled at the Art Students' League of New York, but the active rhythm of life there promptly rekindled his interest in dramatics. Among the many Chinese students in New York at the time, Wen associated closely with Hsiung Fo-hsi (1900–1965) and Yü Shang-yüan (1897–   ), both majoring in drama.[76] In Boston there was also a sizable group of Chinese students. Together they planned the staging of several plays, including the "P'i-pa chi" ["The Lute Song"]. Wen collaborated with Hsiung Fo-hsi in the writing of a one-act play. At the same time he was working on a play in English based on the story of Yang Kuei-fei, the favorite of the T'ang Emperor Ming-huang. What kept him occupied most was stage and costume designing. "I have been so busy that I can hardly breathe," he complained to Liang Shih-ch'iu. "I did not go to a single class last week. This week perhaps it will be the same. But the opening date [of our play] is drawing near, and we have only re-

hearsed one of its five acts. I am doing everything in the art
department all by myself."[77] Unable to concentrate on his painting and too busy to write poetry, for a long period after his
arrival he was completely absorbed in drama. However, the
whirlpool of activities, designing scenes, rewriting scripts, re-
hearsing and staging, did not completely drown the poetic muse
which surfaced to respond to some of the disturbing encounters—
his own strange interludes—as he confided in his closest friends:

> The eye gladdened; touched the heart;
> The meeting is done, let us part.
> Courtly smiles will harden to grins,
> Better end love where love begins.
>
> A lawless shuttle is that of Fate.
> Ere grief is woven, change is late,
> Let us warp and woof remain
> Clean threads from love's freakish stain.
>
> Let us part! our meeting is through,
> Though heart may hunger, heart may rue.
> Your friendship's smile was undream'd of,
> Still less hoped your signs of love.
>
> Thus in after years if again we meet,
> I famishing still, you replete,
> Glad and unshamefaced I'll say:
> "Once we met but did not stay."
>
> "Once we met, our paths converged,
> All currents of my being surged;
> Once we met and parted soon."
> In after years let my heart croon.[78]

Inspired by Eugene O'Neill, he and his friends decided to
form a "Chinese Drama Reform Society"[79] to improve Chinese
drama. Largely because of Wen's interest, the society decided
to start its work by publishing a magazine. Wen had been wanting to do this for a long time, but his plan had failed to material-
ize because his collaborators, members of the Tsing Hua
Literary Society like Liang Shih-ch'iu and Wu Ching-ch'ao
(1901–   ), all had left China for the United States. Now
they came together in the New York area, and Wen applied

himself seriously to the task and went so far as to draft the table of contents for four issues.[80] Originally started with the idea of a journal of dramatics, under Wen's planning the outline looked more and more like a general literary and art magazine. Besides his own poetry, Liang's literary criticism, and Hsiung's plays, the plan included as regular contributors the poets Hsü Chih-mo and Ping Hsin, the novelists Kuo Mo-jo and Yü Ta-fu, the essayist Lu Hsün, the linguist Y. R. Chao, the architect Liang Szu-ch'eng, and the sociologist P'an Kuang-tan. Among the Western artists and writers to be introduced in the magazine were Whitman, Cézanne, Synge, Aubrey Beardsley, and Fenollosa. "Cultural nationalism" was agreed upon as the philosophy of the journal; Wen explained in a letter:

The peril that lies in wait for our country is that not only we will be politically and economically conquered, but our culture also will face ruin. To be culturally conquered is a thousand times worse than any other kind of defeat. Who else besides us can bear the responsibility of turning the tide?. . . .That is why in the first issue Chinese painting, calligraphy, traditional opera, and other Chinese arts will be included. . . .In the fifth issue we probably will discuss the literary renaissance in Ireland.[81]

The Chinese students in the New York area were divided into several groups of which the Chinese Drama Reform Society was one. Two others were the Ta-chiang (Great River) Society and the Ta Shen-chou (Great China) Society.[82] The former had been formed in the summer of 1924 when Liang Shih-ch'iu, Wen I-to, Lo Lung-chi and a few other Tsing Hua alumni then studying in Wisconsin and Minnesota gathered in Chicago and formulated their political platform, including nationalism to safeguard China from foreign encroachment, democratic reform of government to oppose the warlords, and state leadership in economic development toward industrialization to oppose communism. To varying degrees all groups were imbued with nationalism, and dedicated to the building of a stronger, richer, and more glorious China. There was an annual convention of all Chinese students in the eastern United States, which was the occasion for these groups to come into formal contact and compete with one another in membership drives. At first Wen was

merely interested in the cultural activities these groups spon-
sored. Close contact with friends like Lo Lung-chi, whose political interest was ardent, and daily spirited discussion on China's
political problems spurred Wen's enthusiasm until finally he
became an active organizer for the Ta-chiang Society.[83] It was
also planning a magazine, with Liang Shih-ch'iu as the principal
editor. Neither Wen nor Liang, however, had any clear political
program in mind. Wen even admitted in the spring of 1925 that
"up to now the definition of our 'nationalism' still has not been
decided."[84]

Although his heart was never in politics, Wen in New York
was steadily becoming a convinced cultural nationalist. He had
just about reached the decision to give up painting for literature;
yet before he announced it he said he would study and promote
Chinese painting upon his return to China. Between the staging
of plays he read and wrote poetry at night, often all night. The
focus of his literary interest had shifted from Tagore to Sarojini
Naidu, the patriotic poet of India, from Housman to Synge and
Yeats, and from Keats to Whitman. He said to Hsiung Fo-hsi,
"the principal gift with which a poet is endowed is 'love,' love
for his country and his people," which was an echo of his letter
addressed to his brother about two years before.[85] The feeling
he had then about the humiliation of the Chinese in Chicago
now returned to him with greater intensity. He wanted to write
a "series of sketches in blank verse, or like William Ernest
Henley's 'In Hospital,' to depict it."[86] The first result was his
"Laundry Song":

> (One piece, two pieces, three pieces,)
> Washing must be clean.
> (Four pieces, five pieces, six pieces,)
> Ironing must be smooth.
>
> I can wash handkerchiefs wet with sad tears;
> I can wash shirts soiled in sinful crimes.
> The grease of greed, the dirt of desire . . .
> And all the filthy things at your house,
> Give them to me to wash, give them to me,
>
> Brass stinks so; blood smells evil.
> Dirty things you have to wash.

Once washed, they will again be soiled.
How can you, men of patience, ignore them!
Wash them (for the Americans), wash them!

You say the laundry business is too base.
Only Chinamen are willing to stoop so low?
It was your preacher who once told me:
Christ's father used to be a carpenter.
Do you believe it? Don't you believe it?

There isn't much you can do with soap and water.
Washing clothes truly can't compare with building warships.
I, too, say what great prospect lies in this—
Washing the others' sweat with your own blood and sweat?
(But) do you want to do it? Do you want it?

Year in year out a drop of homesick tears;
Midnight, in the depth of night, a laundry lamp . . .
Menial or not, you need not bother,
Just see what is not clean, what is not smooth,
And ask the Chinaman, ask the Chinaman.

I can wash handkerchiefs wet with sad tears,
I can wash shirts soiled in sinful crimes.
The grease of greed, the dirt of desire . . .
And all the filthy things at your house,
Give them to me—I'll wash them, give them to me![87]

Wen's own note to this poem explains that because laundry work
was the most common occupation of the Chinese in America,
Chinese students here were often asked, "Is your father a
laundryman?" Wen, however, did not specify whether he ever
had to answer this question. Instead, he noted the symbolic
significance of washing away someone else's filth patiently and
without complaint, which is another expression of his ideal of
self-sacrifice. In its form and theme, the poem resembles Thomas
Hood's "The Song of the Shirt," and Kipling's assertive rhythm
and Swinburne's insistent alliteration are also quite manifest.[88]

The news of Sun Yat-sen's death reached New York in April,
1925, inspiring Wen to write a long eulogy entitled "The God
of the South Sea," and paint a portrait of Sun for the memorial
service organized by the Chinese students in New York.[89] The
eulogy was a one hundred fifty-two-line poem in which Wen

attributed the acme of wisdom to Sun Yat-sen and ranked him along with Lenin, Gandhi, and Abraham Lincoln. The publication of the poem, however, caused him some doubts. He did not wish to print it in the *Ta-chiang Quarterly* for fear that "it might color the political stand of the Ta-chiang Society, as the poem praises Sun Yat-sen, hence indirectly pats the Kuomintang on the back."[90] He stated no specific reason for his objection to being friendly to the Kuomintang, except that "our *party* wants to raise its own standard. It will not seek anybody's favor nor will it be used by anybody."

Most of the Tsing Hua graduates studying in America sought and obtained extensions of their stays in order to complete the requirements for their degrees, but Wen was an exception. He did not think much of an academic degree and was anxious to return to China to pursue his study of art and literature by himself.[91] In April, 1925, he ended his school life. While waiting for his traveling companion Yü Shang-yüan, he lived with Hsiung Fo-hsi and wrote essays on nationalism in modern American poetry, the prospect of reforming Chinese drama, and his art theories. Conscious of how his recent thoughts affected his poetry, he wrote several in the classical Chinese heptasyllabic quatrain and the *lü-shih* (regulated verse) style:

For six years I learned from the foreign,
I remain unsure about my verses, completed in a strange tone.
Volumes of T'ang masters' works I've read until they are worn ragged,
It's time to halt before a precipice, and return
    to write in the classical mode.

Vague is the direction ahead for the world of art.
Change and renewal require much patient support—
The new hairdo in town admires a bun one-foot high, and yet
The robes of the two kings in the hall are floor-length.
Should we rush to abandon our horses just for
    the chance of striking good fortunes?
Postponing the sacrifice can indeed spare the life of a doomed sheep.
China lacks not varieties of stones from other mountains,
Behold, the glory of Li Po and Tu Fu rises sky high![92]

Because of the classical diction employed in these poems, certain overtones cannot be readily rendered into English with comparable economy of words. The reference to "foreign" in the first line, *chiu-i*, carries the traditional derogatory sense of "nine barbarian tribes." In the second poem, "abandoning horses" refers to an old Chinese legend about losing one's horse and yet in the end the loss results in greater gain; here Wen is questioning whether the Chinese should abandon what has proven value just to gamble on greater gain. The "sheep" story is a turn of an old proverb which suggests that it is not too late to do the right thing even though there has been an interruption, such as his interlude with Western art and poetry.

On the eve of Wen I-to's return to China, to a world so familiar and yet so disconcerting because a new life totally strange to him was soon to begin there, he reflected on his experience in America and realized that the three years had not been passed in vain: His critical and analytical reading of modern Western poetry elevated the art of his own *pai-hua* poetry. Some scholars, such as V. T. Sukhorukov of the Russian Academy of Sciences, regard the poems "Lone Swan," "Remembering Chrysanthemum," and "Red Beads" produced while in America as the very best Wen ever wrote.[93] In the development of the style of his *pai-hua* poetry, the influence of Keats gave way to that of Kipling and Housman. His views on art and literature shifted from spiritual value, through the impressionistic ideal of physical sensations, to naturalism and realism. The cultural patriot in him matured from a purely sanguine Captain Decatur to a relatively more realistic, though still vague, nationalist.[94] His sense of mission in the role he assigned himself changed from creating art and beauty, through crusading for a new literature of high artistic quality, to promoting cultural nationalism. The last was what caused him perplexity, as he wrote:

My sailing date has yet to be set, but not later than June in any case. I still have no idea where to go, and this is a great cause for concern. One thing, however, is certain, and that is to go home. As long as it is our homeland, it does not really matter even if I should drift around in Shanghai as Kuo Mo-jo and Yü Ta-fu are doing now. "The *chün-tzu* (cultivated man of integrity) does not permit his character to be undermined by poverty." The poorer, the more romantic. . . .[95]

So he said, but being a man with a deep sense of responsibility toward his family, the bravado merely served to accentuate his worry. Thus he addressed his farewell letter to Liang Shih-ch'iu, who was to stay on in America:

There is no job waiting for us [he was traveling with Yü Shang-yüan and Chao T'ai-mou] in China; we are but pursuing a dream. . . .[96]

CHAPTER 4

A Poet of the Crescent School (1925-1928) –from Politics to Poetics

If that touch of sunset in the creek
quietly slipped away as it quietly came;
if it wasn't my wish not to keep you then,
that heart of mine was no longer the same.

If once again it's dusk, pale and grey
harboring once again many a bat's wing;
if it wasn't my wish not to think of you then,
I couldn't have thought of anything—anything.

If fallen leaves scurry—so many routed troops,
and from outside my window dark shadows stare;
woman, how could it be thinking of you,
if this heart of mine is no longer there?

If the autumn night is lonesome like this. . .
hey! who's that talking next to my ears?
It's not your voice, woman, obviously not,
if it insists that I be hers, only hers.

Wen I-to, "Chagrin"[1]

I Return to China

IN June, 1925, with his bags full of books of modern Western poetry, Wen I-to returned to his old home at Hsi-shui after exactly three years' absence.[2] The initial excitement of reunion soon gave way to an increasing anxiety about his career.[3] There was not much prospect in China for a creative artist skilled in oil painting. Partly as a matter of necessity and partly because of the decision he had reached in New York about educating his compatriots in art, he joined his friends Chao T'ai-mou and Yü Shang-yüan at the Peking School of Fine Arts where he was made dean of instruction.[4] He brought his wife and daughter to Peking that autumn to start what he hoped to be a settled life. His artistic and dramatic senses spurred him to design an unusual décor for his rooms. After much trouble, he secured enough pitch-black nongloss paper for the wall, banded with a gold frieze, on which he drew the pattern of Han dynasty tomb relief carvings—horse-drawn war chariots complete with ancient warriors in battle dress. For additional adornment, he proceeded to design his own paintings based on the lives and works of his favorite poets. But before he could complete his own small palace of art and poetry, life became unsettled again.[5] Within a year the warlord, Chang Tso-lin, had seized control of Peking and one of his men arbitrarily merged all the public institutions of higher learning in that city; Wen lost out in the ensuing reshuffle of personnel.

Meanwhile, in addition to his academic and administrative duties at the art school, Wen taught a few hours a week at Peking University. Relating himself to the reality around him and developing a life style of his own proved, however, to be a trying task. For a while his interest in politics involved him actively in public rallies and made him envision heroic deeds for the Ta-chiang Society, which were to be dashed by the stark facts of the bloody struggle that culminated in the traumatic Communist–Kuomintang showdown of 1927.[6] Stimulated by the experiences of a returned native, he overcame many distractions to produce the second volume of verse which secured him an esteemed position among twentieth-century Chinese poets. It was, however, his interest in literary criticism which first established his leadership in an entirely new school of modern Chinese poetry, and then led him to reconsider his views and recast his own role in Chinese intellectual movements.

He left New York with a grave sense of responsibility for spreading the Ta-chiang Society's message in China. The other responsible members of the society, Lo Lung-chi, Liang Shih-ch'iu and Wu Ching-ch'ao, all remained in the United States. Wen was the lone evangelist, preaching the nationalism which he had failed to define earlier that year. Shortly before his departure from New York, he and his Ta-chiang friends had agreed on a general declaration of the principles for their society. After several months of discussion, the declaration was finally made public in October, 1925.[7] Although a joint work, the document has the eloquence and zest typical of Wen I-to. The first chapter of the declaration asserts, on the basis of the Darwinian theory of survival, that world history is the story of conflict between imperialistic aggression and nationalism. It cites the Caucasian conquest of the American Indians and the subjugation of African Negroes by the white people to show the pattern of struggle for existence that would soon engulf China if the Chinese should fail to defend themselves. The second chapter analyzes the decline of China's fortunes over the previous one hundred years, quoting Tseng Kuo-fan (1811-1872), Liang Ch'i-ch'ao, and others to prove that the aggressive foreign powers were largely responsible for most of the difficulties China had encountered. It denounces Western economic and cultural enterprises in China as colonialism. Referring pointedly to the Tsing Hua School, it states;

Unenlightened education leaves an evil influence worse than that of lack of education; but Westernized education is still worse than unenlightened education. . . .It is true that nowadays among the students who have studied abroad there are many who were supported by Western missions. . . .[this may speak for the Western interest in aiding Chinese education]. But in reality these educated students with their Westernized habits, speech, writing, views, and thought, are the very ones to imperil China's future because they have forgotten their cultural origins. . . .There is more than one way to carry out cultural aggression. Under the pretext of returning the indemnity funds, certain foreign powers have sought to control the educational and publishing enterprises in China.[8]

The third chapter defines the aim of the nationalism advocated by the Ta-chiang Society as the freedom of a nation to develop itself politically, economically, and culturally.[9] The Ta-chiang Society objected to Western cultural interference, but not necessarily Western cultural influence, in China because the society maintained that there was no absolute good or bad about a culture. Only when the West insisted on its cultural superiority and sought to impose it on China, the Ta-chiang Society would rise to resist it. The society was willing to see a "natural intercourse among cultures in order that they may freely adjust themselves in the normal course of human progress."[10] Finally, the declaration outlines a program of action calling for "domestic reform and resistance to foreign aggression."[11] Arousing a spirit of nationalism, removal of all government leaders too senile to understand the modern world, elimination of Western religious education, and industrialization of China through state socialism to avoid class conflict, were the principal tasks that the Ta-chiang Society urged China to undertake without delay.

This was the political program to which Wen was committed. He participated in different caucuses to promote the Ta-chiang Society, but he ran into strong competition from other political groups. The Awakened Lion (*Hsing-shih*) Society which Tseng Ch'i (1892–1951) and Li Huang (1895–   ) started in France was publishing a journal under the same name to oppose the rapidly expanding Communist influence.[12] In its political program, it closely resembled the Ta-chiang Society, but, as Wen reported to Liang Shih-ch'iu in January, 1926,

Members of the Awakened Lion Society, for example Li Huang, are but bookworms who can only theorize on doctrine. I am afraid the realization of nationalism in China still awaits the Ta-chiang Society. This, Li Huang has admitted.[13]

At this time Wen had decided that the Ta-chiang Society should join forces with the Awakened Lion Society in organizing a Federation of Nationalist Groups in Peking.[14] The principal objective of this federation was to "fight communism." "The Red disaster in China is spreading," Wen told his partisans in America. "Consequently our responsibilities are all the more weighty and the progress of our work all the more difficult. In the near future nationalism and communism will come to a severe collision. I hope our comrades will return en masse ... to take concrete action. Otherwise, the people might become disappointed with us." He reported with enthusiasm that the declaration of his society was favorably received and many people had copied and posted it on their walls as a daily reminder. In March, 1926, the federation held a mass meeting to protest the advance of Japanese and Russian troops in North-eastern China.[15] Wen attended, but he did not play a leading role. His eyewitness account is revealing:

At the meeting many Red devils sneaked in to make trouble. Consequently, no resolution was passed. The nationalists and the false communists exchanged violent remarks across the table like the cross fire over a no man's land. They carried on in this way till late at night, and then resorted to throwing chairs and benches. A free-for-all ensued. . . .[16]

The deteriorating situation in China sustained Wen's enthusiasm for the Ta-chiang cause. The May Thirtieth Incident, ignited by the murder of a Chinese worker in a Japanese textile factory in Shanghai, greeted Wen's return to China in 1925. The next few months were filled with incidents arising from demonstrations staged in most major cities in protest against foreign infringement of China's interests and sovereignty.[17] Antiforeign, particularly antiJapanese, sentiment surged as Japan increased her troops in Manchuria in December, 1925, and as the Chinese effort to negotiate for the abrogation of the "unequal treaties" was frustrated. Some of Wen's students were among the three hundred Chinese who left Japan in anger in January, 1926. Sino-Russian relations were also worsening as a result of the dispute over the Chinese Eastern Railway. Violent disturbances broke out in Harbin in mid-January.[18] Early in March, 1926, Wen witnessed another incident. A Japanese ship clashed with the Chinese at Taku, for which the Japanese held China responsible and demanded an indemnity. On March 18, a mass demonstration was staged in Peking to urge the government not to bow to Japan. Over forty demonstrators died of police gunfire. Meanwhile, the warlords continued to rule their territories according to their individual whims. The government remained completely ineffective. All these circumstances convinced Wen that some kind of nationalistic movement was urgently needed.

II *The Crescent Society and a New Poetics*

These political activities, serious though they were, failed to make Wen forget his other interests. Between academic duties and political meetings, he yearned to return to his poetry writing. Frequently he complained about the distractions that made him neglect literature. At least once he referred to them as *su-shih* (mundane affairs) and sighed, "For nine months I have been back in China, yet I have only written two poems . . . If this is to continue, what should I do?"[19] He sought company among people who were more interested in literature than politics. He opened his house to them, especially those interested in poetry, who promptly made it their regular gathering center. Among them were the members of the Hsin-yüeh (Crescent) Society,[20] who had been holding biweekly dinner meetings to discuss literature. In March, 1926, when Peking was boiling with anti-foreign demonstrations and interparty political controversies, Wen still could not resist the desire to found a "purely literary journal." Financial difficulties prevented the prompt realization of his plan until Hsü Chih-mo (1895–1931), a Cambridge-educated poet of ebullient energy, appeared on the scene. A few days after his visit with Wen, a poetry section, entitled "Shih-k'an" ["Poetry journal"], under their joint editorship was added to the *Pei-ching ch'en-pao* [*Peking morning news*]. In the inaugural editorial of this publication, Hsü described Wen's studio as the background where the idea of such a journal was first conceived and discussed.

I heard that the house of Wen I-to was the paradise of poets. . . .Last Saturday I went there. The three studio rooms were decorated with unusual taste. He fixed all the walls black, highlighting them with a narrow gold strip. The effect was like a naked African beauty wearing only a pair of gold bracelets and anklets. In one of the rooms a niche was carved in the wall, in which was placed, naturally, a sculpture of Venus de Milo about a foot high. . .Against the totally black backdrop, the soft and warm-colored marble statue was rich in dreamy suggestiveness. . .At dusk, shadows would invade the rooms, bringing in footprints of Mephistopheles to walk all over the place. The interplay of light and shadow during the night would present strange images of unrecognizable forms. . . .[21]

Both Hsü and Wen believed that poetry, like music and the other fine arts, was the medium through which man's creativity was to be manifested. Without appropriate expression in poetry, the spiritual revolution and liberation of the Chinese would not be complete. Hsü said that he could feel the air around him to be full of ideas and thought that begged to be put into expression, and that his duty was to construct a suitable form for them, that is, to discover new forms and new rhythms for modern poetry and the other arts. He agreed with what Wen said in the winter of 1923 that the only sign of perfection of essence is perfect form.

As Theophile Gautier, with whom Wen had much in common, had done for French poetry half a century earlier, Wen developed a doctrine for modern Chinese poetry. He theorized on his dedication to poetry and art, which he had expressed in his earlier poems in the *Red Candle*. A poem, he said, must be carved as a sculpture is carved out of a piece of hard stone.[22] In a series of essays published in April–June, 1926, he argued persuasively for the importance of form.[23] "If we compare poetry to the game of chess," he said, "we can easily understand why poetry without form, like a game of chess without rules, must be such a meaningless thing! . . . But most young poets nowadays, in the name of romanticism, regard the ruleless games they are playing as poetry writing." Pursuing his disagreement with the theory of "natural rhythm" or "natural form" advocated by Hu Shih (1891–1962), Wen admitted that there was form in nature, but insisted that very few forms copied intact from nature could be perfect. Perfection in form could be achieved only after much patient chiseling. He quoted Goethe and Han Yü to support his theory that "The greater the artist, the more he enjoys dancing in fetters."[24] That is to say, the greatness of an artist lies in his ability to dance gracefully in spite of the shackles. Moreover, the shackles (form—structural principles) in the hands of a great artist are transformed into effective tools. In this he also found support in Tu Fu's line, "As I grow older I become more particular about poetic rules."[25]

Wen's theory of poetic form stresses mainly the visual and musical effects created by the poetic language. In his typical propensity for structural finesse, he presented a three-point dictum—poetry must possess beauty in three aspects: musical beauty, or the rhythm and melody in a poem; pictorial beauty, or the colors and forms of graphic images bought forth through words; and architectural beauty, or the evenness and neatness of stanza-forms. Making use of the principle of the English prosodic foot, which he had studied with considerable care,[26] he analyzed the stressed and unstressed syllables in *pai-hua* phrases to show the metrical balance that can be achieved in carefully measured lines.[27] Being preoccupied with the graphic and plastic arts, and having mastered the classical Chinese *lü-shih* form, he saw a rich source of aesthetic power in the pictorial quality of written Chinese characters which lend themselves to the architectural structuring of different stanza forms like so many building blocks, each one neat and square.[28] His belief in the convertibility of poetry, painting, sculpture, and music carried him from Gautier's carefully carved *Emaux et Camées* to Mallarmé's graphic *"Un coup de dés jamais n'abolira le hasard."* Although two years later he criticized the forced union of poetry and painting by the pre-Raphaelites,[29] in 1926 he himself planned to decorate his famous studio with three paintings on the themes of three poems by Ch'ü Yüan (343– 290 B.C.), Tu Fu, and Lu Yu respectively, and he completed the one on Lu Yu.[30] With all this emphasis on form, however, he hastened to explain that to find new forms was not to return the newly liberated Chinese poetry to a prison. "The difference between the old and new forms is that the former is a fixed frame into which we are asked to fit all kinds of content and feeling, while the latter is something we must create to suit each individual subject and image."[31] Therefore, with all his respect for T'ang poetry, he would not advocate a revival of writing *lü-shih*, the neatly and strictly structured regulated verse perfected in the T'ang dynasty.

III   *A Persuasive Demonstration*

He demonstrated his poetics in what he called his first most successful experiment, a poem entitled "Dead Water" which became his best remembered work.

Chè-shih/i-kōu/ chüéh-wàng-te/ szǔ-shǔi,
This is /a ditch/ hopeless /dead water

Ch'ing-feng/ ch'ūi-pu-ch'ı/ pàn-tien/ ı̆-lûn.
Light wind/ blow not up/ half point/ ripple

Pù-ju/ tō-jēng-hsieh/ p'ò-t'ûng/ làn-t'ĕh,
Better/more throw some/ broken brass/ torn iron

Shuăng-hsìng/ p'ō-nı̆-te/ shèng-tsăi/ ts'án-kĕng.
Straightforward nature/pour your/ leftover food/ unfinished soup

The scansion he himself suggested shows that in this first of five stanzas,—five quatrains—in "Dead Water," each line contains one trisyllabic and three bisyllabic feet, a pattern maintained throughout the poem. The position of the trisyllabic foot may vary from line to line, but the variation does not impede a sustained rhythmic flow, well puncuated by the uniformly bisyllabic foot at the line's end. The end rhyme maintains an *a-b-c-b* pattern, and though when the Chinese sounds are Romanized according to the Wade-Giles system, *lun* and *keng* in the above quoted stanza seem to be imperfect end-rhymes, they are musically pleasing as an experienced Chinese reader declaims the poem in Mandarin.

It has been said that Wen failed to take note of the lack of fixed stress in Chinese syllables, and that scanning a Chinese line presents insoluble problems.[32] But the words in this poem are all taken from natural Chinese speech which, subject to some variation in individual speech habits, could give each syllable equal stress (except the third of a trisyllable foot, in most cases), or carry stress on the first syllable of each foot, making them nearly all trochaic and dactylic. In the above illustration, all unmarked syllables are usually unstressed, and the circled marks indicate secondary or lighter stress. When properly read, the demonstration shows that Wen's theory works, and his discovery of the important function of binomes in the poetic language certainly has made many students of Chinese poetry aware of what they were unconsciously doing or failing to do. Later, it will be seen that his discovery was to have a lasting influence.

Though Wen did not specifically elaborate on this illustration of prosodic features, he did demonstrate in the single sample above the musical qualities achieved by prosodic arrangements,

including but not limited to the uniform number of feet in a
line and the ringing end-rhymes. There is a pause pattern by
sense grouping (meaning of the language) in each line and
between stanzas—a slight pause between the second and third
foot generally, and a more noticeable pause between each two
stanzas.[33] The last feature is particularly noticeable between the
third and fourth stanzas, which is introduced with a transitional
word, *na-ma*. There is rhythmic repetition of sound units, such
as *sheng-ts'ai* / *ts'an-keng* in the fourth line, repeating the
rhythm of *p'o-t'ung* / *lan-t'ieh* in the third; they are also
syntactical parallels: leftover-food / unfinished-soup and broken-
brass / torn-iron. Then, too, there is rhythmic repetition of
words and phrases, both for reinforcement of certain images
and sound effects. The very first line is repeated at the beginning of the last stanza—the effect is that of a musical refrain
as well as, rhetorically, a concluding statement that goes back
to the theme, indeed the thematic bar of music.

As Wen said that the new form he was advocating must be
wedded to the individual poem's substance, the carefully measured prosody of the "Dead Water" poem works well largely
because the theme is somber, the tone, one of controlled anger,
and the pace smooth but ponderous. For a more lyrical theme,
that of mourning the death of his young daughter, Wen designed a different musical and architectural form:

> Wàng-tiao-t'a/ hsìang i-tuo/ wàng-tiao-te hūa
> Forget her/ like-a-bloom/ forgotten flower
>
> Na chāo-hsía/ tsai huā-pàn-shang
> That sunrise/ on flower-petal
>
> Na huā-hsīn-te/ i-lü hsiāng
> That flower-center's/one-whiff scent
>
> Wàng-tiao-t'a/ hsìang i-tuo/ wàng-tiao-te hūa
> Forget her/ like a-bloom/ forgotten flower

All seven stanzas of the poem follow the same form, with the
same possible scansion, the first and last lines being the same,
three feet each, and two feet in the second and third lines.
That the scansion depends very much on the stress-and-pause

pattern in this poem is quite evident because in some stanzas the lines are so free-flowing and colloquial that the metrical effect can be felt only if they are read with a consciousness of the stressed and unstressed syllables, such as the second and third lines in the sixth stanza:

> Ju-kuo-shih/ yu-jen yao-wen,
> If   there is person ask
>
> Chiu-shuo/ mei-yu na-ko-jen;
> Just say there is no that person

It is very possible to scan both lines into trimeters, but the sense grouping, and the feeling in the poem, call for almost a slurring-over of the second foot in both lines. It's a grief-stricken voice, fighting back tears and trying, almost inaudibly, to dismiss a well-intentioned but nevertheless superfluous question. The refrain effect, at the beginning and end of each stanza, rings a death knell, its sorrow modified only by the mist—

> As a dream in the wind of spring,
> As in a dream, a bell's ring;

—of tears in the eye? or of the evening haze that muffles the sound of the bell?

Even more noticeably demonstrated is the use of the stressed syllables in natural, colloquial speech in the poem "Fei-mao t'ui," which portrays a rickshaw boy, speaking typical Peking colloquial.[34] The neat lengths of the lines, thirteen syllables in every one of the sixteen lines except two, cannot be scanned into regular feet unless the reader grasps the stressed syllables which quite easily define a rather uniform trimetric pattern throughout the poem. One critic has compared this feature with Gerard Manly Hopkins' "sprung rhythm."[35]

In presenting pictorial beauty through his poetry, Wen continued but further refined the colorful images he had used in such poems as "Autumn Colors" in the *Red Candle*. The exhilarating jade-green of the autumn pool in that poem becomes the emerald on the oxidized brass in "Dead Water," and the regal splendor of the imperial palace is now reflected in a putrid open sewer. But the poet, in irony, sees peach blooms on rusting tin cans, and ethereal gauze in floating grease. It is at once the influence of the Western grotesque persuasion as well as the Chinese Buddhist-Taoist perception of beauty in what appears ugly to mundane eyes. In "Spring Light," the berries of a nandina are coral beads; in "Last Day," the "green tongue" of a banana leaf licks the window pane. Here images are also dramatic, when the leaf doesn't just touch but licks. And the little bubbles "chuckle" in the "Dead Water" to become big bubbles; the sunshine in the "Dirge" "pries" open the sleeping (dead) girl's eyelids. In these and numerous other lines the metaphors are fresh, original, effectively appropriate, bringing to the reader stirringly vivid images both still and in motion.

Unlike in his *wen-yen* days, Wen now rarely employed unfamiliar words. "If anyone should ask / Tell him she never existed" is more natural and colloquial than the vernacular in his *Red Candle*, and yet it fits neatly into the strict prosodic scheme of "Forget Her." The expression *i-lun* in the second line, first stanza of "Dead Water" may be considered a rare exception, but even there it does not sound obtrusive. Wen thus lived up to one of his own poetic dicta; namely, that modern speech can and has to be used in the development of a new Chinese poetic language.

IV *Clashing with Prevailing Literary Trends*

On March 13, 1926, Wen presented his doctrine of form in an essay, "The Form of Poetry." The tone, somewhat brash and impatient, clearly reveals that he had been embroiled in a long and drawn-out war of words. "Poetry has never existed without form and rhythm," he said, "this is a universal truth never questioned before by anybody. And yet nowadays all universal truths have to be proven anew before their establishment, right?. . . ."[36] His argument was more rhetorically overpowering than exhaustively analytic, and his examples, brief and perfunctory, as though he was saying—all these have been chewed over before, why go into them in detail once again! The essay, indeed, was a frontal counterattack on the prevailing literary trends since the May Fourth Movement.

When Wen sailed for America in 1922, there was an upsurge of literary activity in China. The formation of the Literary Research Society the year before, followed by that of the Creation Society, marked the beginning of a movement to give direction to modern Chinese literature; heretofore, the new literature movement had been encouraging rebellion against traditional literature without offering anything constructive in its place. The Literary Research Society, with Mao Tun (Shen Yen-ping, 1896–   ) as its spokesman, first advocated a "humanistic realism." Mao Tun declared in 1921:

We are opposed to the "art for life's sake" theory of Tolstoy, and we are also definitely opposed to the "Art for beauty's sake" type of Chinese literature which admittedly divorces itself from life.[37]

Then, to define the purpose of literature and the responsibility of the writer, he said,

The history of literary development in all countries shows that change in literary trends is always such as to enable literature more closely to represent life, to express the feeling of humanity, to voice man's suffering as well as hope, and to fight against the evil forces that hold him in bondage.[38]

The Creation Society, led by Kuo Mo-jo, Ch'eng Fang-Wu (1894–   ), and Yü Ta-fu (1896–1945), all of whom Wen I-to admired, was founded on the Western Art-for-Art's-Sake ideal. "We want to pursue the perfection and capture the beauty of literature," said Ch'eng Fang-wu in May, 1923.[39] The same ideal was expressed by Kuo Mo-jo with greater clarity:

Literature, like the flowers and grass in spring, is the expression of the artist's inner wisdom. As the poet writes a poem, the composer composes a song, and the painter paints a picture, their works are the spontaneous flow of their talents; just as the ripples raised by a spring breeze on the water, they have no purpose of their own . . . Art itself has no purpose![40]

To be sure, elsewhere in Ch'eng Fang-wu's and Kuo Mo-jo's writings in the early 1920's there were already references to the need for literature sympathetic to the unpropertied class, but the predominating voice of the Creation Society at that time was clearly an expression of the Western "pure literature" ideal which this group of writers had acquired during their study abroad, mainly in Japan.

A major controversy in the new literary movement soon developed between those who continued to argue for the independence of literature, and those who increasingly emphasized the social mission of the writer. The latter group gained in strength. Before long, most of the leading writers agreed that literature had a social mission and that the writer must lead rather than follow social and political developments. To this Wen would consent in part, but not completely. But as soon as the other literary leaders turned to the Russian example which seemed to offer a solution to China's problems, Wen with his political sympathies still on the side of the antiCommunist Ta-chiang Society, stood firm to rally his fellow Crescent writers to fight for the cause of "pure literature."

The increasing Kuomintang and warlord pressure[41] speeded the consolidation of the Leftist writers. There was a sharp rise in their influence on the principal publishers and periodicals. The extreme Leftist Sun Society (T'ai-yang She), a small but vociferous group of writers, launched a relentless attack on every writer whose attitude was not clearly radical.[42] When Kuo Mo-jo of the Creation Society first brought up the issue of "revolutionary literature," the Sun Society claimed leadership in this new literary movement. It touched off a race for recognition as the "most progressive and revolutionary" group among the writers. In March, 1926, Kuo Mo-jo said, "the literature we need at present . . . is realist in form, and socialist in content—this I can say with certainty."[43] About a month later he further clarified his new position by writing his celebrated article "Revolution and Literature," calling the youths (with much of the gusto once shown in Ch'en Tu-hsiu's (1879–1942) "Solemn Appeal to Youth" of 1917) to go to "the soldiers, the people, the factories, and the whirlpool of revolution."[44] A series of articles in the same vein appeared, culminating in Ch'eng Fang-wu's "From Literary Revolution to Revolutionary Literature," which exhorted the intelligentsia to band together, denounced neutralism in literature, and urged the writers to grasp dialectical materialism. "Walk toward the proletarian masses," Ch'eng admonished the Chinese bourgeois intellectuals in November, 1927. "Don't worry about losing your chains!"[45] Within a short span of four years, the Creation Society and the trend of modern Chinese literature had reversed their directions completely.[46]

In the literary winds then prevailing, Wen's doctrine of "form" enunciated in May, 1926, was hoisting sail in the opposite direction, because he held that the merit of a literary work should not be judged by its political message. That he was spared the severe criticism of Kuo Mo-jo and Chiang Kuang-tz'u (1901–1931) owed much to the strength of his argument and his poems, but even more to the preoccupation of those "literary revolutionists" with pressing political and social problems, not with strictly literary problems. Those who read Wen's theory most carefully were students of poetry who, since the beginning of Chinese *pai-hua* literature, had been seeking a suitable new technique. They were impressed by Wen's scholarship and encouraged by his own demonstrations in verse. And Wen, in turn, was emboldened enough to predict that the new poetry would soon enter a new constructive stage, as he declared, "We must admit that this 'form' theory is a strong tide in the development of new poetry."[47] In "Drama at the Crossroads," published in June, 1926, he carried his theory further by maintaining that "the highest goal of art is to attain pure form."[48] In its development toward the highest goal of art, drama was hampered by the prevailing "literary thought" with its exclusive emphasis on "moral, philosophical, and social problems." "One can hardly blame the writers," he said; "Literature, particularly dramatic literature, is easily tinted with philosophical and didactic ideas just as odorous matter readily attracts flies." But over-preoccupation with social messages ruined the art of drama, and he criticized the Chinese imitators of Ibsen and Shaw for merely describing "problems" without writing "plays." He was still an adherent of Arnold's tenet that literature "is criticism of life," but "such great critics of life as Shakespeare and Synge did not rely on problem-plays. Furthermore, merely putting a few fashionable polemical phrases into the mouth of a char-

acter is not writing a good problem-play."[49] He was aiming at
the Creation Society writers, particularly Kuo Mo-jo, when he
said:

If one, simply by dragging out such ancient characters as Ch'ü Yüan,
Cho Wen-chün, and Nieh Cheng, and making them ventriloquize
on socialism, democracy, and the emancipation of women, can claim
to be writing drama, . . . then, frankly, we would rather not have
this sort of drama.[50]

Wen suggested differentiating the content (the thought) from
the form of literature (the art of literary writing). He advised
the writer to avoid becoming mired in an ideological bog, but
to strive for literary excellence. In its emphases, this new argument differed considerably from the view expressed two years
before in his essay on Tagore. Then he wanted Tagore to remain
close to the flesh-and-blood physical life of man, to sing his
joys and bemoan his sorrows, to write *litterature engagée;* now,
tired of polemics, he still sought a direct reflection of life in
literature, but without preaching social gospels. He did not
object to the embodiment of social messages in literature; rather,
he opposed writing social messages of no literary quality. This
led him to advise a younger writer in February, 1928, as follows,

Writings that are vague may leave no deep imprint upon the reader,
but writings that are too obvious often leave a bad impression with
the reader. If a piece of writing is to be too obvious, I would rather
have it vague.[51]

He held fast to the supremacy of art in all forms of intellectual
expression. But, no matter how he reasoned with himself concerning the theory of literature, the content-form dichotomy
remained a source of inner conflict which, according to him, was
as serious as the body-soul conflict. Before he found any formula
for merging the dichotomy into a single entity, as he once
did in Keats' beauty-truth equation and Walter Pater's theory
of lyric poetry, he continued to quarrel with himself.

As social dogma without literary art irritated him, so did the
dogmatic attitudes of his contemporary writers. In his view
they were too self-centered, imitating the theatricality and exhi-

bitionism of Byron without Byron's poetic talent. He felt that a poet's attitude should be "tender, restrained, and kind," in conformity with the advice left supposedly by Confucius.[52] Later, Wen refuted such a view completely.

V   *The Conflict between Art and Reality*

Mainly upon these theories rested Wen's leadership among the poets of the Crescent group. Hsü Chih-mo, whose life is synonymous with the Crescent school in the history of modern Chinese poetry, acknowledged Wen's guidance and contribution.[53] Shen Ts'ung-wen (1902–   ), the novelist associated closely with the Crescent group, observed that Wen "has accomplished more than any other modern Chinese poet in the creation of a perfect style . . . many writers are imitating him."[54] Though Wen stressed "form" in his critical essays, the poems written by him in this period reveal an acute sensitivity to current political and social problems. He was extremely perturbed by the ceaseless fighting and the gathering storm of social revolution. The March 18, 1926, incident reminded him of the May Fourth Movement. One of the first poems he wrote after his return from abroad was "T'ien-an Men" ["The Gate of Heavenly Peace" (in Peking where many student demonstrations took place)], in which he let a rickshaw boy describe the apparitions he saw:

Gosh! it really scared the daylight out of me today!
and my legs are still shaking like crazy.
As I looked they kept closing in on me,
otherwise why would I run like that?
Sir, let me catch my breath . . . ah, that thing . . .
can't you see those dark shadows
their heads chopped off, legs broken, so terrible,
still waving white banners, still talking . . .
It's hopeless at this day and age, whom did they think
     they were dealing with?
Even flesh-and-blood humans can't handle it, much less ghosts.
But they insisted on holding meetings, bah!
     Why couldn't they stay quiet-like?
Look, all of them were but little kids from some nice families.
Weren't they only teenagers? Why oh why?

Weren't their heads stabbed by bayonets?
Sir, they say more were killed yesterday.
I bet they were those damn stupid students again.
And would you believe such weird things, in this day and age:
those students all had enough to eat, enough to drink—
not like my second uncle, he died at Yang-liu-ch'ing a year ago,
but that's an empty stomach that'd driven him to join the army,
otherwise who'd want to face Yama, for no reason at all?
Honestly, I never told a lie before in my whole life,
        but I was thinking,
I'd just filled two coppers' worth of oil, a whole ladle-ful,
in the lamp, why I couldn't see the road no more,
        after I took just a few steps?
No wonder Little Baldie was scared stiff and he
advised everybody not to walk by T'ien-an-men after dark.
Gosh! Let's figure it bad luck on rickshaw pullers,
Tomorrow, ghosts will be walking all over the city of Peking.[55]

They were the ghosts of students, victims of clashes between
demonstrators and the police. They seemed to be multiplying
day by day. The glorious homeland that Wen had dreamed of
and longed for while in America was nowhere in sight. His
disappointing "Discovery" was,

I've come, I shout, bursting out in tears of woe,
"This is not my China—Oh, no! No!"
I've come because I heard your summoning cry.
Riding on the wind of time, raising a torch high,
I came, I knew not this to be unwarranted ecstasy.
A nightmare I found. You? How could this be!
This is terror, a bad dream over the brim of an abyss,
But not you, not what my heart continues to miss!
I ask heaven, ask the winds of all directions.
I ask (my fist pounding the naked chest of the earth)
But there is no answer. In tears I call and call you
Until my heart leaps out—ah, here you are![56]

When Hsü Chih-mo painted Wen's studio with words to set
the tone for their joint endeavor, the "Poetry Journal," Wen
wrote in the same inaugural issue an essay on "Literature and
Patriotism" to commemorate the March 18, 1926, incident.[57] He
regarded patriotism as being as important in literature as "love,

the ephemeralness of beauty, the approach of death, and all universal sentiments suggested by nature." The real source of art was great sympathy which, when developed to the extreme, demanded expression not only in words but in action. He saw poetry in the patriotic spirit of the victims of the March eighteenth incident, which he compared to the Sung poet Lu Yu's wish to join the army at the age of seventy. With "cannons rumbling" beyond his window, he could not ignore reality, even when he was predicting that his "Poetry Journal" was turning a new page in the history of Chinese literature.[58] What he saw in reality caused him more despair and disgust. It was in this moment of bitter frustration that he wrote his famous "Dead Water":

> Here is a ditch of hopelessly dead water.
> No breeze can raise a single ripple on it.
> Might as well throw in rusty metal scraps,
> or even pour left-over food and soup in it.
>
> Perhaps the green on copper will become emeralds.
> Perhaps on tin-cans will peach blossoms bloom.
> Then, let grease weave a layer of silky gauze,
> and germs brew patches of colorful spume.
>
> Let the dead water ferment into jade wine
> covered with floating pearls of white scum.
> Small pearls chuckle and become big pearls,
> only to burst as gnats come to steal this rum.
>
> And so this ditch of hopelessly dead water
> may still claim a touch of something bright.
> And if the frogs cannot bear the silence—
> the dead water will croak its song of delight.
>
> Here is a ditch of hopelessly dead water—
> a region where beauty never can reside.
> Might as well let the devil cultivate it—
> see what sort of world it can provide.[59]

This bitter, satirical protest was directed at the chaos and corruption on the national scene, as well as at the environment of the Peking School of Fine Arts.[60] He never liked his administrative job as dean of instruction, for as such, he could hardly avoid involvement in factional disputes over the presidency of the institution. As early as January, 1926, he had started complaining to his friends about annoying rumors that he, Wen I-to, was coveting that post, and he had threatened to resign then.[61] Now, in July, 1926, an arbitrary reorganization of the school by order of a warlord, compounded with the failure of the administration to pay the faculty for several months at a stretch, drove him home to Hupeh. The journey took him through many areas plagued by the fighting between the Northern Expeditionary troops and local warlords. For some time his friends in Peking were concerned about his personal safety.[62] He stayed home until the end of autumn, and then, in response to P'an Kuang-tan's (1898–   ) urging, he went alone to join the faculty of the Academy of Political Science at Wu-sung founded by Carsun Chang (1896–1969), who later with Lo Lung-chi organized the National Socialist Party. The serious illness of his daughter brought him home again that winter. Her death occasioned a number of deeply touching poems, including the well-known "Dirge."[63] In the spring of 1927, an invitation by Teng Yen-ta (1895–1931) brought him to Wuhan to join the department of political affairs in the Left-wing Nationalist government there. He was put in charge of the preparation of propaganda materials, a job which held his interest only about a month. He returned to the Academy of Political Science at Wu-sung, but shortly afterwards the Nationalist authorities in Nanking ordered the academy closed. He then went to Shanghai where he rejoined his Crescent Society friends and started plans for the magazine, *Crescent*. Financial embarrassment forced him to accept a stopgap job in a government bureau at Nanking. He was appointed to the faculty of the Central University, then named the Fourth Sun Yat-sen University, in the fall of 1927, heading the department of foreign languages and literature, and teaching English poetry, drama, and prose.

Thus we see that during 1927, a stormy year that marked a turning point in twentieth-century Chinese history, Wen I-to, like the multitude of his contemporaries, was quite lost and merely drifted along. The reasons behind his choice of a course of action were complex, involving his own temperament, his sense of values, the politics of the time, the endless literary polemics, and his family. In spite of his association with the Ta-chiang Society, he remained, in truth, only a moderate liberal, idealistic, but totally unprepared and unsuited for harsh political realities. When his Ta-chiang comrades returned to China and became swamped with their own affairs, too busy just trying to survive, the Society promptly disappeared and along with it, Wen's political activities.[64] And yet politics would not leave him alone if he continued to publish. After Ta-chiang, politically he had nothing more to say; his antiCommunist stand had been motivated by nationalism, which by now had been preempted by the Kuomintang, and the harsh measures of the Kuomintang against the Communists were more than he could stomach. Weary of the ceaseless polemics and unwilling to be the lone voice in championing his doctrine of form, he grew tired of being identified as a Crescent poet and constantly coming under attack by the radicals; furthermore, even those friends who favored his doctrine failed to speak up in his support. His strong sense of family responsibility heightened his desire for security. If he had felt less attached to his family, he could have become another Yü Ta-fu, or any one of the many creative writers who continued to drift in the buffeting winds of different ideologies in Shanghai. If he had been able to move to the Left, he could have become another Kuo Mo-jo, or even joined forces with Lu Hsün (1881–1936). Since neither was his lot, he chose the relatively neutral haven of teaching where he could avoid compromising his principle to suit either side. But, as his poems revealed, peace of mind was not so easily obtained.

VI   *The* Dead Water—*A Biographia Literaria*

Bringing his jobless, drifting life to a close, Wen sent for his family, settled down, and began to face the serious challenge of teaching literature. In gathering his thoughts, he reviewed his intellectual endeavors of the past three years as recorded in his poems, revised them, and arranged them for publication under the title of *Dead Water*. Literary circles greeted its appearance in January, 1928, with great enthusiasm. The author's mature power of observation and superior technique were immediately recognized. As Shen Ts'ung-wen said,

The author always maintains a crystal-clear vision, gazing at and penetrating everything in life. He never allows himself to be overwhelmed by transient emotional impulses, nor does he avoid looking at the ugly, the base, and the vulgar. . . . He forever gazes at his object, so attentively and carefully.[65]

Chu Hsiang (1904–1933), another noted poet of the Crescent group who had found many faults with Wen's first collection, the *Red Candle,* was now convinced that the years had brought wisdom and maturity to Wen's poems not to be easily outdone by the works of any other poet in modern China. In addition to the technical perfection of *Dead Water,* Chu saw a resemblance between this work and Coleridge's *Biographia Literaria* in that both were coherent records of the authors' intellectual growth.[66] Chu Tzu-ch'ing, a respected professor of literature and an old friend, discussed the theme of patriotism in *Dead Water* and concluded that Wen probably was the only modern Chinese poet who wrote truly patriotic verses *before* the War of Resistance against Japan.[67] The Russian sinologist Fedorenko noted how the cry of anguish became almost unbearable in the anthology; Sukhorukov has observed, "For the first time in the poetry of Wen I-to reality appeared under an allegorical veil, endowing his imagery with a striking force of persuasiveness." Nearly all Japanese scholars of modern Chinese literature recognize *Dead Water* as the peak of Wen's poetic career and the zenith of *pai-hua* poetry in the 1930s.[68]

Designed by Wen himself, the black and gold cover, in keeping with the décor of his first studio in Peking, sets a solemn and intriguing tone for the anthology. The number of poems collected in it, twenty-eight, may not have been merely coincidental with that same number in William Ernest Henley's "In Hospital," which Wen had said in 1925 he would want to imitate, except that *Dead Water* contains rhymed, not blank verse. The poems fall generally into four groups. The prologue, "Confession," reiterates the author's dedication to beauty, while admitting that he has another "self" undetachable from his real world, however ugly it may be:

> Let me not deceive you, I am no poet,

Even though I adore the integrity of white gems,
The blue pines and immense ocean, the sunset on crows'
     backs,
And the dusk woven with the bats' wings.
You know that I love heroes and towering mountains,
And our national flag unfurling in the wind . . . all these
From saffron to the antique bronze of chrysanthemums.
Remember, my food is a pot of bitter tea.

But aren't you afraid?—In me there is yet another man,
Whose thought follows a fly's to crawl in the garbage can.[69]

The first group consists of some poignant commentaries on life,
"You swear by the Sun" is an example which points out the
impermanence of man:

You swear by the sun, and let the wintry geese on the horizon
Attest to your faithfulness. Fine. I believe you completely,
Even if you should burst out in tears I wouldn't be surprised.
Only if you wanted to talk about "The sea may dry up and the
     rocks may rot. . ."
That would make me laugh to death. Isn't this moment while my
     breath lasts
Not enough to get me drunk? What need is there
     to talk about "forever"?
Love, you know my desire lasts only the duration of one breath,
Hurry up then and squeeze my heart, hurry, ah,
     you'd better go, you go . . .
I have long guessed your trick—no, it's not that you've changed—
"Forever" you have long promised someone else,
     only the dregs are my lot.
What the others get is your essence—the eternal spring.
So you don't believe me? But if one day Death produced
     your own signature,
Will you go? Yes, go to linger in His embrace and only
Talk to Him about your undying loyalty.[70]

"You See" stresses the futility of man's sentiment:

Do you see the sun, like a silkworm after its molting in spring,
All day long it spins without end its golden silk-like rays?
Do you see the robins, sun-glow on their breasts,

resting on the telephone pole,
And sleeping mallards parking themselves at the root of
    an old willow tree?

Before you are displayed the treasures of youth,
My friends, why don't you enjoy what's right in front of you;
You have eyes, you should look further at the surging blue peaks,
But never toward your old home way beyond the hills.

When you listen to the linnets singing of spring on trees,
You should wipe away your tears to sing a song with them.
Friends, homesickness is a merciless devil who can
Turn the spring scene before you into a desert.

Look, the spring breeze has unlocked the ice-sealed creek,
And filling half of it with white teeth that rinse themselves
    in murmuring ripples.
And the fine grass, once again, weaves a poem of green, lush green,
As the tiny silvery banners begin to wave on poplar branches.

Friends, when you at last see spring in hometown,
Spring will be old, and man gone.
So, seek not your home—that thief
Will steal your heart, leave you grief.[71]

"The Drum Singer" alludes to something of his personal experience:

I carry a drum, fitted with a leopard skin,
    Drumming on it I've traveled all over the world.
I've sung songs of all kinds, all colors,
    I've also heard applause ringing on and on.

A setting sun lingers under the eaves,
    Tiptoeing in my sandals I step into my hometown.
"How about that song just for you and me?"
    She rushes toward me, in an upsurge of joy.

I know how to sing of heroes, men of destiny,
    And songs for pretty girls and handsome fellows as well.
But if you ask me about our own song, that very one,
    Heaven knows, my heart in panic, I just can't tell.

I swallow my grief, and call her,
    "Bring me my samisen, hurry up, hurry!
That old drum is a bit too noisy, I want
    To pluck out my song on the strings."

I first play a flock of white doves in a wintry forest,
   Their coral claws stepping on a pile of fallen leaves;
Then you listen to autumnal crickets chirping in the rocks
   Which suddenly turns into a spell of cold rain sprinkling
   the wicket door.

The rain sprinkles on, as tears continue to flow . . .
   I call once more, "My wife," and drop my samisen,
"What song can we sing today, what?
   Since all the songs have gone the way of the tears!

"Why? Why can't you also raise your head?
   Ah, what shall we do, what can we do? . . .
Come, come here! I've drawn out your sorrow,
   I must dry it with my very own lips.

"Just let me look at you this way, my wife,
   As the cold banana leaf gazes at the moon beyond
   the window pane.
Let me adore you in silence, in complete silence,
   Though I just can't think of any song to sing.

"Though a sword whittled us into two branches joined at the stem,
   Look, the posture is not twisted, not at all.
My poor thing, please don't doubt me, please,
   I myself never resented the hand that wielded the sword.

"Don't think too much, and I won't ask questions either,
   When the creek has reached the well's bottom,
   whither does it flow?
I know that you will be forever free from all ripples,
   I want you to moisten my singing throat.

"If the last hope is denied the lone skiff,
   If you refuse me, you, my haven!
As I return at dusk, braving the wind and storm,
   Who's my home, my place of rest?

"But, my wife, before you,
   Allow me not to use either samisen or my drum;
We really don't have any songs to sing, as we
   Are neither sentimental lovers, nor heroes among the brave."[72]

"What Dream" and "Don't Blame Me" deal with moments of man's emotional crisis. Both poems are worthy experiments with new forms:[73]

WHAT DREAM

A line of wild geese crosses the sky's river in a hurry,
Their sad songs pierce her heart through,
        "You, ah, yes, you . . ." she sighs,
     "Where are you calling me, where are you?"

With terror under its arms, dusk closes in on her,
Down to the bottom of her heart sinks a heavy pain.
        "Heavens, ah, heavens!" cries she,
     "What does this . . . does this all mean?"

The road is far, the journey, in the dark,
She reels, balancing on the life-death threshold,
        "Ennui, yes, only ennui," she thinks,
     "I must get rid of you, once for all!"

Resolve all over her face—resolved, but calm . . .
A sudden alarm rings—in the cradle, an infant's cry.
        "My child, yes, my baby," she weeps,
     "What kind of dream am I having . . . am I . . .?"

DON'T BLAME ME

     Don't blame me!
This has been, after all, nothing from the start.
People meet, like duckweeds drifting together on water;
Let them part, like duckweeds on water drifting apart.
     Don't blame me!

     Don't ask me!
Tears are held at the eyes' brim.
You need only say one word;
One word will touch them off in a stream.
     Don't ask me!

     Don't bother about me!
Don't try to rekindle dead ashes, I say.
My heart has long given up for fatigue;
Let it stay asleep, let it stay.
     Don't bother about me!

     Don't touch me!
What are you thinking now, what?
We met casually like duckweeds on water;
We should also casually drift apart.
     Don't touch me!

> Don't worry about me!
> From now on, I've added a lock on the bolt.
> Don't knock on the wrong door ever again;
> For this once, say it was my fault, all my fault.
> Don't worry about me!

"The Last Day" and "The Night Song" represent Wen's best in capturing a profound aesthetic experience out of what seems to be weird, grotesque, or even ugly, much as the Tang dynasty poet, Li Ho (791–817), had done before:[74]

THE LAST DAY

The dewdrops sob in the roof-gutters,
The green tongues of banana leaves lick the window panes.
The four white walls seem to back away from me:
I alone can not fill such a big room.

A brazier aflame in my heart,
I quietly await a guest from afar.
I feed the fire with cobwebs, rat dung,
And snakeskins in place of split wood.

As the roosters urge time, only ashes remain;
A chilly breeze steals over to caress my mouth.
The guest is already right in front of me;
I close my eyes and follow him away.

THE NIGHT SONG

A toad shivered, feeling the chill,
Out of the yellow earth mound crawled a woman.
Beside her no shadow was seen,
And yet the moon was so very bright.

Out of the yellow earth mound crawled a woman,
And yet no crack showed itself in the mound,
Nor was a single earthworm disturbed.
Nor a single thread of a spider web broken.

In the moonlight sat a woman;
She seemed to have quite youthful looks.
Her red skirts were frightful, like blood,
And her hair was draped all over her back.

The woman was wailing, pounding her chest.
And the toad continued to shiver.
A lone rooster crowed in a distant village,
The woman disappeared from the yellow earth mound.

The second group of poems echo his earlier preoccupation with
death except that here the idea is less abstract. They reflect his
personal sorrow over the loss of his daughter, as in "Forget Her:"

> Forget her, as a forgotten flower—
> > That ray of morning sun on a petal
> > That whiff of fragrance from a blossom—
> Forget her, as a forgotten flower.
>
> Forget her, as a forgotten flower,
> > As a dream in the wind of spring,
> > As in a dream, a bell's ring.
> Forget her, as a forgotten flower.
>
> Forget her, as a forgotten flower.
> > Listen, how sweetly the crickets sing;
> > Look, how tall the grass has grown.
> Forget her, as a forgotten flower.
>
> Forget her, as a forgotten flower.
> > No longer does she remember you.
> > Nothing now lingers in her memory.
> Forget her, as a forgotten flower.
>
> Forget her, as a forgotten flower.
> > Youth, what a charming friend,
> > Who makes you old overnight.
> Forget her, as a forgotten flower.
>
> Forget her, as a forgotten flower.
> > If anyone should ask,
> > Tell him she never existed.
> Forget her, as a forgotten flower.
>
> Forget her, as a forgotten flower.
> > As a dream in the wind of spring,
> > As in a dream, a bell's ring.
> Forget her, as a forgotten flower.[75]

or as in his "Perhaps—A Dirge:"

Perhaps you are too tired of crying,
Perhaps you want to sleep awhile.
Then I'll tell the owls not to cough,
Frogs to hush, and bats to stay still.

I'll not let the sunshine pry your eyelids,
Nor let the wind your eyebrows sweep.
Nobody will be allowed to awaken you,
I hold a pine umbrella to shelter your sleep.

Perhaps you hear earthworms turning dirt,
Perhaps you hear grassroots sucking water.
Perhaps prettier than man's cursing voice
Is this kind of music you now hear.

I'll let you sleep, yes, let you sleep—
Close your eyes now, tightly.
I'll cover you gently with yellow earth,
And tell paper ashes to fly lightly.[76]

and, in "I Wanted to Come Home:"

I wanted to come home
While your little fists were like the orchids yet to open;
While your hair still remained soft and silken;
While your eyes shone with that spirited gleam;
I wanted to come home.

I did not come home,
While your footsteps were keeping cadence in the wind;
While your little heart was beating like a fly against the
    window pane;
While your laughter carried that silver bell's ring,
I did not come home.

I should have come home,
While a spell of blur covered your eyes;
While a gust of chilly wind put out a fading light;
While a cold hand snatched you away like a kite;
I should have come home.

I have come home,
While little lights shine on you from fireflies drifting;
While near your ears sad songs the crickets sing;
While with your mouth full of sand you stay sleeping;
I have come home.[77]

And "Collect" strikes a disturbing note of defiance of external forces that deny one's fulfillment, very much parallel to the "Red Beads" lines in the *Red Candle*, only much more sophisticated now.

One day if only Fate would let us go!
Don't be afraid; though a dark tunnel's in our way,
Just proceed boldly; let me hold your hand;
And ignore from where rises that gust of chilly wind.

Only remember what I said today, and take care
Of the tenderness, the kisses, and take care of those smiles,
Gather them all up, yes, that's right—remember what I said,
Pick them all up, along with the string of heart-throbs,
          those coral beads.

Poor dear, how you suffer today—one heart longing for the other—
But then I'll let you collect, collect to your heart's desire,
Collect all the gold we are missing today.
All our love, those fallen petals of intense colors,
You'll pick them up, and wear them all.
                    You'll be wearing the halo of love,
As we continue our journey to, who cares, Heaven or Hell![78]

The third group includes some poems which he started writing while in the United States, such as the "Laundry Song," all showing deep sympathy for his pathetic fellow-countrymen. His "Fei-mao t'ui" depicts a sanguine rickshaw boy whose guileless ways and carefree days end when his body floats up in a river:

I say that guy Mercury-footed was really an odd ball,
I bet after a working morning he just had to take the
          rest of the day off.
At least he had to have two or three ounces of that strong stuff,
and then, getting pretty drunk, he'd hang on you, keep talking.
His mother's! Who had the time to fool around with that guy?
"Why's sky blue?" he'd ask you, just because he had nothing to do.
And he'd blow on that damn flute of his—look at him!
wrapped up in a rag of a padded robe, his wife's, perhaps,
and look at how he polished those two lamps on his rickshaw,
and, as he polished them, he'd ask you how many troops
          Ts'ao Ts'ao had.
He never seemed to finish rubbing those lamps and shafts
          of his vehicle.

I said, "Mercury-footed, why don't you polish up your face
    for a change?"
But honestly, Mercury-footed's rickshaw was really polished
    to a high shine,
polished spotless, perhaps as spotless as his own heart!
Hai! That day, Mercury-footed's body floated up in the river . . .
That poor woman, his wife, certainly had died at the wrong time.[79]

The irony of the rickshaw puller's death, when he seems to be indestructibly full of life, is only matched by the pathos suggested in the death, perhaps earlier, of his wife. Unexplained, the poem leaves the tragedy to the imagination of the reader: Did her death cause his suicide out of despair? Did she commit suicide because she was unable to bear the poverty that was the fate of a rickshaw puller. There is certainly no hint at his mistreating her.

"A Crime" sympathizes with an old peddler who trips and spills his fruit basket, spoiling the chance of bringing dinner home to his family:

The old man tripped and fell with his load of fruits,
white apricots and red cherries, all over the ground.
He got up on his feet, still trembling and shaking,
"I know," he muttered, "this is a crime, today."
"Look, old man, your hands are bleeding, look."
"Ah . . . such good cherries, all smashed now!"
"Old man, you aren't sick, are you?
Why don't you say something. Don't just stand and stare."
"I know this is my fault, today,
At the crack of dawn my son started urging me.
He stayed in bed, cursing and fussing
about why I had not started out for the market yet.

"I knew it wasn't too early this morning,
but I didn't think I'd oversleep.
What am I going to do now, what?
What's the whole family going to eat later?"
He picked up the fruits, but they kept dropping,
White apricots and red cherries all over the ground.[80]

The travels in the past three years broadened his indignation over the humiliation of the Chinese in America into a profound compassion for the misery of the Chinese people as a whole. Thus, a picture of his sad motherland, ravaged by civil war and natural disasters, inspired him to write "The Deserted Village" in May, 1927:

Where did they go? How has it come to pass?
On stoves squat frogs, in ladles lilies bloom;
Tables and chairs float in fields and water ponds;
Rope-bridges of spiderwebs span room on room.
Coffins are wedged in doorways, rocks block windows:
A sight of strange gloom that rends my heart.
Scythes lie rusting away in dust,
Fishing nets, abandoned, rot in ash-piles.
Heavens, even such a village cannot retain them,
Where roses forever smile, and lily leaves grow as big as umbrellas;
Where rice sprouts are so slender, the lake so green,
The sky so blue, and the birds' songs so like dew-pearls.
Who made the sprouts green and the flowers red?
Whose sweat and blood is it that is blended in the soil?
Those who have gone left so resolutely, unhesitatingly.
What was their grievance, their secret wish?
Now, somebody must tell them: "Here the hogs
Roam the streets, ducks waddle among the pigs,
Roosters trample on the peony, and cows browse on vegetable
    patches."
Tell them: "The sun is down, yet the cattle are still on the hills.
Their black silhouettes pause on the ridge, waiting,
While the mountains around, like dragons and tigers,
Close in on them. They glance about and shiver.
Bowing their heads, too frightened to look again."
This, too, you must tell them: "These beasts recall days of old
When evening chill approached and poplars trembled in the
    wind,
They only needed to call once from the hilltop.
Though the trails were steep, their masters would help them,
And accompanying them home there would be the scent of hay.
As they think thus, their tears fall.
And they huddle together, jowl against jowl . . ."
Go, tell their masters, tell them,
Tell them everything, do not hide anything.
Ask them to return! Ask them to return!
Ask them why they do not care for their own cattle.
Don't they know that these beasts are like children?

Poor creatures, so pitiful, so frightened.
Hey, where are you, messenger?
Hurry now, tell them—tell Old Wang the Third,
Tell the Eldest Chou and all his eight brothers,
Tell all the farm hands living around the Lin-huai Gate,
Tell also that red-faced blacksmith Old Li,
Tell Old Woman Huang and all the village women,
Tell them all these things, one by one.
Tell them to come back, come back!
My heart is torn by this sight of gloom.
Heavens, such a village cannot retain these people,
Such a paradise on earth without a man![81]

The "heart-rending" sight described in this group of poems disturbed Wen constantly, causing him to ask questions, and even doubt the reason for his existence. These form the themes of the fourth group, which bare his troubled thoughts—the conflict between his love of art and his awareness of the depressing reality around him— as he confessed in "Heart-beat:"

This light, and the light-bleached four walls,
The kind table and chair, intimate as friends,
The scent of old books, reaching me in whiffs,
My favorite teacup as serene as a meditating nun,
The baby sucking contentedly at his mother's breast,
A snore reporting the healthy slumber of my big son . . .
This mysterious quiet night, this calm peace.
In my throat quiver songs of gratitude,
But the songs soon become ugly curses.
Quiet night, I cannot accept your bribe.
Who treasures this walled-in square foot of peace?
My world has a much wider horizon.
As the four walls cannot silence the clamor of war,
How can you stop the violent beat of my heart?
Better that my mouth be filled with mud and sand,
Than to sing the joy and sorrow of one man alone;
Better that moles dig holes in this head of mine,
And vermin feed on my flesh and blood,
Than to live only for a cup of wine and a book of verse,
Or for an evening of serenity brought by the ticking clock,
Hearing not the groans and sighs from all my neighbors,
Seeing not the shivering shadows of the widows and orphans,

And the convulsion in battle trenches, mad men biting their
    sickbeds,
And all the tragedies ground out under the millstone of life.
Happiness, I cannot accept your bribe now.
My world is not within this walled-in square foot.
Listen, here goes another cannon-report, another roar of Death.
Quiet night, how can you stop the violent beat of my heart?[82]

Happy family and quiet academic life could not calm his heart-
beat that quickened at the thought of his country in agony. He
sought reassurance that somehow things would be all right for
China; he was ready to say his "Prayer:"

Please tell me who the Chinese are,
Teach me how to cling to memory.
Please tell me the greatness of this people
Tell me gently, ever so gently.

Please tell me: Who are the Chinese?
Whose hearts embody the hearts of Yao and Shun?
In whose veins flows the blood of Ching K'o and Nieh Cheng?
Who are the true children of the Yellow Emperor?

Tell me that such wisdom came strangely—
Some say it was brought by a horse from the river:
Also tell me that the rhythm of this song
Was taught, originally, by the phoenix.

Who will tell me of the silence of the Gobi Desert,
The awe inspired by the Five Sacred Mountains,
The patience that drips from the rocks of Mount T'ai,
And the harmony that flows in the Yellow and Yangtze Rivers?

Please tell me who the Chinese are,
Teach me how to cling to memory.
Please tell me the greatness of this people.
Tell me gently, ever so gently.[83]

Yao and Shun, legendary sage kings of ancient China, stand as
embodiments of Chinese wisdom. Ching K'o and Nieh Cheng,
two knights-errant whose attempts at tyrannicide during the
Warring States period (8th–3rd century B.C.) represent the
Chinese value of righteousness. The Yellow Emperor legend

speaks for the nobility of the Chinese race. These qualities of China's cultural background are further enhanced by the majesty of the features on her land: the sacred mountains and gigantic rivers. To these symbols of China's superiority Wen I-to dedicated his prayer. He consoled himself with his faith in the cultural tradition of China, which he believed would some day explode into dazzling stars, as he said in "One Sentence:"

> There is one sentence that can light fire,
> Or, when spoken, bring dire disasters.
> Don't think that for five thousand years nobody has said it.
> How can you be sure of a volcano's silence?
> Perhaps one day, as if possessed by a spirit,
> Suddenly out of the blue sky a thunder
>   Will explode:
>   "This is our China!"
>
> How am I to say this today?
> You may not believe that "the iron tree will bloom."
> But there is one sentence you must hear!
> Wait till the volcano can no longer be quiet,
> Don't tremble, or shake your head, or stamp your feet,
> Just wait till out of the blue sky a thunder
>   Will explode:
>   "This is our China!"[84]

Above all, he clung to "A Concept" about China, picturing her as:

> You, a perpetual myth, a beautiful tale,
> A persistent question, a flash of light,
> An intimate meaning, a leaping flame,
> A distant call . . . what are you?
> I don't doubt; the law of causality is ever so true.
> I know: the sea is always faithful to its sprays.
> Being the rhythm one complains not against the song.
> Ah, you, tyrannical deity, you've subdued me;
> You've conquered me, you dazzling rainbow—
> Memory of 5,000 years, please hold still.
> I only ask how to embrace you tightly,
> You, such an untamable spirit, such a beauty.[85]

At last he seemed to have perceived his new ideal of beauty

somewhere in "the memory of the 5,000-year-old culture of
China." Regaining a measure of equilibrium, he said, alle-
gorically, about "Mr. Wen I-to's Desk" in the epilogue to the
volume:

> Suddenly all the still lives speak up,
>   Suddenly everything on my desk starts complaining
> Ink Box groans, "I'm dying of thirst!"
> Dictionary cries of her back soaked in the rain;
>
> Letter Paper hurries up to say her back is bent, aching,
>   The Pen says Tobacco Ashes have clogged his mouth.
> Writing Brush yells because Match has burnt his whiskers.
>   Pencil curses Toothbrush for lying on his leg.
>
> Incense Burner mutters, "These savage Books,
>   Sooner or later I must knock you over."
> Dollar-watch sighs over his bones, rusty for his long sleep.
>   "Wind's blowing, Wind . . . " Manuscript shrieks in alarm.
>
> Brush-dish claims he's there to hold water,
>   How can he swallow stinking, pungent Cigar Ashes?
> The Desk pouts because she gets to bathe but twice a year,
>   But Ink Bottle chimes in to tell her,
>   "I wash you once every other day!"
>
> "What a master! Who's our master?"
>   All still lives start cursing together,
> "If life is so miserable like this,
>   Not to live at all would be better."
>
> The master, a pipe in his mouth, smiles and smiles,
>   "Everything must be content with its own role,
> I have not—never—abused you on purpose,
>   'Order' is not within the power of my control."[86]

VII   *Beginning of His Return to the Classics*

Trusting the greater "order" to the universe, Wen temporarily
halted his internal debate to direct his attention to teaching
during the year 1927–1928. He continued to work together with
his Crescent friends to prepare for their journal, which made its
debut in March, 1928. The inaugural editorial of the journal, at-

tributed to Hsü Chih-mo, who co-edited it with Wen and Jao Meng-k'an (1901–   ), raised the flag of "creative idealism" to oppose the prevailing "radicalism, sentimentalism, and utilitarianism." It proposed to create "a new standard of value" in the midst of conflicting claims.[87] The reaction from Leftist writers was immediate and violent. The Creation Society commented: "We see the wheel of history dragging the Crescent poets toward their graves, and hear their death knell everywhere. ... Their creative idealism is something based merely on whimsical memories and fancy. Their memory can only lead them to work on textual criticism of the *Dream of the Red Chamber,* and their fancy goad them to write love poems, building a Spanish Castle of love, beauty, and profuse colors."[88] The expression "textual criticism" referred to Hu Shih, also a member of the Crescent group, and the term "fancy" referred to Wen and Hsü Chih-mo. Wen's close friend Liang Shih-ch'iu countered the criticism by refuting the connection between literature and revolution, and the theory of the class character of literature. A great debate ensued, bringing in Lu Hsün and his supporters against the Crescent group.[89] Torn between his sympathy for the victims of ugly reality on the one hand and his devotion to belletristic literature on the other, his position became untenable in the incessant quarrels; he withdrew in silence. His only "Reply" was a poem written in April, 1928:

> Shining glories I dare not accept;
> No haloes to crown my head.
> Banners and drums are not my share;
> No yellow earth for the path I tread.
> . . . .
>
> Give to others the pomp of silken robes;
> For me, only hard labor—a joy so real.
> To make me temper songs of plain tunes
> God has promised me a will of steel.[90]

The feeling and style of this poem show the strong influence of Housman, in whom Wen had found a congenial companion for his present mood. He shared Housman's sorrow and pity for his unthinking fellow men. He translated the *Shropshire Lad*

and *Last Poems* and published several selections therefrom in
the *Crescent*, including the following:

> Could man be drunk for ever
> 　　With liquor, love, or fights,
> Lief should I rouse at morning
> 　　And lief lie down at nights.
>
> But man at whiles are sober
> 　　And think by fits and starts,
> And if they think, they fasten
> 　　Their hands upon their hearts.[91]

　Not only Housman's poems and mood, but his devotion to the
classics also seemed to have affected Wen. The "hard labor"
Wen claimed for himself in "Reply" turned out to be a search
for the real China that he had sought in "Discovery," for the
"fascinating myth" in "A Concept," and for the "greatness of the
Chinese" in "Prayer." China's five-thousand-year history and
culture supposedly originating from the legendary sage-kings,
had now become the new object of his quest. Although teaching
Western literature at the Central University, his yearning for
a thorough grasp of the cultural essence of China kept drawing
him back to T'ang poetry. Thus, in the spring of 1928, he once
again took out his unfinished biographical study of Tu Fu, which
he had put aside for over three years. He explained the rationale
of the work in its preface,

Our ancestors of the past several thousand years live in our memory
only as names. We seem to know a little of their lives, but their
faces, voices, thoughts, and the secrets in their hearts . . . all are
vague shadows. We want to remember them, adore them, and worship
them, but how?[92]

Sentimental value was only one factor that sustained Wen's
interest in Tu Fu's works, as he explained by quoting the Ming
dynasty writer Lü K'un, who said: "History is a picture of past
faces. Everyone longs for his ancestors, hence everyone wishes
to see their images. . . ."[93] But Wen also saw a much greater
value and immediate need for a "revival" of Tu Fu, because

Our life nowadays is too petty and self-righteous, too unrefined and undisciplined. I cannot forget Tu Fu, just as there was a time when Wordsworth could not forget Milton.

Wen again thought of Wordsworth's patriotic sonnet "London 1802" which he had quoted once in one of his antiWestern articles written seven years before at Tsing Hua. A merging process of values took place in him; his ideals of beauty–art, love, and patriotism—now came together to be identified with that which lay behind the Chinese classics. This new interest, or rather this rekindled interest with a new significance, loomed larger and larger until it finally outweighed his interest in Western literature, so much so that he changed his job. In the autumn of 1928, he left Nanking for Wuhan University, where he accepted the position of dean of the school of literature and chairman of the department of Chinese literature. He had found a new ideal to which he could dedicate himself, as he once had done to art and poetry. He felt that his conflict was resolved, and that from now on he could resolutely release his creative energy in academic research on the Chinese classics.

CHAPTER 5

Return to the Classics (1928-1938)
–the Excitement of Creative Research

Shining glories I dare not accept;
No haloes to crown my head.
Banners and drums are not my share;
No yellow earth for the path I tread.

Let not conceit gild me all over;
I decline a visit by "success".
My hands push against crushing hassles;
I don't look at dawn which I can guess.

Give to others the pomp of silken robes;
For me, only hard labor—a joy so real.
To make me temper songs of plain tunes
God has promised me a will of steel.

But banners and drums I won't accept;
No yellow earth for the path I tread.
Shining glories I dare not share
There're no haloes to crown my head.

Wen I-to, "Reply"[1]

I Beginning to Teach Chinese Literature

WEN I-to's acceptance of a position as head of the department of Chinese literature at Wuhan University in the fall of
1928 constituted a critical turning point in his life. Occurring
at a time when he was wavering between creative writing and
academic research, between writing modern Chinese poetry and
interpreting classical Chinese poetry, it launched his career in the
latter direction.

His new post required him to review the Chinese classics he
had studied earlier. In this new task he was aided by his col-

league Yu Kuo-en (1899–   ), a specialist in the *Songs of Ch'u,* with whom he soon developed a lasting friendship. Being known as a modern poet and a teacher of Western literature, Wen felt an increasing pressure to prove his scholarship in the Chinese classics,[2] which spurred his research and contributed, in part, to his resignation from the editorial board of the Crescent magazine in the spring of 1929. His biographical study of Tu Fu, started in 1928, led him to compare the annotations of Tu's poetry by past scholars and to ascertain facts about Tu's life by means of historical research. The first result was his "Chronology of Tu Fu," which, though containing no systematic exposition of Tu's thought, was recognized by some critics as comparable to the best of Ch'ing dynasty philological scholarship.[3] Wen used philological tools developed in the Ch'ing dynasty largely because, pending development of his own methods and approach, the Chinese classicists in the 1930's continued to hold Ch'ing scholarship in high esteem. His essay on the *Chuang-tzu,* a much researched classic, stresses its poetry, which is an original and refreshing approach.[4] He discovered two kinds of beauty in the *Chuang-tzu.* One is the beauty, at once simple and mystifying, of the feeling expressed in the text; it tells of "a child's desire to reach the moon, a mysterious disillusionment with the world, as well as an ethereal vision."[5] The other is the beauty of imagery which presents the antique and the quaint with enduring artistic interest, like an ancient bronze or jade.[6] Wen's imaginative approach to classical studies was beginning to take shape.

The serenity of his life was soon invaded by another storm of campus politics. He issued a statement in which he said that his job to him was like "the rotten mouse to the phoenix"—an allusion to a story in the *Chuang-tzu.*[7] The school administration tried but failed to persuade him to stay. He left Wuhan late in spring and all through that summer he stayed at his Hsi-shui home, working on T'ang poetry. In September he joined the Tsingtao University (later renamed Shantung University) faculty as dean of the school of arts and letters and, again, head of the department of Chinese literature. He taught T'ang poetry, the history of Chinese literature, and English poetry. He enjoyed heartily his lecturing, often letting loose his poetic imagination in the classroom in defiance of academic conventions. Once he told his English poetry students, "I wish this were not a classroom, but a lawn; then while I am lecturing, you could smoke cigarettes, sip tea, or even smoke opium, which doesn't matter at all."[8] Among his closest students were Tsang K'o-chia (1904–   ) and Ch'en Meng-chia (1911–1968), whose interest in modern poetry drew much of Wen's attention. When they asked why he himself stopped writing poetry, Wen sighed and said that he could not do it any more. Insistence on perfection inhibited him; absorption in research channeled his imagination in a different direction; both factors seemed to be responsible for the drying up of his poetic well. Furthermore, the conflict between his dedication to poetic excellence and his sense of duty toward society and his country—a conflict he never quite resolved—set him apart from the other Crescent leaders, and the gap between his ideas and those of Hsü Chih-mo and Hu Shih steadily widened.[9] Yet on the other hand, he could not agree with the literary tenets of the "revolutionary literature" school of Leftist writers who were increasingly popular. It made him unhappy to be continuously identified with the Crescent school that seemed conservative, even backward, and was losing its audience every day.[10]

II The "Miracle"—His Last pai-hua Poem

His interest in modern poetry never really subsided; when other priorities forced themselves upon him, he grudgingly suppressed creative writing, which, like his favorite metaphor of the volcano, lay dormant only for a time before its next explosion. A person of his sensitivity simply could not stop feeling and responding to the world and the people around him. At times strong surges of emotion would overwhelm him, but only momentarily, for he was not free from inhibitions imposed by his upbringing, and he would, as Liang Shih-ch'iu put it, "nip his own feelings in the bud" before they had a chance to bloom.[11] One such truncated outburst of feeling had resulted in one of Wen's unpublished English poems;[12] this time it led to his "Miracle," a powerful piece of free verse with exquisite and colorful images and a well wrought form that do justice to his own doctrines. It is his last and possibly best *pai-hua* poem:[13]

> Never have I sought the red of fire, nor the black
> Of the Peach Blossom Pool at midnight,
>   nor the plaintive tune of a lute,
> Nor the fragrance of roses. Never have I loved
>   the proud dignity of a leopard.
> The tenderness I longed for, no white dove could offer.
> I never wanted these things, but their crystallization,
> A miracle ten thousand times more miraculous than them all!

The forty-nine line poem descends upon the reader with a crushing rhythm at the beginning, impelling him to rush on almost breathlessly. Then a slight pause, followed by a much subdued, somewhat plaintive, rather quiet even flow of explanatory narrative,

> But, this soul of mine being so famished, I simply cannot
> Let it remain without food. So, even trash and dregs
> I have to beg for, don't I? Heaven knows I am not
> Willingly doing this, nor am I too stubborn, nor too stupid.
> Only I cannot wait for you, wait for the approach of that miracle.
> I dare not let my soul go unsustained. Who doesn't know
> How little these things are worth:

It ripples on until the next crest,

> A tree full of singing cicadas, a pot of common wine.
> Even the mention of misty mountains, valleys at dawn, or glittering
>   starry skies,
> Is no less commonplace, most worthlessly commonplace.
>   They do not deserve
> Our ecstatic surprise, our effort to call them in touching terms,
> Our anxiety to coin golden phrases to cast them in song.
> I, too, would say that to burst into tears because of an oriole's song
> Is too futile, too impertinent, too wasteful.
> Who knows that I *have* to do it: this heart is too hungry,
> Forcing me to make believe, to use coarse cereals for fine viands.

> I am ready to confess, the moment you—
> The moment that miracle occurs, I shall at once abandon
>   the commonplace.

Never again will I, gazing at a frostbitten leaf,
    dream of the glory of spring blossom.
Never will I squander the strength of my soul
    in peeling the stubborn rocks
In vain search for the sheen of jade; just give me a miracle,
I shall never again whip the "ugly" for the meaning
Of its opposite. In truth, I have long been tired
Of these doings, these brain-wracking implications.
I only ask for a plain word, jewel-like, radiating
Luster. I ask for a whole, positive beauty.
Not that I am so stubborn or stupid that I cannot imagine
The angelic face behind the fan when I see a fan.
So—

Several such waves lead the rhythmic movement up to a
crescendo,

I will wait for no matter how many incarnations—
Since a pledge has been made, also an unknown number of
Incarnations ago—I'll wait, without complaint, only quietly wait
For the arrival of a miracle. There must be such a day.
Let thunderbolts strike me, a volcano blast me, the entire hell
Turn over to crush me . . . Afraid? Have no fear for me, as
No gusty wind can extinguish the lamp of the soul. To have this
Body turned into ashes is nothing because that is precisely
My one moment of eternity—a divine fragrance, a most mystifying
Silence (the sun, the moon, and all the stars are halted in their
Revolutions, even time stands still), a most perfect peace . . .
I hear the sound of a door latch, suddenly,
And from afar comes the rustling of a skirt—
    that, then is the miracle—
In the half-opened golden gate, there you are, crowned with a halo.

Much discussion of the "Miracle" followed its release in the
Poetry Journal, which was revived in 1930 by Hsü Chih-mo
who claimed that it was he who had midwifed this miracle
because he had threatened Wen with, "No work from Wen
I-to, no *Poetry Journal!*"[14] Others insisted that the miraculous
display recorded another eruption of Wen's volcano, releasing
the fireworks of his typical zeal in seeking beauty, color, and
the mystery of life. Still others saw Wen's willingness to keep

on "breaking the stubborn stones in search of jade" as a reference to his patient research in the classics, to his diligent digging in "the pile of moth-eaten papers" in search of aesthetic values. All these speculations were not unfounded, but central to them all was the emotional static in his otherwise tranquil academic life in Tsingtao—a jolt severe enough to cause him, a family man, to send his wife and two children home in the summer of 1931 to Hupeh while he himself returned to live alone in a desolate dormitory fronting an abandoned graveyard![15]

Once again Wen demonstrated his theory about good poetry writing, and once again he argued against the prevailing literary trend, in two essays on poetic criticism published at about the same time as the "Miracle."[16] He continued to champion the importance of structural perfection and unity.

He remained diligent in his research. In spring 1932, Yu Kuo-en joined him at Tsingtao, sharing the same apartment house with him. Their enthusiastic discussion of the *Songs of Ch'u,* however, was interrupted by a controversy on campus. According to Wen's student Feng I (pseudonym of Chao Li-sheng; dates unknown), Tsingtao University was under the control of four different government offices, each favoring its own faction in the faculty. Using a certain curricular requirement as a pretext, the student body, which favored the local government authority, agitated to expel the university president, Yang Chen-sheng (1891–   ), Wen's former schoolmate at Tsing Hua.[17] The situation became so explosive that police guards had to be posted around Wen's house to protect him. But Wen stood firm and remained calm, refusing to change the requirement.[18] Liang Shih-ch'iu related Wen's action in the incident: the usually pro-student Wen I-to this time felt he had "with tears in his eyes, to order the execution of Ma Su," referring to the famous episode in the novel *Romance of the Three Kingdoms,* and he did support the expulsion of several militant student leaders.[19] By that time Wen had been personally postered on campus as "the ignorant and incompetent Wen I-to,"—a most unfair charge in view of his diligence, productivity, and popularity among most students, but then his imaginative approach to literary research, and his unconventional style of lecturing, could have incurred the objections of conservative elements.

III   *Back at Tsing Hua*

In September, 1932, he returned to Tsing Hua, which had grown into a university. As professor of Chinese literature, he lectured on T'ang poetry and the *Songs of Ch'u*. He moved his family into a faculty house on the campus, put in a lawn, planted bamboos, and acquired an aquarium of goldfish. All these he tended to personally. For the first and only time in his life he had a measure of real peace and comfort. Without any administrative responsibility and free from distraction, he devoted his attention to the *Songs of Ch'u*. Before long he acquired the distinction of being a leading "Peking School" scholar on the campus. He acknowledged the label proudly, because it set him apart from those "Shanghai School" intellectuals deeply involved in politics, such as Lu Hsün and Kuo Mo-jo. A very popular lecturer, Wen was called a Taoist hermit on the campus, with his perennial black robe, black bushy hair, and always a stack of thread-bound rice-paper notebooks. He preferred to meet his classes at night, and his classroom was always too small. Outside the window, auditing students stood four or five deep. Upon his entry, he would say, "Drink heartily and learn the 'Li Sao' by heart—only then one can be a true scholar,"[20] intoning each word with feeling as if he were a Taoist priest invoking gods at the beginning of a ritual. He would offer cigarettes to his students, light one for himself, and begin his lecture. His skilful presentation of the Chinese classics was refreshing and dramatic. Often with his audience spellbound, and himself carried away by his discussion, the class would continue overtime till very late hours.

His friends wondered why he chose to be a "Peking School" scholar, burying himself in old books, often for days without even looking at the newspaper. His answer was that his interests had been too diverse. For fear that he would accomplish nothing at all, he had decided to concentrate on one subject at a time as the Western scholars of literature did.[21] Underneath the serenity of his academic life, however, his mind was constantly troubled by a sense of failure which he revealed on September 29, 1933, to Jao Meng-kʾan, his former Tsing Hua schoolmate and Crescent collaborator in publishing poetry journals. He said that the memory of his past few years (apparently referring to his frequent changes of jobs and his groping for a career) was very painful. He had discovered his own shortcomings, of which the worst was inability to adapt himself to the environment, consequently he could not modify his poetic tenets to suit the prevailing trend. He turned "inward" because he found that it was impossible for him to develop his "outward" expression, and he was greatly comforted by the evidence of his success in academic research. He listed his eight research plans at various stages of completion. They included extensive exegetical, philological, and biographical studies of the *Book of Poetry*, Tʾang poetry, and the *Songs of Chʾu*.[22] As he explained later, these plans were the groundwork for his ultimate task of explaining the social, cultural, and historical significance of these classics.

Thus his concentration on academic research seemed to be the best compromise between his ultimate ideal—discovery of beauty in Chinese culture—and his circumstances. With his health impaired by a weak stomach, and five young children to care for, he felt, as did many of his fellow teachers then at Tsing Hua, inclined to cling to the peace and security provided by that well-endowed school.[23] Recognition of his classical scholarship came promptly, and in the safe aerie of a classical scholar, he looked down upon the political mire in which the "Shanghai School" intellectuals were wallowing. No wonder Professor Chi-chen Wang of Columbia University, also Wen's Tsing Hua classmate, found Wen's bookcases crowded with only Chinese classics in 1935.[24]

There must have been moments when he reflected on his youthful aspirations and felt guilty about his present retreat, as he indicated in a statement made to the graduating class of 1933.[25] He compared the education of the students with the basic training of recruits in the army. "When does a soldier feel that he has fulfilled the obligation of a soldier?" he asked the students. Merely to take part in combat was not enough; a soldier must wait until he had been totally defeated, badly

wounded, or even killed, before he could thoroughly grasp the
meaning of being a soldier. He exhorted them to strive for their
ideal until they returned with wounds and scars all over them.
This statement recalls one of his early poems in the *Red Candle,*

> I only wish to lose to you
> My body and soul,
> Both in their entirety.

But Wen himself did not stay in the battle over new poetry; he
did not go down fighting as he asked his students to do. To
rationalize his retreat he had to apply himself to research with
feverish diligence and vigor. When his old schoolmate Ku
I-ch'iao (1902–   ) invited him to serve in the government
in 1938, he declined, saying that he wanted to realize his long-
cherished ambition of writing books.[26] "If we know our direction and each do our own utmost, we will arrive at the same
destination by different routes," Wen replied. He had come to
believe firmly in the value of his contribution through research.

IV *His Contributions to Classical Studies*

The results of his research in these ten years were three major
studies on the *Songs of Ch'u,* three on the *Book of Poetry,* and
over ten articles on the ancient lexicon *Erh-ya.* These were
significant philological contributions which show much orig-
inality and insight.[27] A combination of creative imagination
and philological knowledge enabled Wen to make many new
discoveries about the meanings of certain doubtful passages.
The word *hung* in the "Hsin-t'ai" (forty-third poem in the
Book of Poetry), for example, has been traditionally accepted
as "wild goose." The authoritative Han dynasty scholar Cheng
Hsüan had said so; the Sung Dynasty philosopher-scholar Chu
Hsi had said so. Arthur Waley, accepting the tradition, translated the two lines (first and second, third stanza) as:

> Fish nets we spread;
> A wild goose got tangled in them.[28]

Wen did not dispute the traditional interpretation of the theme which suggests disappointment and frustration in one's effort to seek something—a lover, a sweetheart, an ideal marriage partner, who turns out to be a wild goose rather than good fish, as the traditional interpreter puts it. But Wen wondered why a high-flying wild goose got snared in a fishing net in water. Furthermore, contrary to the traditional interpretation which seemed too forced to Wen, the traditional symbolism of the wild goose is actually something grand, handsome, and noble, not a source of bitter disappointment.

Wen treated the word *hung* exhaustively; by citing twenty-five sources, all Chinese classics, including the *Historical Records, The History of Han, The Book of Changes, Commentaries on the Spring and Autumn Annals,* and such lexical studies as *Erh-ya* and *Shuo-wen,* Wen came to the conclusion that the *hung* is actually a toad, a generally despised creature. Before reaching this conclusion, Wen took us on a long and fascinating philological journey. He first established that the ancient *hung* sound was sometimes pronounced *gung* (or *kung* in W-G Romanization), and the words pronounced with a "g" initial were often interchangeably used with those having an "l" initial. Not that the Chinese could not distinguish these two sounds, Wen added, but rather these sounds used to carry a common diphthong initial, "gl" which, in subsequent phonetic evolution, became separated into "g" and "l." In this last analysis, Wen acknowledged his indebtedness to Lin Yutang (1895–1976).[29]

Wen's new interpretations of the texts exerted a great influence on his fellow scholars.[30] Kuo Mo-jo lauded Wen for correcting some of those "2,000 year old errors."[31] These studies also revealed Wen's increasing interest in cultural anthropology. In order to understand ancient poetry, he began to study ancient Chinese society, folklore, and mythology. His first product was an essay on the legend of the Shen-nü (Goddess) of Kao-t'ang, which was published in October, 1935.[32] He started his search for the identity of the goddess from the "Hou jen" ["Waiting for him," one hundred fifty-first poem in the *Book of Poetry*], where he interlaced six pages of internal evidence to establish the connotation of fish as women, and the numerous references in the same book to physical hunger as a metaphor for sexual hunger.

Then he compared an earlier "Hou jen" song attributed to a woman who fell in love with the legendary sage-emperor, the great flood-fighter Yü, to arrive at the meaning of the later poem: a girl waiting for her lover. Then Wen brought in the Han dynasty poem, Sung Yü's "Kao-t'ang *fu*" and through epigraphical and etymological research, supported by historical and geographical evidence, arrived at the conclusion that the goddess dreamed of by the King of Ch'u in the "Kao-t'ang *fu*" was just another version of the same woman who, according to legend, fell in love with the Great Yü.

What did the twenty-seven-page study teach us? Wen's answer was that much of ancient Chinese legends, songs, and mythology was inseparably intertwined with the primitive ritual practice—still observable among the aborigines in China—of celebrating the union of the male and the female. Next to sex, food, being the most important concern of primitive peoples, became intertwined also with the worship of a progenitress, the goddess who propagated the Chinese race. Hence the entire host of symbols, the rain (needed for agriculture), the clouds, the rain-promising rainbow, etc., all became related to the life-bearing and life-generating female sex. Only prudish traditionalists such as the Sung dynasty philosopher Chu Hsi, said Wen I-to, would try to hide these facts behind euphemism and impose far-fetched allegorical interpretations on the *Book of Poetry*.

Applying his newly gained understanding of ancient Chinese society to the *Book of Poetry*, Wen next demonstrated how the "Fou-i" poem (the eighth), traditionally regarded as one of the most insipid in that ancient anthology, actually vibrated with the pathos, expectation, and excitement of the women berry-gatherers.[33] The "Lang-po" (one hundred-sixtieth poem), after Wen's detailed exposition, became a clear, vivid caricature of a rotund nobleman, complete with orange-colored shoes and lower garment, black upper garment, cap, and sash. Wen even amassed enough evidence to substantiate his speculation that the "narrator" of this caricature was none other than the nobleman's wife.[34]

Encouraged by the exciting results of his study, his hands itched to return to his painting brushes; he wanted to illustrate the *Book of Poetry* with his own paintings and to create a book of all books.[35] He wanted to make up for what he had missed in designing his own poetry books. The joy and satisfaction in this kind of creative research made him completely ignore the tumultuous political scene and the imminent military disaster in North China in the mid-1930's. Although always sympathetic toward his students,[36] he maintained silence when an incident similar to the May Fourth Incident occurred on December 9, 1935. He was so engrossed with his study of the ancient script, which contributed much to the solid basis of his research, that in the summer of 1936, in spite of already difficult travel conditions, he ventured a tour of the Anyang archaeological excavation sites and the area of Loyang where Tu Fu had spent many years.[37]

Upon his return, he told his restive students to remain calm: "Of course China must resist Japan in order to survive, and your demonstrations to urge the government to take action are entirely praiseworthy. However, as I passed through Loyang on my recent journey, I realized that the government had some preparation there. The national situation is very different from what we see here around Peiping. Therefore I think we should not be completely disappointed with the government."[38] Then he told his students that they were "more important than the soldiers," and that to serve their country they should apply themselves to tasks more difficult than merely going to war.[39] To the dismay of his old friends who had admired his vigorous expressions of patriotism ten years before, he seemed to have completely abandoned most of his earlier ideas.

But disturbing events relentlessly forced themselves upon Wen. The beginning of the Japanese offensive in July, 1937, made him wonder if he could forever cling to his old books. As he hurriedly packed a few of his important manuscripts to catch a train with his family on July 19, he met his student Tsang K'o-chia at the station. Tsang asked him about his valuable library, whereupon he replied, "Miles upon miles of our country's territory are being lost to the enemy, how much are a few old books worth?"[40] His original plan to spend his sabbatical leave writing in peace was dashed. When Tsing Hua decided to move south, it asked for volunteers among the faculty to go along. Wen postponed his leave and, after accompanying his family back to Hsi-shui, rejoined the university at its temporary campus outside the city of Changsha. He recalled later that at first the shock had stirred the students and faculty, and made them wonder why the government had not declared total mobilization so that they could join the armed forces to contribute directly to the war effort. As the days went by, it became obvious that there would be no such opportunity for them. The faculty began to resume teaching and life regained a semblance of normality. Besides occasionally gathering to talk about the war situation, they spent their leisure hours climbing mountains and sightseeing.[41]

Their temporary peace lasted only a month or two. The rapidly deteriorating military situation brought anxiety to everyone, particularly the restless students. Some of them quietly left school to join the various "resist Japan" organizations; others went to the Communist capital at Yenan; not a few found their way back to the rear of the enemy lines where they worked with scattered groups of guerrillas. Wen no longer talked about the greater importance of study as compared to joining the army; he merely looked at his dwindling classes and sighed. Nanking fell in December, 1937. The victorious Japanese began to threaten Changsha. Once again the school had to flee. The subsequent journey turned out to be an eye-opener for Wen, who, at the end of the trip, began a new phase of his life.

CHAPTER 6

Revival of Early Interests (1938-1943)

When a gentle breeze lifts the cloud-robe of the night,
When one by one the bare branches stand still, upholding the sky,
When dawn paints its pale blue all over the fields,
When sunrise spreads the joy of a new day's birth;
    You walk in the spaciousness of a wintry day,
    Leading your children, big, medium, and small,
You all arrive at the side of a river, clear and shallow,
To bathe your faces with the chilly water,
    Let the drops string pearls on your long beard.

When the oil lamp shines on your face, gaunt and lean,
    When sleep creeps around your tired, tired eyes,
When children go to bed, filing by your desk,
When quiet settles in your room upstairs in a small house;
    You carve a smile on the stone—
    Like a star sparkling on the horizon,
Your long hair stands straight up, defiant,
As night chill pierces your thin cotton robe,
    Let your chisel's sounds reach a lonesome remoteness.

        Ma Chün-chieh,[1] "Poet Wen I-to"[2]

I The Long Trek to Kunming

IN organizing the next exodus—to Kunming, about one thousand miles overland to the south, the university arranged trains for the girl students, the less hardy boys, and the faculty, to go to Haiphong in Indo-China and thence northward to Kunming via the Yunnan-Indo-China Railway.[3] The rest of the students, including a few undaunted girls, were grouped into platoons and companies, with the help of the military instructors who had been at the university, to prepare for the trip on foot. They welcomed the cotton military uniform issued them, since most

135

of them had little to wear anyway, and military hiking equipment replaced their own meager luggage. They even welcomed a "commander," a lieutenant general offered them by the Hunan Provincial governor. Wen I-to and seven other faculty members volunteered to walk with them, which immediately turned the march into a potential learning experience. A geologist and two biologists planned specimen-collecting activities; two professors of chemistry supplemented the mobile science curriculum. Wen I-to and two other professors of Chinese literature formed teams for cultural and ethnographical studies. Three engineering students gathered up some signal corps equipment; they became the radio crew. The military instructors took charge of security and supervised the vanguards scouting for the route and rest stops ahead. It was a motley but excited column marching off on February 19, 1938, bidding farewell to Changsha where they had quartered themselves for about a year.

Once on the journey, the constant company of the young and vigorous, the hard but satisfying physical exertion, and the countryside and village people, opened up a new world to Wen. The memory of his own student life returned to rejuvenate him, making him an enthusiastic captain of the group. There were more than old memories; there were fresh stimuli. They all had read and committed to memory the fourth-century poetic essay, "Peach-blossom Spring," by T'ao Ch'ien (365–427), but when they came upon that very legendary place on March 2, none of them could recognize it. Wen was moved to give an extemporaneous lecture on the legend and the volumes of poetry inspired by it, thus adding another evening by a bonfire on a riverbank (the Yüan River, a tributary to the fabled Tung-t'ing Lake) to the marchers' memory. They trekked for days through the territories of the Miao tribes, some hostile, mostly friendly, still others even staging songs and dances to greet them—a column of what must have seemed to the local people "heavenly soldiers" from out of the world. They talked well, knew just about everything that was going on through their mobile radio team. On March 26, colorfully costumed Miao performers charmed them into dancing with them on a school playground nestled in a mountain gulch outside Huang-p'ing, about one hundred miles into eastern Kweichow Province. The teachers and students responded with their own choral songs of the War of Resistance against Japan. Their Miao hosts and hostesses challenged them to a contest of downing the local brew; quite a few of them ended the evening totally inebriated. Wen did not dance, but helped himself liberally to the liquid refreshment, and talked excitedly with his team of folk song gatherers about what they were hearing, himself busily taking notes and drawing pencil sketches. To the marchers, mostly urban-bred students, the evening was enchanted, and its magic rippled among them on and on, throughout the journey, quite in spite of the blistered feet, upset stomachs, and waves of fever that at times threatened to turn typhoid.

The marchers made sidetrips to visit sights of scenic beauty and legendary charm, and Wen I-to always had a story about what they were viewing to liven up the trip. The string of daily discoveries and excitements, however, was not altogether unmarred by tension and unhappiness. In the midst of breathtakingly beautiful hills and vales, pillboxes stood as silent reminders of the constant threat of banditry, and perpetual mementoes of the Communist-Kuomintang battles that had raged in those areas only three years before during the historic Communist Long March. Clusters of shanties housing half-starved villagers dotted the landscape, even right next to the utopian dreamland of "Peach-blossom Spring." On mountain trails trudged human beasts of burden, dwarfed under heavy loads of salt and coal. Opium poppies covered many valleys; and school children still recited the *Four Books* like a catechism while kowtowing to the tablet of Confucius. In some villages near the Yunnan-Kweichow border, the residents were so poor that even girls of seventeen or eighteen had no trousers to wear.[4] Wen I-to wrote lengthy letters to his family at Hsi-shui, giving a detailed description of the scenes he witnessed.

And among the student marchers themselves it was not always a gala celebration either. Long days of hard marching over rough terrain brought out short tempers. On April 11, they arrived at An-nan near the western Kweichow Province border. The sturdier were still relishing their memory of the sight of the greatest waterfall in China, the Huang-kuo-shu Falls, seen only two days before, but the more easily fatigued could no longer

hide their travel-weariness, and all of them were hungry. Somehow the usually efficient vanguards with the mess service had
not stayed ahead of the column that day, and no food or
lodging had been arranged for them. The students looked in
vain for their teacher-advisers, only to learn that they were at
a reception given by the magistrate. Enraged, the students
staged a sit-in in the magistracy. Wen I-to heard the commotion
and walked out of the dining room. "We have been in this thing
together," he said, visibly agitated. "If there is still someone
among us who could have knowingly created an unhappy situation like this, that person could not have been human!" Whereupon he sat down, joining the students for the rest of the night,
without dinner or sleep.

After sixty-eight days, the group reached Kunming. What he
had seen en route, the beautiful as well as the ugly, and the
opportunity to think without books, changed his attitude considerably. First, there was a return of the interests of his younger
days which drove him to new activities. He helped to direct
plays, arguing excitedly with the students on technical and
literary points.[5] His associates all remarked that he had become
a different person. Secondly, his sympathy for the humble and
the lowly was deepened, and he acquired an appreciation for
the simple, the natural, and the primitive, quite contrary to his
earlier doctrine of poetic refinement.[6] In a preface he wrote in
May, 1939, for the anthology of over two thousand songs collected by Liu Chao-chi, one of his students on the journey,
he said,

When a group of country folk catch your side glance as they walk
down a city street, your impression of them is that they are stupid,
slow, timid; never can you imagine the pride implanted in the heart
of every one of them. What the men among them envision is:

> Yellow rust gathers when the sword is not whetted,
> Your back hunches if you don't stand straight, chest out.

(a folksong from An-nan)

What the women among them enjoy is:

> The dainty, the refined, ah, how disgusting!

We die of love for those tough-skinned farmer boys.
You, my man, are an old farm hand,
Not a pale-faced dandy, not an effete false snob.

(a folksong from Kweiyang)

And of course they, too, want material comfort like everybody else,
but they disdain the timid, secretive acts of theft:

When we eat we choose big heads of cabbages,
When we love we pick big chiefs of gangs;
At midnight, in sleep, we hear the swords sing,
Then we'll wear silk, and our men, brocade.

(a folksong from P'an-hsien)

And which of you city dwellers have the guts to talk and think
like this:

I love you in life and I love you in death,
I fear not my legal husband, should he be right here;
I'll face the judge as though he were my parent
And settle in jail as I'd sit in a garden.

If you say this is primitive or savage, you are quite right. What we
need now is precisely the primitive and the savage. We have been
"civilized" too long. Now that we are driven to a point of no return,
we have to . . . let loose the animal nature that has lain dormant in
us for several thousand years, to bite back. War is not a civilized
gesture . . . [If we cannot face this test] we would have to admit
that we are a people, born emasculated, not fit for existence on
earth. . . . [7]

His admiration of the true and intense, even violent, feeling
expressed nakedly in poetry was carried into his study of T'ang
poetry. In 1941 he reviewed the development of the *kung-t'i*
(palace style) poetry of the Liang and early T'ang dynasties.
The "decadent" sentimentality that dominated the poems describing a court life of wine, women, and song infuriated him
and made him welcome the northern vitality of Yü Hsin's (513–
581) *fu*. He praised Lo Pin-wang's (?–684) long poems that
carved tragic romances in bold relief, regarding them as effective
cures "to revive the paralyzed hearts and souls" of Lo's time.

Wen, however, compared Lo Pin-wang's poetic revolt to a storm
which Wen believed should not, and indeed did not, last long
before poetry returned to its proper serenity and purity.[8]

In all of Wen's classical studies, particularly in those on T'ang
poetry, which he had never stopped reading since childhood, he
pursued a systematic approach leading to an understanding of
the background of the works, first through a textual study to
ascertain the correct reading (the task of removing the encrustations on the classics he described in his Tsing Hua days), and
then through an exegetical investigation to arrive at reliable
meanings of the text. As Professor Tamotsu Sato has observed,
Wen I-to always looked for an understanding of how the ancient
writers lived. Wen used the philological tools developed by
traditional scholars but went beyond their pedantic concerns.
With his ability to perceive the darker side of human life and
the human mind, Wen went deeper into T'ang poetry than, for
example, Su Tung-p'o had done eight hundred years before him.
Wen succeeded in breaking out of the framework of classical
studies dictated by Confucian values.[9]

II   Resurgence of Patriotism

Thirdly, his patriotism resurged, expressing itself in various
ways. It spurred him to quarrel with his colleagues whenever
they expressed pessimism regarding the war.[10] During the long
trek, many of the participants grew long beards which they
shaved off upon their arrival in Kunming. To show his confidence
in China's cause, Wen vowed to keep, and did keep, his black
beard until the day of victory. Patriotism also strengthened his
sense of mission that had, at least partly, motivated his research.
Now, he worked with renewed fervor, often for days with very
little rest. Because he often refused to interrupt his work to see
his friends, they nicknamed him "Master Why-don't-you-come-
downstairs-for-a-moment."[11] "The mystifying beauty behind
China's history of five thousand years" seemed to have come
within his reach as he envisaged his ultimate work—a comprehensive study of the nature and characteristics of Chinese society
through its cultural and literary development. Toward this end
he began to integrate his study of ancient Chinese history and

the results of his ten years of philological and exegetical ground-work. But the peace and serenity of Tsing Hua, now renamed Lienta, were no longer there.[12] First there were frequent air-raids; he was once wounded in the head and another time he and his family were almost killed.[13] Then poverty quickly caught up with the university people when spiralling inflation reduced their salaries to below subsistence level. Even the travel expenses of his wife and children became a great problem.[14] Upon their arrival in Kunming, he had to borrow rent money and a few chairs to provide them with a place to live. For safety and economy they had to move frequently, from apartments in Kunming to cheaper places in nearby villages. In 1941, after his brother had joined him to teach French poetry at the university, Wen's family of eight, together with his brother's family of three, shared two rooms in the Ch'en-chia-ying village north-west of Kunming. The rooms were immediately above a pack-horse station. They all slept on the floor. In the morning he rolled up his bedding and swept the floor while his wife cooked break-fast. He even developed a theory on how to sweep the floor without sprinkling water, which would cake the dust on the floor, and yet keep the dust from flying all over. Short rations reduced their three daily meals to one and a-half. Meat and fat had long disappeared from their diet. Wen bore these hardships stoically and cheerfully, often reassuring his family that it was only fair for them to put up with some such inconveniences after the good life they had enjoyed in Peking. He repeatedly reminded them to be patient, for victory was near and good days would return soon. He walked several miles to school three or four times a week, and he took pride in his rugged health tempered by the long trek.

He snatched time between family obligations and distractions to do his research. Two things happened that helped him greatly. One was his long-awaited sabbatical leave of 1939–1940 which he spent in a small city called Chin-ning, about twenty-five miles southwest of Kunming. Upon his return, he had completed a study on the *Book of Changes* and organized two new courses —the history of Chinese literature and ancient Chinese legends. The other was the establishment of the Tsing Hua Research Institute headed by Fung Yu-lan (1895–   ) in 1941. Being in charge of the Chinese literature section of the institute, he had a little more time for research. Moving his family (the sixth time in three years) to share the quarters of the institute at the Szu-chia-ying village, he found an environment somewhat more conducive to concentrated study. There was a slight improvement in his living. For the first time in months his wife could afford to serve tea late at night to him and his associates still engrossed in academic discussions.[15] Added to the encouraging developments was the award granted him by the National Scholarship Evaluation Commission for his exegetical work on the *Songs of Ch'u* started back in 1936.[16] During the last period of Wen's academic career, his effort was directed at a synthesis of the results of his research, revolving around the *Songs of Ch'u*, the *Book of Poetry*, and life in ancient China.

III   *The* Songs of Ch'u—*and Ch'ü Yüan*

Wen had two interests, developed simultaneously but separately, in the *Songs of Ch'u*: the literary value of the poems and the historical role of the poet, Ch'ü Yüan (343?–290? B.C.).

In 1941 he had already completed three substantial philological studies of the *Songs of Ch'u*. He now proceeded to give an overall view of the aesthetic and sociological value of the poems. Using the "Chiu-ko" ["Nine songs"] as an example, he analyzed its eleven sections for the light they shed on life and ideas in ancient China.[17] He explained that the theme song was intended to propitiate "the Supreme Emperor of the East," the patron deity of the state of Ch'u. The other songs were dedicated to nature divinities whose geographical origins coincided exactly with the description in the "Li-yüeh chih" ["Essay on rites and music"] in the *Ch'ien Han shu* [*History of the former Han dynasty*].[18] The places ranged from the northern state of Chao to southern Ch'u, and, as one moved south, one could notice that the tone and images of the songs showed increasing liveliness and sensuality.

Wen stressed the significance of the cultural traits of the various parts of ancient China as reflected in the "Nine Songs," but he disagreed with many scholars who believed that the *Songs of Ch'u* was merely a document faithfully recording the religious ideas prevailing at the time. He held that even the Ch'u people enjoyed the "Nine Songs" as literary and artistic expression, and watched them being performed on stage. To reenact the "Nine Songs" in a way they might have been presented in the third century b.c., he wrote "A tentative Interpretation of the Ancient Opera Chiu-ko." With his arrangement, he succeeded in breathing life into the ancient poems and restoring their aesthetic appeal. The settings he designed are imaginative and produce an intense poetic effect, especially the scene for the "Shan Kuei" ["Mountain spirit"] song:

Under the thick shadowy foliage of a bamboo grove on a hillside there is a cart drawn by a leopard. The animal has a bright orange coat; beside it lies a fox. . . . Behind the bamboos in the background we can see Goddess Peak, towering like a screen and forever hiding itself in the clouds and mist—the most beautiful and bashful among the Twelve Peaks of the Wu Mountain. The monotonous chirping of insects in the woods sounds like buzzing in our ears. Suddenly a voice splits the silence, "It seems there is someone over there, in that fold of the hill." And the echoes, like countless concentric ripples on water, spread wider and wider toward the cliffs on all sides— "The hill—the hill—the hill—." A bat swishes by, and from the tall grass below the hill rises a rustling sound. . . .[19]

Complete with detailed description of the *dramatis personae* and full stage directions, Wen's arrangement makes the entire sequence of eleven songs meaningful and enjoyable even without translating the original esoteric text into modern vernacular. His operatic version starts with a Prologue, which traditionally has been identified as a song dedicated to the Supreme Emperor of the East (or Great Monarch of the Eastern World, or the greatest of all gods commanding from the East). In the prologue the King of Ch'u appears in full regalia to greet the arrival of the gods. (See Prologue, *supra*.) In the midst of male and female voice choruses, the image of the Supreme Emperor appears briefly in the sky to open the rest of the sequence.

The second scene features the Lord of the East, a red-faced bearded god who ushers in the sun and orchestrates the young farmers, men and women, working in the fields. There are songs and dances celebrating their productive labor, but no particular erotic emphasis, with the solos all by a male voice. The scene closes at the end of the day when the sky darkens.

The Lord Amid the Clouds follows. It is evening, and the young women selected from the Kao-yang clan, which Wen I-to has identified as the same *dramatis personae* involved in the legend of the Goddess of Mt. Wu (See pp. 131 *supra.*), appear in their best finery to dance around a flagpole, somewhat suggestive of a May Dance, waiting for the god's arrival. The women are there to repay the god for his favor in granting clouds and rain for the crops throughout the year. An orgiastic banquet greets the god; a pause on a darkened stage represents the god-human union; and a stage full of grieving women weep over the departing god who rises into the cloud.

Hsiang Chün, or the Princess of the Hsiang and *Hsiang Fu-jen,* or the Lady of the Hsiang, traditionally the third and fourth in the song sequence, have been upheld by other scholars as addressed to two female spirits. In Wen's version the two songs are combined into the fourth scene. *Hsiang Chün,* instead of being the Princess of the Hsiang River, appears as the Lord of the Hsiang (a god? a chieftain? of the region), who, accompanied by a prince (his son?), arrives on an island to be greeted by a group of women. In the first half of the combined song, the Lord of the Hsiang finds the one woman who has been waiting and searching for him. In the second half, the prince finds his. The scene closes with a group dance, all the characters pairing off two by two.

The Big Lord of Lives, or the Greater Master of Fate, is a black-robed god with a huge entourage of marine creatures. Here Wen is utilizing the traditional Chinese mythology of the five agents and the *yin-yang* combinations, black being the correspondence of water. The god chases after a bevy of beautiful women cavorting in the vale and catches one, and the rest of the women surround them to dance in celebration, with all the marine creatures joining in. The god and the selected woman sing in duet, the rest form a chorus, until sleep due to fatigue interrupts the pace. The god wakes first, picks a flower and puts it in the hand of the woman, who wakes up forlorn because he and his entourage have left, visible only in the distant clouds.

The Little Lord of Lives appears with a child (a girl) of five or six. The setting is semi-tropical, luxuriant with flowers and plants. One of the women in the garden takes the child and entices the Lord to follow her, finally, into the room—leaving the child in the garden to play with the other young ladies. There is again the sorrowful parting after union, but only the Lord and the chosen woman sing solo parts.

The River God sits, naked to his waist, on a white tortoise that floats in water. The scene is a tableau, and only a duet between one of the white-garbed young women and the River God is heard. The next scene opens on the Mountain Spirit, a bewitching young female spirit dressed in flowers and vines, who sings a duet with a handsome prince. The color key to the setting is red, which presents a dazzling contrast to the rising white fog. After a rainstorm the fog swallows up the Mountain Spirit.

The Epilogue, or Envoi, returns to the scene of the Prologue. Like a regular finale, all the characters are on stage; flower-bearing girls pass their fragrant charges from one to the next and they dance by the altar in the middle, with the King of Ch'u and his immediate entourage at the end of the procession. The curtain falls in the midst of choral singing and shouts of "Long Live the King!"

All the scenes confirm Wen's perception of the "Nine Songs" as a shamanistic dance depicting man-god communications— all except the second from the last scene (Epilogue), which is *Kuo Shang*, or the Spirits of the Fallen. Against the backdrop of a corpse-strewn battleground at sunset, dancers holding swords, spears, and battle drums circle their fallen comrades in a rather primitive, tribal ritual. Solemn-faced spectators join in the chorus. In his study, "What Are the 'Nine Songs'?" Wen has explained the Spirits of the Fallen as belonging to a category different from but on a par with the other eight gods or goddesses—counting both Hsiang spirits as two, but excluding the Supreme Emperor because he is in the overall Prologue. Wen argues that the eleven pieces may have evolved at three different periods in the cultural history of China, but there is no reason why the Ch'u poet could not have organized them into a single performance which, in fact, is what Wen believed.

Wen I-to's interest in Ch'ü Yüan the poet was more directly linked to a continuing controversy. Until the twentieth century,

most scholars of the *Songs of Ch'u* had been concerned with
the identity of Ch'ü Yüan and what poems he wrote; modern
interest in Ch'ü Yüan, however, centered on the personality
and ideas of the poet. Kuo Mo-jo, having propounded a theory
about the pattern of development of Chinese society, asserted
in 1942 that Ch'ü Yüan's thought was "people-oriented."[20] Lin
Keng, whose contribution to an understanding of the *Songs of
Ch'u* has been regarded as both important and original, insisted
that when Ch'ü Yüan spoke of *min* (people), he meant "human
beings" in contradistinction to "heaven."[21] Lin believed that
Ch'ü had no concept parallel to our modern "common people"
or the "masses." Wen I-to, however, only stressed the significance of Ch'ü Yüan's death as symbolic of man's struggle for
life with honor.[22] Although always an admirer of Kuo and
interested in Kuo's writings, Wen early in 1943 still did not see
much value in arguing about whether Ch'ü Yüan was a revolutionary. His interest in Ch'ü Yüan the man remained in the
symbolic role Ch'ü played in the history of all mankind. As he
said, at Ch'ü Yüan's time, man had already progressed from
fighting and dying merely for food. Honor had already become
important, so much so that Ch'ü preferred death to disgrace.

IV   *The* Book of Poetry—*a Sociological Approach*

Wen's continued study of the *Book of Poetry* followed an
approach which was more sociological than purely literary. He
felt that he had brought his exegetical and philological work
on this classic to a conclusion and that he was ready to attempt
a broad interpretation of the poems.[23] As he explained, his
earlier textual study was an effort to "bring the poems to modern
times." Now he would attempt to "roll back three thousand
years" and bring the modern reader back to the ancient society
in which these poems were written and sung.[24] The first step he
took was to group the *feng* poems into three major categories:
marriage and courtship, family life and conjugal love, and social
life. Each group was subdivided into those from a man's viewpoint and those from a woman's viewpoint. In his commentaries
Wen stressed the importance of sexual rites and festivals in
ancient China, but he did not share Granet's view that these

songs were sung in contests at village mating festivals.[25] Wen apparently developed his interpretation without the benefit of Western sinological scholarship during these years,[26] and yet his system yielded significant insight as shown, for example, in his treatment of the poem "Ju-fen" (tenth), which distinguished itself from earlier interpretations by accomplished scholars, both East and West:

> The bream is showing its tail all red;
> The Royal House is like a blazing fire.
> Though it be like a blazing fire,
> Your parents are very near.[27]

This is James Legge's rendition of the last stanza of "Ju-fen" which, in his reading, becomes "the affection of the wives of the Joo (Ju), and their solitude about their husbands' honor." The "Royal House" refers to the Shang. The "blaze" symbolizes the difficulty the House experienced under the "tyranny of Chou." In this reading, Legge was following Chu Hsi closely. Chu Hsi, in turn, followed the Later Han scholar Cheng Hsüan. The traditional interpretation is based on a *Tso Chuan* precedent; the allusion of a bream's red tail suggests that one is harassed or imperiled. Hence Legge states that the poem describes "the wife of a soldier (or officer), rejoicing in the return of her husband from a toilsome service."

But other problems remain. How does the last line "Your parents are very near" fit in here? The traditional annotators assert that this line suggests an excuse for the scholar to accept official appointment under Chou rule, in spite of the fact that this would mean severing his allegiance to the Shang dynasty, because he "has to support his parents!" They quote the *Hou Han shu* [*History of the Later Han dynasty*],[28] which describes Chou P'an, a scholar of integrity, who rejected but, after reading this poem, finally accepted the appointment as a *Hsiao-lien* (a modest rank) in order to offer his mother a better living.

Arthur Waley translated the same stanza into:

> The bream has a red tail;
> The royal house is ablaze.
> But though it is ablaze,
> My father and mother are very dear.[29]

He believed that here the returning husband is speaking, and the fish with a "bleeding tail" is the symbol of a ruined kingdom. Thus he grouped the poem with those of "warriors and battles."

Wen I-to first established, with the support of abundant, persuasive philological evidence that fish was a common metaphor in ancient Chinese literature, usually used by a girl to refer to her beloved or ideal mate. There was no special significance about the "red tail," unless the observation that the bream's tail turns red during the spawning season be taken literally. The "royal house" was a misinterpretation of "a member of the noble family," or simply "my lord." "Ablaze," or "burning" could have a less prudish meaning than what Chu Hsi assigned it. Hence the poem became a plain love poem:

> The bream with red tail—
> My lord is desperately passionate;
> He is passionate, yes, but—
> My parents are around![30]

In studying the metaphors and symbolism, represented by the Chinese term *yin-yü*,[31] in the *Book of Poetry*, Wen I-to found that they belonged to two types: the first type was the symbolical or allegorical; the second type conveyed the meanings of commonly used words by means of homophones. They were sociologically important because they strengthened the magical character of the divinations recorded in the *Book of Changes*, and were extensively used in every aspect of life in ancient China, from diplomatic negotiation to courtship. The fish metaphor was also the subject of a larger study[32] in which he assembled evidence from numerous classical works and folksongs to prove that fish had always been a Chinese symbol of fertility and love.

V   *The* Book of Changes—*a Historical Emphasis*

In his study of ancient legends, Wen also had moved from philological explanation, exemplified by his study of the Goddess legend in 1935, towards a combination of historical, philological and sociological approaches.[33] His study of the legendary origin

of the Chou royal house, completed in January, 1940, showed
his increasing emphasis on the historical approach.[34] His impressive work on ancient legends can be represented by the study
of the Fu Hsi myth published in 1942,[35] in which he analyzed
in great detail forty-nine legends of the flood and the genesis
of man, and compared many graphic and glyptic representations
of Fu Hsi. His sources included classical records and the oral
traditions of the ethnic minorities in Southwest China, Central
China, Indo-China, and Central India. He reached several conclusions. First, Fu Hsi and his legendary mate Nü Kua were
originally totem symbols appearing as two snakes intertwined
in the sexual act. That early Chinese culture had had totemic
elements was seen in the pre-Han practice of tatooing among
coastal peoples and in surviving folk rituals in many parts of
China, such as the dragon boat festival and the dragon dances.
The snake or snakelike symbol was the totem of the strongest
tribe in ancient China which absorbed other tribes, including
their totem attributes. The result was the legendary dragon,
with its horse head, eagle claws, fish scales, and snake body.
The most primitive Chinese peoples regarded the intertwined
dragons as their ancestors. Secondly, the dragon identity of Fu
Hsi and Nü Kua was subsequently humanized and they became
brother and sister before their marriage. The legend prevailed
and was accepted in all parts of China till the Later Han, but
a growing sense of decorum in Han times caused the elimination of the incestuous element from the legend. Thirdly, the
legends of wars between the ancient kings and spirits were
actually tribal wars that had acquired mythological coloration
through the years. Most of the leaders in these battles were
connected with the dragon tribe. The flood legend that existed
in some areas was partially influenced by the actual experience
of inundation of certain tribes located near the rivers. Fourthly,
etymological and other evidence was elicited to support the
hypothesis that Fu Hsi and Nü Kua were the gourd which,
according to many Miao legends, gave birth to the first man
and woman. Later, when the flood legend became assimilated
in the genesis myth, the same gourd became the vessel which
saved, as did Noah's Ark, the progenitors of mankind.

Wen's study of the ancient legends was an evaluation of their cultural significance without becoming involved in the question about the historical persons in the legends. In this he escaped Maspero's criticism.[36] Wen's speculations on the ancient totemic society of China are highly regarded by other scholars interested in ancient China.[37] His study of the *Book of Changes* followed a similar pattern of development. The work he published in December, 1939, was an exegetical and literary study, which attempted to discover poetry in the symbolism of the *Book of Changes*.[38] His 1941 study focused on life in ancient China.[39] He extracted three kinds of data from the book, pertaining respectively to economic life, social life, and religious and moral concepts. What he discovered in this incomplete study was not so much factual information on ancient Chinese society as the usefulness of this approach which was, as Kuo Mo-jo has said, revolutionary in the history of Chinese scholarship on the *Book of Changes*.[40] Furthermore, the ninety items which he explicated revealed that these seemingly obscure and esoteric references were no more than plain statements about daily life, from the seasonal care of domestic animals to the difficulties of travel.

VI *An Original Thought on Chinese Painting*

Many of his classical studies made strategic use of epigraphical research techniques, which, together with his explorations of the origins of man's cultural expressions, led him to rethink some of his ideas about the graphic and plastic arts. He had ignored traditional Chinese painting when he was trying to master the Western technique of oil painting in America; now he found genuine accomplishments by the Chinese painting masters of old, but almost as an accident, an aberration.

Strictly speaking, he said, "painting is a fantastic expectation, a self-contradictory ideal" because it has been trying to create three-dimensionality with a medium confined in two dimensions. It's really a dead-end street. Knowing that the form captured on paper, if indeed it could be done, had to be an illusion, the Chinese artist consciously used lines to allude to the existence of form. Wen even asserted that lines were man's optical illusions, a necessary foil in order to perceive form—an illusion of the real form. Finally the Chinese artist gave up trying to simulate form altogether, and that's where Chinese painting, relying upon lines, joined Chinese calligraphy. "The accomplishment of Chinese painting with its powerful expressiveness in lines, has been nothing short of the miraculous," said Wen I-to, "but as painting it has departed from the main subject too far already. In this sense who can say the very success of Chinese painting is not its doom?"[41]

VII *History of Ancient Chinese Literature*

Extensive study of the classics and their historical background led Wen to synthesize his findings in preparation for the writing of a history of ancient Chinese literature. He began a draft of the book in 1939, and continued to work on it while teaching a course on this subject in 1940. In the first and only published chapter, he discussed the origins of Chinese literature.[42] His thesis, supported by a mass of philological evidence, was that spontaneous expression of feeling in the form of wordless songs preceded written verses. The first rhymed verse was written to record events, to make them easier to memorize, rather than to express feeling.[43] The sense of the word *chih* in the classical definition of poetry *shih yen chih* had shifted from "remembrance" to "record" and finally to "will or ambition."[44] The evolution of the sense of the word coincided with a change in the role of poetry from the epical to the lyrical. It was only after prose had been developed to record history more effectively that poetry was released to join what had been wordless lyrical songs. Consequently, one finds remnants of history, or epic-type story poems, as well as the lyrical *feng* poems in the *Book of Poetry*, the most ancient anthology of Chinese verse, in which the elements of song and poetry had achieved a perfect balance.

It was a start towards a comprehensive history of Chinese literature for which his plan took definite shape only after the last change in his basic views and attitudes in 1943.

CHAPTER 7

A Political Crusader (1943-1946)
–Impassioned Speeches in a Tortured Voice

A medieval age drags its fox's tail,
Hurrying to create a holocaust that spreads and spreads;
Nero on the balcony, his face lit by happy thoughts and happy smiles,
"Ha, finally I've burnt the whole of Rome!"

Highrises rising high on the money of the rich and mighty,
While the butchers dream of subduing the entire universe;
Only a bunch of dried twigs now, the people's bodies;
"Not enough! Tighten the rope harder on their necks!"

Isn't truth poetry's goal, ultimate goal?
Doesn't learning anchor itself on reality?
Thus you walked out of the Palace of Art

Joyfully joining the masses in the street,
To reveal the power of your soul in combat:
"The moment we've stepped out, we don't think of stepping back!"

Yü Ming-ch'uan, "Mourning My Teacher Wen I-to,"[1]
Kunming, July 1946

I *A Dramatic Story*

THE last period of Wen's life is a dramatic story of a well-educated man driven by the brutality of war and the abuses of an authoritarian government to risk his life for a political cause. The causes he championed—democracy and the cessation of civil war—were not new, but his discovery of them was. Since the beginning of the twentieth century, Chinese intellectual leaders had been demanding political reform and national unity in about the same terms as those used by Wen shortly before his death, but a different time and a different national pathos added a

152

dramatic impact to Wen's role seldom before so deeply felt by the educated Chinese.

Pondering over the changes in Wen's attitudes, we realize that his crusading spirit was but a new manifestation of the same dedication to an ideal which he had shown in his earlier career as a creative poet. The Romantic search for beauty continued to hold him in its magic spell. In the midst of his feverish political speech-making and pamphleteering, he would take time out to work on his operatic arrangement of the "Nine Songs." Plagued by dire poverty, he would literally sell his shirt to see a motion picture which depicted the life of a Polish composer who died for his music.[2] He would join, even lead, the students in demonstrations against police gunfire, but he would also persuade them to end their strike to avoid prolonged interference with their study.[3] He remained an idealist full of righteous indignation, not a revolutionist equipped with a practical program of action. His caustic criticism of Chinese traditions was not based on a thorough understanding of Chinese society, because he was, to the very end, basically an imaginative poet, not a social scientist. The change in his attitudes, therefore, was mainly an emotional response to the rapidly deteriorating political, economic, and military situation during his last years.

II *The Background*

The situation in China, worsening year after year since the War of Resistance began, had become particularly disheartening around 1943. Against the earnest hope that the expanding Pacific front would force the Japanese to ease their pressures on the Chinese front, the important cities in Central, South, and Southwest China were falling rapidly into Japanese hands.[4] A Japanese force penetrated Western Yunnan province, and by the end of 1944 had all but occupied the entire province of Kwangsi. The American participation in the China Theatre, which had momentarily raised Chinese morale, brought disillusion after the Stilwell episode.[5] Apathy and despair became epidemic, while the few who tried to maintain their confidence in China's future found their efforts increasingly desperate. Hostilities between the Kuomintang and the Communists flared up from time to time

along their common borders. There was constant mutual acri-
mony; each accusing the other of perpetuating the civil war
under the pretext of fighting the Japanese.[6] To counteract
growing popular sympathy with the Communists in Yenan, the
Kuomintang government intensified its police measures. Censorship was strict, and any criticism of political corruption and in-
efficiency was dealt with as treason. The minor political parties,
which had reemerged from underground upon the formation of
the so-called "united front"[7] in 1937, were kept under close
surveillance by the Kuomintang. As the situation worsened, these
parties became more and more restive. Partly motivated by their
belief that a compromise must be found to break the Kuomintang-Communist deadlock, and partly encouraged by the American interest in a democratic China, they formed in 1940 a
Federation of the Democratic Political Parties of China which
grew and in 1944 changed its name to the Democratic League
of China to include interested individuals without party affilia-
tions.[8] Among the principal components of the League was the
Chinese Youth Party, with which Wen I-to had had some acquaintance in 1925. One of the top leaders of the League was
Lo Lung-chi, Wen's former classmate at Tsing Hua. The avowed
purpose of the League was to mediate the conflict between the
Kuomintang and the Communists in order to consolidate China's
war effort under the direction of a coalition government. The
Kuomintang, unwilling to relinquish its one-party rule, regarded
any suggestion of a compromise with Yenan as a pro-Communist
effort to undermine its control. Consequently, the Kuomintang
resorted to harsh measures to suppress the League. The leaders
of the League were frequently jailed,[9] and after Hong Kong and
Kweilin were occupied by the Japanese, its publications could
circulate only in Kunming.

Kunming during the Second World War was one of the few
intellectual islands where, in sharp contrast to the rest of the
country, the strange game of Chinese politics allowed a certain
measure of intellectual freedom. The Yunnanese authorities, who
had never wholeheartedly accepted Chiang Kai-shek's leadership, were partially successful in resisting Nationalist attempts
to seize control of that province.[10] Although the semi-autonomous
status of Yunnan was steadily weakened as more Yunnanese

troops were ordered out of the province and Chiang's troops sent in, the Yunnanese governor Lung Yün (1888–1962) and the Yunnanese garrison commander of Kunming were able to restrict the activities of the Nationalist secret police. It was under these favorable conditions that the League could be active in Kunming and the students there could feel free to express their dissatisfaction with the Nationalist government.

Kunming was also a place of sharp contrasts where the disintegration of China's economy was dramatically revealed. The ranks of the local wealthy were swelled by an influx of rich refugees. Until the Burma Road was cut off, imported goods continued to bolster the city's appearance of prosperity. Yet the Yunnanese living just beyond the city wall remained miserably poor, just as the streets outside the financial district remained unpaved. When Wen I-to's university moved in, it was given permission to level a few acres outside the city to construct temporary shelters for classrooms. Penniless and homeless, most of the students crowded into straw huts that had no flooring. When it rained, the roofs leaked and the students slept in mud holes.[11] After class, many joined local water carriers and janitors to eke out a living, but there were others who made a fortune overnight by taking to the Burma Road to join the smugglers. Always remembering Wordsworth's line, "Ennobling thoughts depart when men change swords for ledgers, and desert the student's bowers for gold," Wen was grieved by those who yielded to temptation, and openly criticized his colleagues for moonlighting with business firms to augment their academic salaries.[12] He himself resisted the pressure until May, 1944, when his monthly salary could feed his family of eight for only ten days; then he agreed to teach a few extra hours a week at a local middle school, which paid him a picul of rice a month.[13] In addition, he yielded to the suggestion of friends that he take up seal-carving for fees. His artistic discipline, his knowledge of the ancient script, and his scholarly reputation assured him a ready market. Although he had to work long hours at night with a chisel that ruined his hand for sensitive calligraphy, the income helped with household expenses. That the most drastic change in his political attitudes took place in 1944 when his financial situation was actually somewhat better than it had

been since he left Peking, seems to indicate that personal pri-
vation was not a decisive factor.

III   Reasons for His Change in Political Outlook— the Abuses of Civil War

Three main factors seem to have led to a change in his political
outlook at this time: a compelling sense of urgency to do something about the political situation; the influence of his associates,
both faculty and students; and the rebellious strand in his
character which was not entirely divorced from hero worship.
No matter how much his mind was absorbed in research, his
heart was always with the younger generation and he basked
in the midst of their admiring, worshipful faces. His own children, for whose education he had to borrow money from all
possible sources, were growing up. As early as 1938, some of his
students had already gone to Yenan to join the Communists,
while others had joined the Nationalist army. Beginning in 1943,
there was talk about drafting college students for military
service. The grim prospect of his own son fighting, not necessarily against a foreign invader, but very possibly on one or the
other side of the Kuomintang-Communist conflict, haunted him.
The pitiable army conscripts he saw around Kunming confirmed
his fear and fired his anger.[14]
    He had been walking to and from school, and he often saw
conscripts being herded along the highway under army guard.
All in tatters, they were roped together to prevent escape. Some
of them, too ill to walk, were whipped mercilessly. Others were
left to die by the roadside. In a voice choking with emotion, Wen
discussed this situation with his students one day in the spring
of 1944, "We must do something about it. Everytime I look at
the bodies on the roadside I myself feel tortured. . . . Look at
those who are still tied with ropes and being dragged along;
their legs are only about this big,"[15] he closed his index finger
on his thumb to show his students. He went home that day, still
trembling with anger and muttering, "This is too inhuman!" His
wife tried to calm him by saying that the problem was too big
for him to worry about alone, whereupon he retorted, "If I

don't do anything about it, nobody else ever will!"[16] His feeling
of desperation was strengthened in the summer of that year when
one of his nephews in the Nationalist army stopped in Kunming.[17] The young man told Wen about the misuse of soldiers
and corruption in the army. Many recruits died of disease because American-donated medicines more often went to the black
market than to the sick soldiers, and there was little hope that
those who survived would ever be sent to fight the Japanese.
These stories destroyed Wen's last shred of confidence in the
government. He stayed home for a week to think through the
problem and decide on a future course of action. When he returned to the campus, every trace of his former tranquillity was
gone. At the July seventh (Marco Polo Bridge incident) anniversary assembly, he challenged the chairman who urged the
forum to keep its discussion academic. "Is today the time to talk
about academic learning... when we all are starving?" said
Wen. "The May Fourth Movement was started by us students, so
was the December ninth (1935) movement. Now is the time for
us to do it again!"[18] When he was invited by military commanders to participate in a discussion a month later, he shocked
them by saying, 'I used to maintain my last hope in the army.
Now you have told me that militarily there is also no way
out.... There seems to be only one thing left—revolt!"[19]

But how was he, who had closeted himself with old books
for nearly twenty years, going to revolt? He found a ready
answer in the program of the Democratic League. In the autumn
of 1944, he joined the League. His first act was to help his
friend Lo Lung-chi organize a mass rally on National Day,
October 10. Unidentified but organized hecklers attempted to
interrupt the program. The Yunnanese police, and Wen's impassioned plea for the people of Kunming to rise and defend
themselves, finally overpowered the hecklers.[20] The incident made
Wen a hero, and at the same time a hated enemy of the Kuomintang. Now that he had emerged as an idol of the nation's
students—something he perhaps always subconsciously wanted
to be—he was convinced that his choice of active participation in
politics was the right one. He gave up writing academic mono-
graphs almost completely for political pamphleteering. In December, 1944, he helped the League found the *Min-chu chou-k'an*

[*Democratic weekly*] in which he published many of his political essays.

A second factor in this decision—the influence of his associates—was also related to his preference for the company of younger and more active people. The faculty and students of the National Southwest Associate University (Lienta) were sharply divided on political issues, with the majority, in varying degrees, sympathetic with the Left. Wen's feeling and ideas quickly identified him with that group. He remained close to the students, helping them to organize poetry clubs and study projects, and spending much time arguing with them on political questions.[21] Among the faculty his close associates now included:[22] the historian Wu Han (1909–1966?), who later became Vice Mayor of Peking and a target of attack at the beginning of the Cultural Revolution; the political scientist Chang Hsi-jo (1889–   ), a member of the standing committee, the Fourth Chinese People's Political Consultative Conference in 1964; the chemist Tseng Chao-lun (1903–   ), who had been with Wen on the long trek into Yunnan; and the sociologist P'an Kuang-tan, whose house in Shanghai had been Wen's shelter during his jobless days in 1925. Ch'u T'u-nan,[23] head of the history department of Yunnan University with a long record of Leftist activities, and Li Kung-p'u (?–1946),[24] who, as a leader of the National Salvation Association, had been jailed in Shanghai in 1936, were also Wen's frequent visitors. With Wu Han's encouragement, Wen began to expand his interest in a reappraisal of China's history. He reviewed Kuo Mo-jo's analysis of ancient Chinese society and traced Kuo's theorem to Marxist writings, including Mao Tse-tung's works, which he secretly borrowed from Wu Han and other Leftist friends. Wen reviewed Lu Hsün, and through Lu Hsün he further read up on Plekhanov, Lunacharsky, and Gorky, until he was moved to declare, "In Peking we used to denounce Lu Hsün, scorning him for being a Shanghai-school writer. Now I must repent before him. We were wrong, Lu Hsün was right. . . . We sought to be clean and aloof, but our cleanness and aloofness have got our country into this mess. Some say now I am associating with political people. Yes, it is precisely these people with whom I want to associate. . . ."[25]

A third important factor—the rebellious strand in his character —can be clearly noted in his violent reaction to pressures to silence him. As his criticism of the government became sharper, he embarrassed the school, which had been attempting to maintain a neutral position, and brought upon him mounting political pressure. A popular lecturer, he drew large crowds and became so controversial that prudent people began to shun his company. Rumors spread that the university would dismiss him.[26] But his attitude at faculty meetings was all the more militant when he defended student demonstrations and openly challenged Kuomintang apologists. The university did not dismiss him, but he lost his second job at the local middle school in January, 1945. This kind of political pressure provoked the "explosion of the dormant volcano" in him,[27] and led to a change in his outlook on Chinese literature, the historical role of Ch'ü Yüan, and Chinese ideological traditions.

IV   *Chinese Literature—a Record of Enslavement*

The starting point of his new views on Chinese literature was a change in taste. In 1939, immediately after his long walk to Kunming, he began to express admiration for the primitive man's lust for life, and he complained that traditional Chinese culture drained the fighting spirit of his people. Now, in his T'ang poetry classes, the adoption of a sociological viewpoint caused him to stress more than ever before, the social significance of Tu Fu's works. In the fall of 1943, when it was suggested that he collaborate with Robert Payne in editing English translations of modern Chinese poetry, he gladly accepted the task. In the course of the project he discovered the young poet T'ien Chien (1914–   ).

T'ien Chien was a newcomer whose style showed the influence of Mayakovsky.[28] After reading T'ien Chien's works, Wen was so delighted that he brought a selection of them to his class to read to his students. He said that when Professor Chu Tzu-ch'ing first showed the poems to him, he wondered how they could be poetry, but he read them again, and then said to himself, "Isn't this the sound of the drum?"[29] The drumbeat in T'ien's poems, such as the "People's Dance,"

Look!
Their
Vengeful
Force,
Their
Vengeful
Blood,
Their
Vengeful
Songs. . . .[30]

inspired Wen to write an essay praising the young poet as "The Drummer of Our Time."[31] He regarded the drum as the ancestor of all musical instruments and the drumbeat as the most authentic rhythm of life. The complexity of modern music, in his view, had developed from the simple monotone of the drum. Similarly, poetry had developed from short trisyllabic or quadrisyllabic meters into the complex rhythms of modern poetry. The process toward complexity and refinement was progress, but the same process, unfortunately, also weakened human feelings to the point where the delicacy of much modern Chinese poetry revealed only a tired, consumption-ridden spirit. As opposed to this kind of poetry which sang only in "half-notes," Wen felt refreshed to hear the "unpretentious, forceful, and savage drumbeat" of T'ien Chien's poems. His reaction was that of a person who had too long closed his windows to enjoy "the square-foot of peace within the four walls" and was now suddenly brought face to face with reality. The drumbeat had been rumbling at least since 1935 when the December ninth student demonstration in Peking started the debate on the "Literature of National Defense" and led to the establishment of the literary "united front" in China.[32] In 1935 he was sympathetic with the students but refused to associate with the Left-wing writers headed by Lu Hsün. Now his students applauded heartily at his frank and sincere admission of his change of heart.

In such a mood, Wen was easily irritated when younger associates reminded him that he was "burying himself in a pile of worm-eaten papers." In anger he wrote to his former student, the young poet Tsang K'o-chia, on November 25, 1943, "Nobody hates the old worm-eaten papers as much as I do, but precisely because I hate them, I am compelled to find out all about them. You accused me, without any basis in fact, of being a bookworm; you don't know that I am, on the contrary, the mothball that kills bookworms."[33] This may be true of Wen's work in 1943, but it certainly was a belated and dubious rationalization of his decision fifteen years before to study Chinese classical literature. Then he had begun with the purpose of searching for beauty in poetry; now he found fault with those traditions embodied in the classical literature, and believed that he had finally diagnosed the cultural ailment of China, which he planned to discuss in a comprehensive history of Chinese literature. In the proposed book he intended to trace the character and development of Chinese literature, and then to point out the correct direction of its future development. He did not live to finish the book, but an introductory essay and outline clearly reveals these theses.[34]

He was now convinced that all existing cultures would eventually merge into one world culture, and that all national literatures would similarly fuse into one. Although the paths of their individual historical developments differed, their basic direction was the same, that is, a movement toward an accurate reflection of the life of the common people. Chinese literature began with lyrical poetry which, from ancient times, had exerted a decisive influence on Chinese society. But Chinese poetry gradually isolated itself from the life of the common people, ran its course, and completely spent itself in the Northern Sung Dynasty (960–1125). Thereafter, it turned from poetry to the novel and drama, or from aristocratic to popular literary forms. It had to return to life of the common people to rejuvenate itself,[35] and contributing to this return were, at different times, two stimuli—Buddhism and Christianity. Wen believed that Chinese literature should follow the main trend of world literature, lest China be left behind. Modern poetry must "obey the command of the time," observe the rise of the novel as a signal, and develop a new language, new forms, and new ideas rooted in the life of the common people. To encourage young Chinese poets to be bold in innovation, he cited the examples of Juan Chi (210–263), Meng Chiao (751–814), Wordsworth, and Whitman, who all suffered the ridicule of their contemporaries only to emerge as the standard-bearers of a new poetry.[36]

Elsewhere, Wen explained that man would continue to free himself from social and spiritual bondage.[37] Literature, which expresses the life and aspirations of man, would also follow the same course. The Chinese literary tradition, developed and maintained by Confucian literati, was not free because the literati often wrote under subtle but always effective political and social restrictions. Wen urged the modern Chinese writer to strive for the control of his own destiny, and not to be content with half-freedoms. Coming from a recognized scholar of classical literature and at a time when there were more people in China conscious of their lack of intellectual freedom than ever before, Wen's words had a strong appeal.

Wen realized the perpetual conflict between the absolute freedom of the poet's mind, which was what he championed now, and the poet's responsibility toward his society. It was, essentially, the same conflict between "pure literature" and "social literature" which troubled him throughout his life. Thus, while he criticized Kuomintang censorship as well as political interference with literature in Russia,[38] he acknowledged the need for some check on the "irresponsible propaganda" of poets and other writers. But the government should never be permitted to impose restrictions on writers; only literary critics could assume the responsibility of appraising the social significance and aesthetic value of literary works. It is quite clear that in his mind only people with his own qualifications could perform this important service to man and society.

His belief that literature should directly reflect the life and aspirations of the common people supported his position that the modern Chinese writer should actively participate in the struggle of the common people for a better life, freedom, and democracy.[39] The belief also gave him comfort when he put aside his academic research to write political essays, and indicated a return to "actual practice" which he had advocated in his Tsing Hua School days. After trying for years to ignore occasional criticism of him as an ivory tower poet, Wen now felt greatly relieved because he could criticize caustically those arm-chair writers who closed their eyes to war, misery, and the pulsating tragedy of life in China.[40]

V   *Final Judgment of Ch'ü Yüan—the First Chinese People's Poet*

The emotional element in his new views on literature was in harmony with the national pathos and his own inner mood. The same emotional climate conditioned his final judgment on Ch'ü Yüan. There had been, since the beginning of the twentieth century, a growing sentiment in China to honor Ch'ü Yüan as China's first and foremost patriotic poet, which culminated in the designation of the legendary date of Ch'ü's death, the 5th of May, as Poet's Day in 1941. On that day in 1944, someone made public an iconoclastic study of Ch'ü, describing him as something of a court jester, a parasite, and a plaything of the king.[41] Among the evidence cited were some of Wen's studies of the *Songs of Ch'ü.* To clarify his own stand in the ensuing debate, Wen made two specific points.[42] First, he maintained, Ch'ü occupied a position similar to that of a court jester, but this was not of his own choosing. Being born into a family of the decadent nobility, tradition demanded that he live on the king's bounty. He was a slave as were all the king's subjects. Like others who for generations had been accustomed to their lot, Ch'ü knew of no other way to live. In view of these circumstances, Ch'ü's position, despicable though it might seem to a modern scholar of integrity, actually deserved more sympathy than contempt. Second, Ch'ü Yüan's sorrow over the loss of royal patronage was in the very same tradition of all the ancient sages who "felt lost without seeing the king for three months."[43] That his complaint was not quite the same as the selfish jealousy of the ladies of the royal harem could be seen in his concern for the misery of his people. Ch'ü grieved more for the peril to his country caused by the rejection of his advice than for a personal loss of political influence. Wen concluded that in the sense that Ch'ü expressed discontent on behalf of the people and warned the king, his heart was with the people and his act revolutionary. Ch'ü deserved to be called the first "people's poet."

Wen's argument, in reality, had been anticipated by Kuo Mo-jo and Lin Keng.[44] In 1942, Kuo and Lin had crossed swords on the meaning of the word *min* ("people") in the *Songs of Ch'u.* Kuo interpreted it as "common people" in contrast to the

nobility; Lin took it to be "man" in contrast to "heaven." At
that time Wen was not interested in this argument. But by 1944
the Marxist definition of "people"—the economically exploited
and politically suppressed—had become more widely accepted
by Chinese intellectuals than ever before. Scholars specializing
on the *Songs of Ch'u*, like Wen, felt a compulsion to reinterpret
Ch'ü Yüan's loyalty to the king as loyalty to the state, and to re-
identify the interest of the state of Ch'u with that of the common
people of Ch'u. This was exactly what Wen did, and he was
given credit for originating the ringing phrase "people's poet,"
which has ever since been quoted by all Chinese Leftist writers
on the subject of Ch'ü Yüan.[45]

VI   *Criticism of the Chinese Character and Tradition—*
Conservatism, Selfishness, and Hypocrisy

The same emotional compulsion prompted him to reap-
praise Chinese traditions, measuring them against his new
ideal—a happy and democratic China in a happy and democratic world. In doing so, he consciously or unconsciously
adopted the views of people whom he had known at different
times in his life. Under the influence of the deepening crisis
and Marxist social theories, he discovered the importance of
the common people and the urgency of improving their material
life. He came to feel that there was something basically wrong
in the Chinese concept of, and attitude toward, life. Comparing
this attitude with that of the West, Wen came to the conclusion
that the lack of a religious faith was principally responsible for
China's retarded condition.[46] His argument followed these lines:
the Westerner, with a religious outlook that accepts the existence
of an anthropomorphic and omnipotent god, can identify his
ideals with his god, deify his patriotism, science, even personal
love, and defy failure because he believes in eternal life. Such
a religious attitude explains why Puritanism contributed to the
growth and prosperity of America. Religion possesses that
"magic power" which can summon the latent power of man to
deal with a crisis, as has been well demonstrated in the West.
In contrast, the Chinese, lacking a faith in eternal life, developed

the Confucian philosophy of moderation to justify their efforts to compromise with reality, to find contentment in a "life between hunger and death." With intense feeling, Wen denounced his countrymen as creatures without "love, hate, sympathy for their fellow men, or a desire for truth." He said that the philosophy of the ancient Chinese sages, though cast in beautiful terms, was no more than a camouflage for the mediocrity, cowardice, and pettiness of the Chinese character.

There had been parallels to Wen I-to's line of thinking. It was to foster a religious attitude and promote modernization among the Chinese that the reformer K'ang Yu-wei (1858-1927) proposed to establish Confucianism as a state religion. His disciple Liang Ch'i-ch'ao supported the proposal and the reasoning behind it. Upon close comparison, however, one notes a major difference between Wen's idea and those of K'ang and Liang. K'ang felt that China needed a code of behavior, a standard of moral conduct, to rid herself of corruption, before any good government could be established.[47] Liang Ch'i-ch'ao, in his earlier days, carried K'ang's ideas further to champion the preservation of *K'ung-chiao* (Confucian doctrine; Confucian religion) because, in his view, it was the "national essence" of China.[48] In 1902, Liang reversed his position and argued for the need to enrich the Confucian doctrine with advanced Western ideas.[49] Liang abandoned his effort to promote unadulterated Confucianism as a religion for China, but he continued to urge his readers to adopt what he considered to be the rational and practical elements in Confucian teachings in order to save China. Throughout, K'ang and Liang persisted in one thing— stressing the rationalistic character of Confucianism to show that it was worthy of consideration in an age of science, and using Confucianism to prop up a national morality that was crumbling under the weight of decay, apathy and the impact of western ideas.[50] At different times, they felt that the Chinese needed a religious attitude which would inspire them to dedicate themselves to duty.

Wen I-to also felt that by acquiring a religious attitude the Chinese could become more conscientiously interested in the reconstruction of their country, but the driving force behind such a movement, he believed, would come from something akin to a blind faith in an omnipotent god, and in life eternal. Wen's argument thus differs markedly from that of K'ang and Liang. Wen's reference to the role Puritan attitudes played in the economic development of America sounds Weberian, but there is no clear evidence that Wen was familiar with Max Weber's works. Wen's reference to the "mysterious latent power" of man to meet a challenge shows traces of the Bergsonian idea of "inner self," and he had some knowledge of that French philosopher. The basic point of departure in Wen's argument is his conception of man's fundamental attitude toward life. He cited the lack of a true religion among the Chinese to explain their lack of a sense of permanent values, and their habit of avoiding difficulties. Wen's argument is on a plane different from, and more sophisticated than, that of K'ang and Liang. K'ang and Liang read Confucius, and Wen read K'ang and Liang, and now Mao Tse-tung and Lu Hsün; all three men were motivated by an urgent sense of need to find a formula to cure China's ills. In a time of deepened national crisis, Wen's solution had a greater emotional appeal.

In the same spirit Wen criticized the familism in Chinese tradition.[51] He blamed the emphasis on *hsiao* (filial piety) for the underdevelopment of a spirit of patriotism and a feeling of community among the Chinese. He was alarmed by renewed interest in antiquity among learned circles in 1944, and warned his readers to beware of the survival powers of Chinese traditions which resisted advanced Western ideas.[52] In his view, China must adopt advanced Western ideas in order to survive. He criticized the Confucians for their self-centered conservatism which helped to maintain the status quo and blocked social progress.[53] He went so far as to call the Confucians thieves, because, as he saw it, they selfishly capitalized on man's instinctive desire for order to establish and maintain a rigid social order that perpetuated their privileged status.[54] Completely reversing his earlier view on Taoism and dismissing the worth of its poetic vision of life, Wen now observed that during periods of crisis in Chinese history, it had thrived as a form of silent protest, but, in doing so, it had degenerated into various forms of irresponsible behavior, and it became something worse than a sham when Confucian officials appropriated it as a reputable escape from responsibility. Mohism, as a body of formulated doctrines, went down in early defeat when it attempted to compete with Confucianism for the dominance of Chinese society, but Wen saw something of the Mohist spirit preserved among the rebels and bandits in Chinese history.

Wen's theories, expressed in essays or speeches hastily written in an atmosphere that was hardly conducive to calm reflection, show more signs of emotional reaction than careful analysis. There is much facile analogy, indiscriminate use of politically biased terms, and sweeping generalization. They also show the influence of Kuo Mo-jo's analysis of Chinese society and the Marxist interpretation of history. But there are things note-worthy about these writings.

During his last years, Wen was clearly enamored of economic determinism; he even indicated that he intended to re-study Chinese history and the history of Chinese literature from the viewpoint of dialectical materialism. But his understanding of Marxism was superficial and, if he had lived to carry out his plans, it is not likely that he would have been able to resolve the conflict between economic determinism and his basic idealist convictions. He seems to have accepted Marxism merely as a convenient formula to cure China's physical ills, and to have believed that as soon as peace and prosperity were attained, man would cease to be materialistic in his outlook. This kind of dualism has its roots in Chinese historical thinking which tends to divide history into *sheng-shih* (times of peace and prosperity) and *luan-shih* (times of chaos), and to assign different values to them respectively. In times of peace, the Chinese have tended to accept a basically Confucian view of man, regarding him as more spiritual than material; in times of trouble, they tend to favor a basically Legalistic view which treats human responses to the material forces as almost purely mechanistic. Without being aware of the fundamental conflict between such views, Wen I-to followed a pattern of dualistic thinking for which the Chinese also find sanction in the saying attributed to Confucius that only when man has sufficient food and clothing will rites and righteousness prevail.

The way in which Wen used a Marxist framework to interpret Chinese culture may be imperfect, but his training lent his arguments a literary quality that is at once fresh and imaginative. He gave an intensely emotional and eloquent expression to what most Chinese intellectuals believed to be the most urgently needed thing in China—a drastic departure from tradition. His was a simple truism, one which had been expressed by numerous reformers since the last years of the nineteenth century. But the emotional intensity of his argument, and the emotional intensity with which his audience responded to it, made the difference.

In his criticism of Chinese traditions, Wen demonstrated that he had acquired the pithy, biting, and poignant qualities of Lu Hsün's prose style. He put those qualities to good use when he turned to comment directly on pressing political and military problems. Referring to wartime profiteers, he compared the street scene of Kunming with the pink cheeks of a tubercular patient at an advanced stage of illness, and warned against a "terrible complacency."[55] He accused the newspapers of white-washing corruption and insulting the people's determination to fight to the last.[56] He satirized the megalomania and self-worship of Chiang Kai-shek.[57] To his students in the army he said that Chinese intellectuals, including himself, should realize their debt to the people. If the Chinese army were looked down upon by their Western Allies, the blame should go to the intellectual minority who monopolized education.[58]

He bitterly criticized the Kuomintang, and occasionally used the word "revolt" or "revolution" in his impassioned outbursts, but he never seriously considered a violent overthrow of the Nationalist government. As he once did in the early 1920's, he again identified his romantic ideal with a utopian world order cast in the old Chinese concept of ta-t'ung (great uniformity; great harmony); only now he saw this ideal world order in the Marxist context, because his interest in a ta-t'ung society had been recently rekindled by Mao Tse-tung's works. Without any practical knowledge of social and political revolution, Wen was attracted by the naive vision of a perfect classless society where men are equal and free,[59] and the urgency of the situation in China made him momentarily forget his reservations about Russia. Consequently, although he was ready to risk his life for his ideals, he continued to abhor war and violence. He accepted bloodshed as necessary only in China's struggle against Japan, and he refused to believe that Chinese unification and progress had to be bought with human life. Hence, his sincere acceptance of the program of the Democratic League which centered on an immediate cessation of the civil war and peaceful, democratic reform of the government. Mainly because of these convictions, and only partly due to political pressure, he seldom talked directly about the Communists, except on a few occasions when he hinted at his approval of what he heard about Yenan.[60] Beneath his changed attitude toward Chinese traditions, Wen I-to retained his dedication to a romantic ideal. But most of his contemporaries saw only the surface change. Even his old friend Lo Lung-chi asked him if he anticipated a fourth change, after he had gone through three changes in his life—poet, classicist, political crusader. Wen's answer was that, having found the right path, he would never change again.[61] Unfortunately, he did not live long enough either to prove or disprove these words.

VII   *The Last Days of Wen I-to—the Volcano's Final Eruption*

The leaders of Kunming's citizenry gathered on June 28, 1946, to listen to the Democratic League explain its position in the voice of its star performer, Wen I-to. After about ten minutes of analysis of the current situation and a description of the evolution of the League's political philosophy and platform, Wen said,

Let us today publicly and formally extend our hands to you, my distinguished friends. Please take a good look at them: they are the hands of bookworms, powerless even to hold a chicken still. They can't possibly and they are unwilling to threaten anybody, and precisely because of that they are also unwilling to submit to the threats of others. They are the hands of the penniless poor; they can't possibly and are unwilling to buy anybody with money, and precisely because of that they won't be bought by anybody. . . . Don't be afraid of them. If you don't believe me, just smell them, there is no stench of blood on them. . . .

As he dramatically extended his hands toward the audience, showing a quantity of chalk powder, he added,

You see, these hands that have been holding chalk for all our lives, we can hold them open for you to inspect any time. This snow-white chalk powder is precisely their symbolic color. I declare again, please don't be afraid. These are clean hands . . . and we extend them to you![62]

The eloquence and power of Wen's speeches drew growing crowds until the Nationalist government could no longer ignore him. In July, 1944, soon after he began his severe criticism of the government and castigated the military commanders, word went around that he had been blacklisted by the secret police. His friends and devoted students became concerned for his safety. One evening in August, 1944, Wang I, an instructor of Chinese literature at the university, went to his apartment on the second floor of the K'un-hua Middle School building.[63] Besides two beds and a makeshift table, the room was bare. With a piece of steamed bread in one hand and the other hand polishing the surface of a stone seal he was carving, Wen greeted his visitor with his usual kind smile. "This is my second job," he said after swallowing a bite of bread while motioning to his visitor to sit on the bed. "We depend on small handcraft industry like this to live now," he smiled again. There was an awkward silence. Finally Wang mustered up enough courage to say, "I am coming to you as a student, to ask you to take better care of yourself. There are too few people who uphold the truth now; we cannot afford to lose you." Wen stared at him for a long while. Tears came to his eyes. "This is a matter of an individual's attitude toward life," he replied. "I have come to feel that too many young men nowadays are too cold. . . . A man must have heart and blood. . . . I don't understand politics, but is today the time for us to worry about our personal safety? I appreciate your concern very much. But I still want to be a man, and I still have a conscience."

Wen continued to make speeches and write political criticism. The Japanese surrender brought great excitement to Kunming. Upon hearing the news, Wen immediately went to a nearby barbershop and had his rich, bushy beard shaved. The threat to his life did not dampen his jubilation. He repeatedly told his family and friends that soon a political solution would be reached and peace would be restored to China, and then he could return to his research.[64] But his optimism was premature. On October 3, 1945, Nationalist troops stormed Kunming, escorted the Yunnanese Governor Lung Yün to a waiting airplane and installed a new governor, Li Tsung-huang (1888-?), who had ruthlessly suppressed a student demonstration in Kunming in 1928. The new garrison commander, General Kuan Lin-cheng (1905–   ), also Chiang's loyal lieutenant, immediately issued orders prohibiting all "communist-inspired" antigovernment activities and expression. Defying these orders, the students in Kunming gathered on the evening of November 25, 1945, to commemorate the 1915 Yunnan Uprising. Wen was one of the speakers. Nationalist troops surrounded the campus and opened fire to disperse the students. But the meeting proceeded and concluded with a demonstration march in which Wen, for the first time in his life, participated. This was the beginning of a series of conflicts between students and garrison troops, leading to the December 1, 1945, incident in which four students, including a girl, were killed, twenty-five wounded, and much university property destroyed. With bitterness Wen denounced the government action as "black terror" and described that day as "the darkest day since the overthrow of the Manchus."[65] Although he was told that the garrison commander had set a price on his head, he became more vociferous than ever as the students continued to hold meetings.[66] On February 17, 1946, he addressed another student rally organized to celebrate the First Political Consultative Conference held earlier that month in Chungking. The rally also demanded government action to punish those responsible for the February tenth incident in Chungking in which Kuo Mo-jo and Li Kung-p'u were wounded. Again Wen participated in the demonstration that afternoon.

Late in June, 1946, the 184th Division, which was composed mostly of Yunnanese and was then stationed in southern Manchuria, revolted in protest against the continuing civil war. The news caused the Kuomintang to tighten its control and surveillance over Kunming, turning it into a city of terror. Another change of garrison commanders did not ease the tension. The new commander, a General Huo, supported a mysterious "Chinese League for Democracy and Freedom" which distributed posters identifying Wen, Lo Lung-chi, and Wu Han as Communists.[67] In the pro-Nationalist press of Kunming, there appeared a continuous flow of vilifications leveled at Wen, one of which sarcastically suggested that Wen drown himself in the Kunming Lake à la Ch'ü Yüan.[68] Friends urged him to leave. Professor Fung Yu-lan, the noted philosopher, tried to persuade him to go to America with him, but he declined. The University of California at Berkeley extended an invitation but he again declined.[69] He wanted to go back to Peiping with his students as soon as he could wind up the League's business in Kunming. By the end of June, 1946, most of the students and faculty had left, including Wen's close associate Wu Han.

Li Kung-p'u, the League's national chairman, arrived in Kunming to plan future League activities with Wen. Because Li had been a marked target, his presence only added to the tension. Confirming rumors of a plot on the lives of League leaders was the unexplained presence of suspicious individuals in the area of the League's office and Wen's apartment. Then a strange woman, faking mental derangement, visited Wen's house to mumble predictions of Wen's imminent death. A frightened and seriously ill Mrs. Wen ordered their eldest son, Wen Li-ho, to stay with his father at all times; she also ordered the gate to their compound kept locked, and no stranger was admitted after dark.[70] In the morning of July 11, the last group of students departed; that same evening Li Kung-p'u was assassinated at a street corner a few blocks from Wen's apartment.[71] The next morning, as Wen rushed to the emergency hospital to see the dying Li, anonymous posters appeared in the streets charging the Communists with Li's murder. Late that night, while Wen was preparing statements for the press and petitions to government authorities, a friend went to his house to inform him that he was, with absolute certainty, next on the list.[72]

"It has come to this now," with a calm smile on his face Wen said to the concerned friend. "If I don't go out to look after things, how am I to face the dead?"

Wen continued to take charge of the League office and went ahead with plans for a memorial service for Li on July 15. On that day, after Li's widow, too grief-stricken to finish speaking, was helped off the podium, Wen spoke,

We all know that, only a few days ago, the most despicable, the most shameless incident occurred in Kunming. What crime had Li Kung-p'u committed to deserve such an ending in unconscionable hands! . . . Today I want to know if there are more secret agents here, right here. Step up, you, tell us, tell us why you killed Li Kung-p'u. . . .

In an emotion-choked voice he went on to deliver a scathing indictment against the assassins, and praised the youth of Kunming for standing up against oppression,

You, reactionaries, you try so hard to alienate us from our friends. What shame! You think now that Lienta has moved away and the students have dispersed for the summer, you think we are powerless now. But, secret agents, you are wrong! Look at the thousand and more young people gathered here, our arms linked together. We, the young generation of Kunming, shall not tolerate your reckless action. . . . We are not afraid of death, we are constantly ready to follow in Li Kung-p'u's footsteps. The moment we step out of this door, we won't think of stepping back![73]

The meeting, frequently punctuated by sustained applause, broke up at noon.

A few minutes after five in the same afternoon, as Wen emerged from the office of the *Democratic Weekly,* he fell under a shower of bullets.

CHAPTER 8

Conclusion

You are a roar of fire.
Lighting up even the abyss' bottom,
Guiding the youth
To find themselves from despair.

You are a roar of fire,
Spotting the demons,
But destroying yourself
To let a New China rise from your ashes!

Chu Tzu-ch'ing, "Mourning Wen I-to"[1]
August 16, 1946

FEAR and silent grief gripped the few participants in Wen's
funeral. There was no impassioned speech like the one Wen
had made for Li Kung-p'u only a few days before. Nobody dared
refer to his death as a murder and nobody demanded justice.
Surviving members of the Democratic League in Kunming found
refuge in the U. S. Consulate compound. Several students, still
waiting for transportation out of Kunming, walked furtively by
the deserted gate of the campus and exchanged whispers as they
passed in front of the faculty quarters. But outside Kunming,
in the wartime capital of Chungking and elsewhere, the educated class soon recovered from the initial shock and bom-
barded the government with messages of protest. Columbia,
Harvard, and New York University educators also responded
with open letters urging the American government to reconsider its China policy. The Nationalist authorities went through
the motions of an investigation, but the result did not satisfy
an angered populace. The League was denied participation in
the official investigation, or in the trial of two alleged assassins.
Though two executions resulted and the court declared there
174

was no evidence of government involvement in a possible conspiracy, the League's own investigation placed the responsibility upon the Yunnan Garrison Command. The American Consulate in Kunming filed its own confidential report implicating the KMT government of an elaborately planned undertaking.[2] The storm raged, and in no small measure contributed to the waves of student strikes in 1947 which gained intensity with the impending political, economic, and military collapse of the Nationalist regime. The Communists capitalized on Wen's death and placed him on the level of Lu Hsün. Chou En-lai in a public speech in October, 1946, said that both Lu Hsün and Wen I-to were "the most loyal beasts of burden serving the people";[3] he compared Wen's last determination to "be a slave of the common people" with Lu Hsün's famous epigram.[4] Insured of martyrdom, Wen's name glowed brighter each day. In August, 1949, even Mao Tse-tung was moved to cite him as one who "had backbones . . . who chose to fall rather than bow before the assassins' guns . . . and who pounded on the desk [of a scholar] and rose up [a warlike hero]!"[5] And Mao urged writers to immortalize Wen in poetry and prose because he deserved a place among the titans of Chinese history. Public commemorative services were held, and eulogistic essays and reminiscences poured forth in every publication except official Kuomintang organs; these demonstrations were renewed on every anniversary of Wen's death for many years.[6] A noted author, Ch'üan Mo, made his life into a movie script in 1959, to which a nationwide readership responded with enthusiasm.[7] Wen Li-ho, who was wounded at the scene of the assassination offered suggestions for the improvement of the script. Twenty years later, in June, 1978, Peking announced preparations to film Wen's life story under the title, "P'ai-an sung" [Ode to the desk-pounder], referring to the line of praise once uttered by Mao Tse-tung.[8] In the memory of modern Chinese intellectuals, Wen now looms large as a model for them to emulate.

Thus ended the career of a leading modern Chinese intellectual whose life, as ordained by Keats, was not written on water but cast in bronze. On it he had inlaid several jewels, such as his "Sheath of the Sword." His poetry will continue to be read, and it will continue to exert a palpable influence on future

Chinese poets. Even in the post-Cultural Revolution era, the verses of many poets reflect Wen's sensitivity to rhythm and follow the direction he indicated—adaptation of the tones and styles of native folk songs. His "Sunshine Rhymes" influenced many successful younger poets, such as the worker-writer Li Hsüeh-ao, who acknowledged the benefits he gained from Wen I-to's example, as, for instance, in his using one rhyme throughout his long poems in *Ying-hsiung sung* [*Ode to heroes*, 1973]. There is more evidence on nearly every page in the *Poetry Journal*, which was revived after 1976.

Wen's prosodic theory has furnished points of departure in every debate on the direction of China's new poetry when ideology ceases to be the only subject for discussions. The latest debate stimulated by Wen's ideas started in 1959 and reverberated through the first half of the 1960's with Ho Ch'i-fang (1911–1977), the director of Chinese literary research, the Academy of Science, as the chief proponent. Chu Kuang-ch'ien (1898–   ), Tung Ch'u-p'ing, and Wang Li, among many others, joined in the debate which, as may be expected, ended inconclusively.[9] But everyone agreed that Wen I-to had convinced later poets of the advantages to be gained from the skillful and conscious use of musical elements native to the Chinese language.

The imaginative approach and refreshing style of presentation of Wen's classical research have also blazed new and promising trails. Minor imperfections notwithstanding Wen succeeded in breathing life into the often labored but erudite world of classical scholarship.[10] His lectures on the *Book of Poetry* and his interpretations of the *Songs of Ch'u*, sometimes couched in conversational terms, possess a charm that is every teacher's envy and every student's hope. He initiates the discussion in straightforward terms with no clearing of the throat, as though he had been engaged in conversation with the reader for some time. The effect is one of a sharing cf confidence with the reader, whereby he effortlessly draws the latter into the discussion. It is an art many later scholars tried to emulate but few achieved.[11]

His essays of political and social criticism embody his total being, visceral and rational; they are the pained, though eloquent, voice of a man with an honest and thorough commitment. They may not be the most shining among the jewels on his crown, but their glitter remains undiminished when viewed in historical perspective and with an understanding of his own intellectual development.

His own development went through clearly marked stages. The first stage was his formative years when he was a student at the Tsing Hua School. During those years he was attracted to, and overwhelmed by, many Western ideals which partially alienated him from his native tradition. Toward the end of this period, however, he was already partially repelled by the school's overemphasis on the material aspects of Western culture and drawn back to his own native traditions by a youthful sense of national pride. The second stage was distinguished by the life he led as a modern poet, during which time he quite successfully synthesized many Western and Chinese ideas on literary criticism and creative writing. His attitude was sympathetic to the Western tradition, but antagonism mounted as he became increasingly sensitive to China's position in the world. The running dispute among his contemporaries who subscribed to different sets of foreign ideas made him weary. A resurgence of interest in the aesthetic value of classical Chinese literature, together with the attraction of a peaceful academic life, initiated the third stage of his life. As a scholar of the Chinese classics, he refrained from discussing Western ideas. What may seem to have been an escape into the Chinese past was actually a time of contemplation and sorting out of ideas, of careful avoidance of superficial comparisons between the Chinese and Western traditions. His efforts to understand the development of Chinese society and his anger at the continuing chaos in China brought a close to this third stage and ushered in a period of violent reaction against many aspects of the Chinese tradition. The last stage of his intellectual development was characterized by a resolute acceptance of many Western values.

These stages in his intellectual development represent changes in outlook which involved centrally, his views of man, of man's relation to society (mainly of the Confucian persuasion), and of man's attachment to his country (or patriotism).

From traditional Chinese thought he had acquired the idea

that man is something more than material. Man may not be able to escape from material forces and physical laws, but he is distinguished from material things by his *ling* (spirit).[12] Wen's idea of *ling* may have been subsequently influenced by the Western idea of soul, but important differences between the two ideas remained. To him, *ling* is that which distinguishes love from carnal desire, and that which enables man to recognize right from wrong. It cannot defy material forces, but with it man, though defeated, is not conquered. *Ling* is the creative fire in man which may explode at any time. It is noble and beautiful because it is what distinguishes man from beast.

But his contact with Western thought caused a substantive modification of this view of man. He was impressed by the Darwinian concept that man was but a combination of material elements, and that life had no profound meaning beyond the effort to survive. He accepted Darwinism in spite of the conflict it created with his earlier views. The conflict continued and was never completely resolved at the time of his death. At different stages of his life, one or the other view would dominate his thinking. When he was in college, he believed in the absolute validity of the theory of *ling*, because he felt that the world had progressed far enough, or had become civilized enough, for man to be able to put aside the fight for survival. So he accepted Kropotkin's doctrine that man's desire for art surged forth spontaneously when his material needs were satisfied; he even found support for this idea in Confucian sayings. After seeing poverty and misery at their worst in 1938–1943, however, he was no longer so certain that man's struggle for existence was over. Thus, when economic determinism drew him back to the Darwinian concept of man in his last years, he admitted that man had, first and foremost, physically to fight for his own material survival; other values were of secondary importance.

The conflict in his mind produced, with varying degrees of clarity and success, a dualism: man's physical needs versus his *ling*, a parallel to but not an equivalent of the Western dualism of body and soul. The twain never met on harmonious terms, and Wen's dualism came to the fore at different times as a clash between pure literature and social literature, betwen imagination and reality, and between his emotional self and his rational self.

The Confucian concept of man's relationship to society prescribes that the greatest man is he who dreams of and works toward an ideal order, and that the highest goal of life is to make the great way, or the true way, prevail, so that peace and plenty will obtain on earth, and man thus attain a nobler life. Wen took this idea for granted in his younger days, but he never seriously considered it as a personal goal until he became more aware of the national predicament. When he was a starry-eyed youth of eighteen totally absorbed in lyric poetry, he talked blithely about the "transmission of the sage's way and the king's way." At twenty-five, acquaintance with the stark contrast between China and America made him think about devoting his life to the education of his fellow countrymen through art, but he promptly abandoned the thought. From the age of thirty to forty, the idea of serving his fellow men, if still in his mind, was submerged in his intense preoccupation with literary research. After forty, it reemerged in a new utopian image which he identified with the Western ideal of democracy and the Marxist ideal of a perfect social order free of strife. From passively dreaming of a Confucian utopia to actively working toward a Marxist classless society, the dramatic change in Wen I-to's attitude was largely due to a changing vision of how man can best serve society.

Most of his critics and hagiographers have tried to make his patriotism his prime virtue, but few have noted the various elements that constituted the love he had for his country. In his student days, his patriotism was inspired by the stirring verses of Yüeh Fei, whose loyalty was dedicated to the emperor, and by the poetry of Lu Yu, which expressed indignation against foreign invaders. But nineteenth century English Romanticism attuned him to other aspects of human compassion and devotion. Except for a brief period when he championed the cause of the Ta-chiang Society, Wen I-to's patriotism was submerged during his mature life. When his attention was finally drawn to politics, what actually lay behind his patriotic sentiment was mainly a simple but deeply-felt sympathy for the plight of his fellow countrymen.

Underlying the many changes in his intellectual outlook were two constants, or absolutes: a belief in the beauty of Beauty and in the beauty of China's cultural traditions. In his early life he was trained to appreciate the aesthetic quality of lyric poetry and painting, but the idea that beauty is a permanent value on the same level with truth and virtue did not occur to him until he discovered Keats. His quest for ideal beauty led him first to pursue the perfection of color, form, and imagery in poetic and graphic expression that could arouse man's noblest sentiments; his love was the muse who breathed life and music into words. When he returned to classical Chinese literature, he identified this abstract concept of ideal beauty with the aesthetic values of the Chinese classics, and with the "mysterious beauty" of Chinese culture, which he defined in vague but passionate terms. Finally, as he turned to political pamphleteering, he also identified his sense of ideal beauty with the beauty of the land, which was threatened by war, and with the impoverished but lovable common people, who were victimized by continuing chaos. And he responded by championing the cessation of civil war and reform of the political and social order. However frequently he may have changed his ideals, the underlying and energizing idea remained unchanged. As Wu Han has said, "All Wen I-to sought through his life was beauty,"[13] true and perfect beauty wherever he could find it.

His conviction about the permanent value of the Chinese cultural tradition also remained constant. He stated it in different terms at different stages of his life, but he never really rejected it altogether. The idea had been inculcated in his early schooling when he saw, in addition to their aesthetic values, the universal principles embodied in the Chinese classics, which are, after all, manifestations of ancient Chinese culture. In his mature years, he ceased talking about the universal principles of the sage-kings, but he clung to a belief in the permanent aesthetic values of classical Chinese literature until his death. Even after he attempted to adopt a sociological approach to the study of Chinese culture, and still later accepted the Marxist frame of historical interpretation, what he sought was but a new interpretation, not a total rejection, of the values of China's cultural tradition. In his last years he talked about the "cultural ailment" of China; he denounced the Confucians; he claimed that he had emerged from his "pile of moth-eaten papers;" but he maintained that the Chinese historical experience would retain its glory if only he could restudy it and retell it from a different viewpoint, and he continued to uphold Ch'ü Yüan and Tu Fu as models of behavior, particularly Ch'ü Yüan. His commitment to Chinese cultural traditions, to Tu Fu and Ch'ü Yüan, was never a result of pure reason; even in his early writings he objected to the so-called scientific reexamination of China's past advocated by Hu Shih. To Wen, it was unthinkable for one to assume an emotional detachment from one's cultural background, and he himself chose to plunge back into it with intense personal feeling.[14]

The path Wen I-to charted in his intellectual development traces the general pattern of the shaping of the modern Chinese mind. Chinese and Western ideas were fused into many different constructs by members of his generation, and certain of these were more dynamic, more coherent, and more enduring than others. One of them was the synthesis of Western Romanticism and Confucian utopianism. The Romantic attitude toward life which Wen I-to acquired from Keats and Byron made Wen believe that to live is to live intensely. The Byronic Romanticist acknowledges that life is short and the most must be made of it, but his sense of the ideal fullness and richness of life is the opposite of that of a hedonist. The latter hurries to "fill the cup" because "the leaves of life keep falling one by one;" the former rushes to accomplish something of value before the sands run out. The latter attitude led Wen to strive relentlessly for personal accomplishment, to "burn himself to ashes like the wick of a candle," or to "explode like a volcano." The explosion of the volcano in him awaited the proper moment which came when he fused the Romantic ideal of individual fulfillment with the Confucian ideal of the world order. The Confucian ideal urges man to make prevail the ancient sage-king's way, the attainment of personal perfection which finds expression in an ideal social order. In the last years of his life, Wen I-to accepted the Marxist version of *ta-t'ung* (the great uniformity), dedicated himself to it, and fought for it with zeal. Only in intense conflict could he feel the excitement and real significance of living. As he said in his *Red Candle*, "You must 'burn' before there can be light;" Lu Hsün also left a well remembered motto to Chinese youth: "If you have a bit of heat, you must radiate that much light."[15] The attitude has much to do with the readiness of many young Chinese intellectuals to sacrifice everything to their chosen cause.

Closely linked to the fusion of Western Romanticism and Confucian utopianism is that of Romanticism and populism, in which the Romantic admiration of the primitive lust for life and of the savage drumbeat merges with the cult of the common people. In Wen's early life the dictum had been "what the sages said;" in his last years the mandate became "what the people want." From Confucian utopianism to populism, the shift was indeed rapid. This metamorphosis, however, was not incomprehensible, because the Chinese concept of *min* (people), as we have noted above, is flexible enough to accommodate a variety of interpretations, and among the Confucian teachings, particularly those of Mencius, there is enough emphasis on the importance of *min* in the *chün-min* (king-subject) relationship to make the ideological shift relatively easy.

The importance of a national emotional climate in the process of personal ideological change is well demonstrated in the case of Wen I-to. Wen and his contemporaries shared a sense of urgency which intensified with each setback China suffered and with each scene of human misery they witnessed. Even when Wen I-to was, on the surface, content with academic research, he avoided reading the newspapers simply because he could neither smother the sense of urgency nor bear it with indifference, and it propelled him from one set of ideals to another. While vacillation is clearly noticeable in his case, the lives of many intellectuals of his generation show similar movements from one philosophical and ideological extreme to another. In every case, the prevailing emotional climate was a crucial factor.

The fluidity and flux of the modern Chinese mind found clear reflection in Wen I-to. After the collapse of the old Confucian value system, the Chinese intellectual had no fixed values to cling to, no accepted traditions to live by, and no opportunity carefully to construct a new ideological system. Time was precious, serenity unattainable. Wen I-to and his contemporaries were not "system builders;" their efforts only mirrored a desperate quest for a new ideological system, or theories hastily contrived from disparate strands of Western and Chinese traditions, to explain history, society, and man's position in the universe. This desperate search, as Wen I-to's life history clearly testifies, is the breath and spirit of the intellectual life of twentieth century China.

Envoi

a

A scholar you are, yes, but aren't you concerned
    about your own safety?
You just cannot feel unashamed, staring at the thousands
    weeping on the roadside.
Your mind made up, you are willing to risk stepping
    on the tiger's tail.
Your lofty virtue thus established, we look up to you
    to boost our morale.
Then, Red flags had just pointed out the much harassed road,
Now, history should portray such a spray of blossoms,
    defiant of heavy snow.
You will remain with us as long as the righteous spirit
    of the universe remains,
Together with the clouds and the moon you'll radiate your
    divine quality.

Year after year I think of those days and my mind goes
    far, far away,
When cicadas sing, rice ears swell, and swallows soar in the sky.
The fallen petals on the ground still suggest your painter's palette,
And surging waves that reach up to heaven remind us of you in anger.
Now the "Dead Water" is gone—a highrise building's replaced
    the Dragon Ditch,[16]
As poetry flourishes like spring flowers in the garden of arts.
I want to tell you all these things, but where can I find
    a stellar messenger?
Here I pour a libation in the direction of Yunnan in the south.

> Jao Meng-k'an, "Remembering My Late Friend Wen I-to
> in a Summer Night,"[17]   July 1962.

b

New China News service, Nanking Dispatch, July 16, 1957:—
184

Ts'ai Yün-ch'i, who had actively participated in the murder of the patriots Wen I-to and Li Kung-p'u, was sentenced to a ten year term in prison by the Intermediate People's Court, Yen-ch'eng District, Kiangsu Province, on July 6. . . .

"Thirteen Years Ago Today,"[18]
New Evening News (Hong Kong, July 16, 1970)

Notes and References

Acknowledgments

1. Sato Tamotsu, "Wen I-to to Toshi" ("Wen I-to and T'ang Poetry"), *Kindai Chugoku no shiso to bungaku* (*Literature and Thought in Contemporary China*) (Tokyo: Tokyo o daigaku bungakubu Chugoku bungakukenkyu shitsu, 1967), p. 589. Hereafter cited as Tamotsu Sato. Also see *Jen-min jih-pao* (*People's Daily*), July 20, 1956, p. 8; and footnote 23, Chapter 6 below.

Preface

1. See Chapter 8 below, and the list of events testifying to Wen's enduring fame in Yü-ming Shaw, "Wen I-to: The Early Life and Writings of a Modern Chinese Intellectual, from 1899 to 1933," unpublished paper, University of Notre Dame, 1974, pp. 1–2. Hereafter cited as Yü-ming Shaw.

Prologue

1. Reconstructed from my memory of the site (I lived for three years in a rooming house just about a block from the murder scene), from Wen Li-ho, "Pa-pa yü tz'u chi-hsiang" ("A Detailed Account of My Father's Assassination"), *Wen I-to hsien-sheng szu-nan chou-nien ch-nien t'e-k'an* (*Memorial Issue: on the First Anniversary of Wen I-to's Death*), Ch'ing-hua chou-k'an she (The *Tsing-hua Weekly* Editorial Office), 1949, pp. 10–12. Hereafter cited as *Memorial Issue*, and the journal, as *THW*.

2. Chu Tzu-ch'ing, et al., eds., *Wen I-to ch'üan-chi* (*The Complete Works of Wen I-to*), 4 vols., Shanghai, 1948, Section *chia*, pp. 305–34. Hereafter cited as *CW*. This work does not include all of Wen's writings.

3. Interview with Wen Chia-szu and his family on March 25, 1973, in Peking.

Chapter One

1. Hsi-shui, formerly known as Ch'i-shui.
2. Original name, I-to (also-many); styles, Chia-hua and Yu-san;

187

changed to To upon enrollment at Tsing Hua; upon the suggestion
of P'an Kuang-tan, started using I-to (one-many) in October, 1920,
in school publications, and formally adopted it after his return from
the United States.

3. Wen accepted this legend. See *THW*, No. 73 (April 17, 1916),
p. 11.

4. Shih Ching, *Wen I-to ti tao-lu* (*The Path that Wen I-to Chose*)
(Shanghai, 1947), p. 1. Hereafter cited as Shih, *The Path*. The
author of this work was Wen's student, distant relative, and close
associate for many years.

5. *Hu-pei t'ung-chih* (*The Gazetteer of Hupeh Province*) (Shanghai, 1921), pp. 3206, 3246, 3251; To Ch'i, ed., *Ch'i-shui hsien chih*
(*The Gazetteer of Ch'i-shui*) (n.p., 1886), chüan 12 *passim*.

6. Mien Chih (pseud.), *Wen I-to* (Hong Kong, 1949), p. 25
(Hereafter cited as Mien, *Wen I-to*.) The work seems comparable
to, but shows minor discrepancies with, Shih, *The Path*.

7. Facsimile of Wen's handwritten letter dated Oct. 16, 1923,
Chicago, in Shih Ching, *Wen I-to* (Hupeh, 1958), Frontispiece. Hereafter cited as Shih, *Wen I-to*.

8. Shih, *The Path*, p. 2.

9. Li Wen erh lieh-shih chi-nien wei-yüan-hui (The committee
for the Memorial Service for the Two Martyrs Li Kung-p'u and
Wen I-to), ed., *Jen-min ying-lieh* (*The Heroes and Martyrs of the
People*) (n.p., n.d.), p. 376. Hereafter cited as *Heroes and Martyrs*.
The committee apparently included Kuo Mo-jo, Wu Han, and others
sympathetic with the Democratic League. This work, possibly published in 1946, includes numerous articles on the assassination of Li
and Wen.

10. *CW*, Section *keng*, p. 78.

11. *Heroes and Martyrs*, p. 375.

12. *CW*, Postscript by Chu Tzu-ch'ing, p. 5; Chu, Tzu-ch'ing,
Chu Tzu-ch'ing hsüan-chi (*Selected Works* of Chu Tzu-ch'ing)
(Peking, 1952), p. 162. Hereafter cited as Chu, *Selected Works*.

13. *CW*, Chronology, pp. 31–32.

14. Wen frequently quoted Su Tung-p'o's works. See *CW*, Section
ting, p. 255. The translation of these two lines is from Hans Frankel,
"Poetry and Painting: Chinese and Western Views of Their Convertibility," *Comparative Literature*, IX, 4 (Fall 1957), p. 289.

15. Elsewhere this institution is referred to as the Tsing Hua
College, but when it was founded, it was more of a preparatory
school, composed of two divisions, the High School and the Middle

School, of four years each. It was not expanded into a university until 1928.

16. Mien, *Wen I-to*, p. 11.

Chapter Two

1. *CW*, Section *ting*, p. 69.

2. Liang, Shih-ch'iu, *T'an Wen I-to* (*About Wen I-to*) (Taipei, 1967), p. 3. Hereafter cited as Liang, *About Wen I-to*. Liang points out the error in *CW*, Chronology, p. 31, that Wen's English deficiency set him back a year, and then at the end of his ninth year he stayed on for one more year, making it a total of ten years. Wang Chi-chen also recalls that Wen enrolled at Tsing Hua beginning in the fall of 1912.

3. For the early history of the Tsing Hua School, see *Ch'ing-hua i-lan* (*A Glance at the Tsing Hua School*) (Peking, 1926), pp. 9–12; *Kuo-li Ch'ing-hua ta-hsüeh i-lan* (*A Glance at the National Tsing Hua University*) (Peiping, 1932), pp. 3–6; and *Kuo-li Ch'ing-hua ta-hsüeh nien-k'an, 1933* (*The National Tsing Hua University Yearbook, 1933*), pp. 7–9.

4. *THW*, Special Supplement, No. 1 (June 26, 1915), pp. 40–42.

5. *THW*, Special Supplement, No. 2 (June 1916), p. 20.

6. P'an Kuang-tan, "Students and Servants," *THW*, No. 185 (April 24, 1920), p. 27.

7. *THW*, No. 87 (Nov. 15, 1916), p. 22.

8. *THW*, No. 20 (Dec. 7, 1916), p. 20; No. 97 (Feb. 22, 1917), p. 24. The typical topics are: "Should China remain agrarian or industrialize?" "Which should China stress today, economic progress or moral education?" and "Should there be free marriage in China?" *THW*, No. 82 (Oct. 11, 1916), p. 20. "Will there be a war between Japan and the U. S. in ten years?" *THW*, No. 86 (Nov. 8, 1916), p. 24. "Is the library more important than the gymnasium?"

9. For the subjects of these lectures, see *THW*, Nos. 87 (p. 20), 88 (p. 18), 78 (p. 18), 85 (p. 19), 95 (p. 22), 97 (pp. 15–18), 103 (pp. 17–18), and 100 (pp. 20–21), respectively and in that sequence.

10. *THW*, No. 89 (Nov. 30, 1916), p. 17.

11. *THW*, No. 86 (Nov. 8, 1916), p. 16.

12. Wen's letter to Wang Chi-chen in Peking, dated August 11, 1918, mailed from Hupeh.

13. Interview with Wang Chi-chen in New York City, February 4, 1978; Liang Shih-ch'iu, *Ch'iu-shih tsa-i* (*Miscellaneous Reminiscences in the Autumnal Studio*) (Taipei, 1971), pp. 31–32. Hereafter cited as Liang, *Miscellaneous Reminiscences*.

14. *THW*, Special Supplement, No. 1 (June 26, 1915), p. 41.

15. *CW*, Chronology, p. 33.

16. *Ibid.*, p. 34.

17. *Ibid.*, p. 33.

18. *Ibid.*, p. 37. Also, see James J. Y. Liu, *The Poetry of Li Shang-yin* (Chicago, 1969).

19. In 1915 and early 1916, only three lead articles did not deal with stale moral exhortations, and these were: "Ch'ung-pai ying-hsiung" ("Hero Worship"), *THW*, No. 50 (Oct. 3, 1915), pp. 1–3, which stresses the importance of worshipping China's own heroes; "Hsüeh chan" ("The War of Learning"), *THW*, No. 57 (Dec. 1, 1915), pp. 1–3, which urges the promotion of Chinese culture to compete with Western cultural expansion; and "Chung Hsi tzu-li shuo p'ing-i" ("On the Theory of Cultural Independence of China and the West"), *THW*, No. 64 (Jan. 19, 1916), pp. 1–3, which defends Chinese familism.

20. In the fall of 1916, the establishment of the Confucian Society at Tsing Hua inspired a number of chauvinistic comments in support of the organization. See *THW*, No. 84 (Oct. 25, 1916), pp. 1–2; No. 87 (Nov. 15, 1916), pp. 8–13; No. 88 (Nov. 23, 1916), pp. 1–3; and No. 89 (Nov. 30, 1916), pp. 7–11.

21. "Erh-yüeh-lu man-chi" ("Random Notes of the Two-month Hut"), *THW*, No. 81 (Oct. 4, 1916), p. 14, and other installments in subsequent issues. These are the notes which Wen took while studying classical Chinese works during his two-month summer vacations at home.

22. "Lun chen-hsing kuo-hsüeh," *THW*, No. 77 (May 17, 1916), pp. 1–2.

23. "Chih yu-jen shu," *THW*, No. 97 (Feb. 22, 1917), pp. 9–10.

24. *THW*, No. 77 (May 17, 1916), p. 2.

25. For the theory of "practice" of these scholars, see Liang Ch'i-ch'ao, *Chung-kuo chin san-pai-nien hsüeh-shu shih* (*The History of Chinese Learning in the Past Three Hundred Years*) (Taipei, 1956), pp. 53 ff., 79–80, and 106. Also see David S. Nivison, "Knowledge and Action in Chinese Thought Since Wang Yang-ming," Arthur F. Wright, ed., *Studies in Chinese Thought* (Chicago, 1953), pp. 124–25.

26. "Hsin chün-tzu kuang-i," *THW*, No. 92 (Dec. 21, 1916), pp. 1–2.

27. Over four hundred were said to have attended the founding ceremony of the Confucian Society. See *THW*, No. 86 (Nov. 8, 1916), p. 15. During 1911-1921, the peak enrollment of Tsing Hua was

about six hundred-sixty. See *A Glance at the National Tsing Hua University*, p. 4.

28. "Pien chih" (On Temperament), *THW*, No. 101 (March 22, 1917), pp. 1–2.

29. *THW*, Nos. 77 and 78 (May 17, 24, 1916), pp. 4–6, 7–8, respectively.

30. "Chieh p'ien hsin" ("Warning against Over-emphasis on the New"), *THW*, No. 103 (April 5, 1917), pp. 1–2.

31. *CW*, Chronology, p. 34. *Ch'ing-hua hsüeh-pao* (*The Tsing Hua Journal*), started in 1916 as a quarterly, was also edited by students but with faculty participation. Hereafter this journal will be cited as *THJ*.

32. "Hsüeh-sheng tui shih-chü kan-hsiang" ("The Students' Reflections on Current Affairs"), *THW*, No. 90 (Dec. 7, 1916), pp. 1–2.

33. *CW*, Chronology, p. 34. Representatives of Tsing Hua students attended the meeting at Peking University on the afternoon of May 5, 1919. See *Wu-szu yun-tung wen-chi* (*Essays and Documents on the May Fourth Movement*) (Hupeh, 1957), p. 175. On the afternoon of May 6, 1919, Tsing Hua students joined the demonstrating groups in Peking. See Hua Kang, *Wu-szu yun-tung shih* (*History of the May Fourth Movement*) (Shanghai, 1952), p. 115.

34. Mien, *Wen I-to*, p. 17; Shih, *The Path*, p. 13; Shih, *Wen I-to*, p. 4, describe Wen's circumstances at the time. The first time Wen joined in any mass demonstration was on Dec. 25, 1944, in Kunming, shortly before his death. See *CW*, Chronology, p. 77. Chou En-lai was among those students stirred to action by the May Fourth Incident.

35. Liang, *Miscellaneous Reminiscences*, pp. 33–34.

36. *THJ*, IV, 6 (June 1919), p. 50.

37. P'an Kung-chan, *Hsüeh-sheng chiu-kuo ch'üan-shih* (*The Complete History of the Students' National Salvation Movement*) (Shanghai, 1919), p. 128. The author of this work participated in the May Fourth demonstrations in Shanghai. Also see *THJ*, IV, 8 (Sept. 1919), pp. 78–79.

38. *THJ*, IV, 6 (June 1919), pp. 52–53.

39. "Tzu-chih yü pei-chih" ("To Govern Oneself and to Be Governed"), *THW*, No. 223 (Sept. 15, 1921), p. 4.

40. "Chung-wen k'o-t'ang ti chih-hsü i-pan" ("The General Situation of Order in Chinese Classes"), *THW*, No. 214 (April 1, 1921), p. 21.

41. "Lü-k'o-shih ti hsüeh-sheng" ("The Hotel Guest-like Students"), *THW*, No. 185 (April 24. 1920), pp. 22–23.

42. "Mei-kuo-hua ti Ch'ing-hua," *THW*, No. 247 (May 12, 1922), pp. 3–4.

43. The last two lines, quoted from Wordsworth's sonnet, "London 1802," and many other key words are given in English in the original article.

44. Shih, *Wen I-to*, pp. 4–5, gives this version. According to *CW*, Chronology, p. 36; Shih, *The Path*, pp. 14–16; and Mien, *Wen I-to*, pp. 18–20, the controversy centered on an extra examination imposed on the graduating class, presumably to penalize those who participated in the May Fourth demonstrations. In a letter to me dated April 2, 1959, Professor Chi-chen Wang of Columbia University, who was Wen's classmate, said that the first version is correct. Professor Liang Shih-ch'iu also confirmed the first version.

45. "Hui-fu ho-p'ing" ("Restoration of the Peace"), *THW*, No. 226 (Nov. 19, 1921), p. 16. For his argument against both extremes, see *ibid.*, pp. 17–19; and "Ch'ing-hua chou-k'an ti ti-wei" ("The Position of the *Tsing Hua Weekly*"), *THW*, No. 223 (Sept. 15, 1921), pp. 2–3. In the latter essay, he even expressed distrust of the "irresponsible and irrational" character of the masses.

46. "Tu fei chi," *THJ*, IV, 6 (June 1919), p. 53.

47. These arguments are referred to in "P'ing pen hsüeh-nien chou-k'an li ti hsin-shih" ("A Critique of The Modern Poems Published in the *Weekly* during This School Year"), *THW*, Special Supplement, No. 7 (June 1921), p. 8.

48. *THW*, No. 191 (Sept. 24, 1920), pp. 23–24. Later this poem was rewritten and greatly improved, *CW*, Section *ting*, pp. 56–59.

49. Yokoyama Eizo, " 'Wen I-to to sono shi' no ichikisatsu" ("A Study of 'Wen I-to and His Poetry' ") *Yamaguchi daigaku bungakukaishi;* (Yamaguchi, 1961), pp. 4–5.

50. For instance, the "feng-i" in the second line.

51. "The Lesson of Time," "Dusk," "Impression," "Beauty and Love," and "Love's Storm," all are included in *CW*, Section *ting*. The title of the last poem has been changed to "Storm."

52. *THW*, Special Supplement, No. 7 (June 1921), pp. 9–10. The line is quoted from a poem by Su Tung-p'o.

53. *Ibid.*, p. 16.

54. *Ibid.*, p. 11.

55. Wen himself had been studying the technique of classical Chinese poetry without interruption. See *CW*, Chronology, pp. 36–37; *THW*, Special Supplement, No. 7 (June 1921), pp. 20–21.

56. *THW*, Special Supplement, No. 7 (June 1921), p. 23.

57. These views are expressed in his articles: "Ch'u-pan-wu ti feng-mien" ("The Cover-designs of Current Publications"), *THW*, No. 187 (April 24, 1920), pp. 19-25, in which he discusses the artistic quality of the cover-designs of magazines; "Cheng-ch'iu i-shu chuan-meng-

che ti hu-sheng" ("Calling for Professional Artists"), *THW*, No. 192 (Oct. 1, 1920), pp. 1–6; "Tui-yü Shuang-shih-chieh chu-tien ti kan-hsiang" ("Thoughts on the Double-Ten Celebration"), *THW*, No. 195 (Oct. 22, 1920), pp. 15–17; and "Tien-ying pu-shih i-shu" ("The Motion Picture is not Art"), *THW*, No. 203 (Dec. 17, 1920), pp. 14–24.

58. Here Wen anticipated the debate on "science and philosophy of life" which began in China in 1923.

59. "Huang-chih t'iao-kao" ("Bulletins on Yellow Paper"), *THW*, No. 198 (Nov. 12, 1920), p. 18.

60. Published in September, 1923, by the T'ai-tung Book Co. of Shanghai, the cover was a disappointment to Wen, who had wanted to make it attractive, but the cost factor forced him to compromise. It has a blue border with rather plain red letters on white background. The title poem, also the preface, was composed in the fall of 1922 in America. The first three sections, forty-one poems excluding the prefatory verse, were written while still in China, all except "The Sheath of the Sword" which seems to have been completed in the United States. The last two sections, twenty poems (or sixty-one poems if we count the Red Bead series not as one poem) were done in America. Here we are discussing only his pre-American poems. For its cover, see Hui An, *Shu-hua* (*Book Talk*) (Peking, 1963), p. 28.

61. Written Feb. 28, 1921, first printed in *THW*, then in *CW*, Section *ting*, pp. 66–67.

62. *CW*, Section *ting*, pp. 86–87.

63. Newell F. Ford, *The Prefigurative Imagination of John Keats* (Stanford, 1951), p. 5; Chapter I, *passim*.

64. These comments are in a letter in which Wen criticized a collection of verses, Wang Ching-chih, *Hui-ti feng* (*The Wind of the Orchid*). *CW*, Section *keng*, pp. 25–26.

65. See his letter to his wife (date questionable), in *CW*, Section *keng*, pp. 59–67.

66. *CW*, Section *ting*, p. 79.

67. *Ibid.*, p. 75.

68. *Ibid.*, pp. 40–47.

69. *Li T'ai-po ch'üan-chi* (*Complete Works of Li T'ai-po*) (Taipei, 1956), chüan 8, p. 1. *Lun-yü* (*The Analects*) (Taipei, Commercial Press), p. 135.

70. All these poems are found in *CW*, Section *ting*, pp. 40–90.

71. *Ibid.*, p. 82.

72. Chao Chia-pi, ed. *Chung-kuo hsin-wen-hsüeh ta-hsi* (*A Com-

pendium of Modern Chinese Literature). 10 vols. (Shanghai, 1935–1941). Hereafter cited as *Compendium*. Vol. 8. Preface by Chu Tzu-ch'ing, pp. 4–6.

73. Wei Fa, "P'ing Hung-chu" ("On the *Red Candle*"). "Hsüeh Teng" in *Shih-shih hsin-pao* (*New Current Affairs Daily*), November 27 and 28, 1924. Chu Hsiang, "P'ing Wen chün I-to ti shih" ("Comment on the Poetry of Wen I-to"). *Hsiao-shuo yüeh-pao* (*The Short Story Monthly*), XVII, 5 (May 10, 1926), pp. 63–74. (Hereafter cited as Chu Hsiang, "Comment on Wen.")

Chapter Three

1. K'o Chung-p'ing "Ai Shih-jen Wen I-to" ("Mourning Poet Wen I-to"), *Ts'ung Yenan tao Peking* (*From Yenan to Peking*) (Peking, 1950), pp. 26–32.

2. *CW*, Chronology, p. 37. There is a photograph of Hsiao-chen, taken about the time of their wedding, in the section of illustrations, *CW*, Vol. I.

3. Letter to Liang Shih-ch'iu, in *CW*, Section *keng*, p. 3.

4. Liang, *Miscellaneous Reminiscences*, p. 45, reveals that Liang himself was not too eager about going to America, and he discussed his reservations with Wen. It seems that Wen did not share the same reservation.

5. Letter written on board the ship to his Tsing Hua friends, in *CW*, Section *keng*, pp. 7–8.

6. *Ibid.*, p. 8.

7. The story he read was "Tsui-ch'u chih k'o" ("The First Lesson") by Tung-shan, pen-name of Chang Po-ch'i, in *Ch'uang-tsao chi-k'an* (*Creation Quarterly*); see *Compendium*, V, pp. 462–70; X, p. 470.

8. Hung Shen wrote an account of how the Japanese police searched his fellow Korean travellers. *THW*, No. 84 (Oct. 25, 1916), p. 25. A similar story appears in *THW*, No. 85 (Nov. 1, 1916), p. 8.

9. A leader of the Democratic League in the 1940's, Lo later joined the Chinese Communist government as a minority party spokesman. In 1957 he came under fire for his alleged Rightist activities, but he was not harmed and by the spring of 1958 the pressure was removed.

10. *CW*, Chronology, p. 38.

11. At this time Lo had already left Chicago for the University of Wisconsin. *CW*, Chronology, p. 42.

12. *CW*, Section *keng*, pp. 20, 22.

13. *Ibid.*, pp. 24–25.

14. *Ibid.*, p. 71.

15. *CW*, Section *ting*, p. 39.

16. In these few poems, Wen seems to have used the term "soul" in the way the writers and translators of English literature liked to use it at that time.

17. Feng Hao, comp., *Li I-shan shih* (*The Poetry of Li I-shan*). (Taichung, 1956), p. 332.

18. *THW*, Special Supplement, No. 7 (June 1921), p. 16.

19. Controversial views on Li Shang-yin's role in the history of Chinese poetry have been noted by many scholars, e.g., Professor James R. Hightower of Harvard. It is true that Li, in his earlier days, imitated Tu Fu, and there is ample evidence of Tu's influence on Li's works. But the subsequent development of Li's poetry departed from Tu Fu, and Li is better remembered as a leader of an entirely new school of poetry.

20. Liu Ta-chieh, *Chung-kuo wen-hsüeh fa-chan shih* (*A History of the Development of Chinese Literature*). (Shanghai, 1958), II, pp. 149–52. (Hereafter cited at Liu, *History of Chinese Literature*.)

21. *CW*, Section *keng*, pp. 22, 27.

22. *CW*, Chronology, p. 42.

23. Letter to Wu Ching-ch'ao, *CW*, Section *keng*, p. 18. Kai-yu Hsu, *Twentieth Century Chinese Poetry* (Cornell, 1970), pp. 51–52. Hereafter cited as Hsu, *20th C.*

24. Wen studied Arnold quite thoroughly. It is significant to compare Wen's attitude with that of Arnold as analyzed by Lionel Trilling: "He himself (Empedocles) cannot support a life limited to reconciliation and compromise; he yearns for the absolute, and his own resolution is to flee from choked, circumscribed existence by flinging himself into the crater of Etna. It is not entirely suicide of escape. The act is done in ecstasy and is, as it were, the affirmation of human desires by merging with the All and mingling with the elements, much as the devotee of the Bhagavad Gita desired absorption in the All. As Empedocles commits his last act the song of Callicles rises again up the slope of Etna: he sings of Apollo and the Muses." *Matthew Arnold* (New York, 1949), p. 88.

25. "Chien-hsia," *CW*, Section *ting*, pp. 48–55. Wen quoted the first section of Tennyson's "The Palace of Art" as the epigraph for this poem. In doing so Wen quite ignored the theme of Tennyson's long poem which the author himself described as "embodying my own belief that the Godlike life is with man and for man." Wen took the first section and dwelt literally on the theme that the artist can build a "palace of art" in order to dwell in it—to breathe, live and die happily in the midst of its splendor.

26. *CW*, Chronology, p. 39. Wen has a serious interest in Fletcher and the group of modern American poets identified as the "Imagists."

According to Amy Lowell, who impressed Wen greatly when they met in Chicago, imagism is "a renaissance, a re-birth of the spirit of truth and beauty in the New Movement of American poetry." *Tendencies in Modern American Poetry* (New York, 1917), p. 237. Wen most probably referred to Fletcher's poem "The Vowels" when he talked about the sense of color. "The Vowels," again according to Lowell, is an imitation of, but much superior to, Rimbaud's "Voyelles." *Ibid.*, pp. 291–95.

27. "Ch'iu lin," later the title was changed to "Ch'iu se" ("Autumn Color") in *CW*, Section *ting*, pp. 106–10. Hsu, *20th Century*, pp. 52–54.

28. The "Weaving Goddess" who resides across the Milky Way from the "Ox Herder."

29. "Se-ts'ai" ("Colors"), *CW*, Section *ting*, p. 113.

30. "T'ai-p'ing-yang chou-chung chien i ming-hsing," *CW*, Section *ting*, pp. 95–96.

31. Letter to Wu Ching-ch'ao, *CW*, Section *keng*, pp. 11–18. The poems enclosed are "T'ai-yang yin" ("The Sunshine Rhymes") and "Ch'ing chao" ("A Sunny Morning"), *CW*, Section *ting*, pp. 102–104.

32. "Ku-yen," "Wo shih i-ko liu-ch'iu," "Ch'iu shen-le," *CW*, Section *ting*, pp. 92, 97–98, and 110, respectively.

33. "I chü," *ibid.*, pp. 104–06.

34. "A Lament under the Great Wall," *Ta-chiang chi-k'an* (*Ta-chiang Quarterly*) (July, 1925), pp. 24–32.

35. "I Am Chinese," *ibid.*, pp. 97–99.

36. *CW*, Chronology, p. 39.

37. *Ibid.*, p. 40.

38. *Ibid.* The story of Kuo Mo-jo can be found in his *Collected Works*, V, pp. 260–64.

39. *CW*, Section *keng*, p. 77. His brother, Wen Chia-szu, later became professor of French literature at the National Tsing Hua University.

40. *Ibid.*, p. 75.

41. Mien, *Wen I-to*, pp. 25–26; Shih, *Wen I-to*, pp. 20–21.

42. *CW*, Section *ting*, pp. 120–25. The title of the poem is "Hung-tou."

43. *Ibid.*, p. 118. There were outbursts of affectionate expressions among Wen's letters to his wife, delivered or undelivered. One such example is in *CW*, Section *keng*, pp. 59–60. It is a straightforward, passionate love letter which, if fallen into the hands of a third party, such as Wen's conservative father, could understandably cause Wen much embarrassment in view of the social conventions of those days. The date of the letter, however, seems faulty. If it is July 16, 1937, his

wife was still with him and they were hurriedly packing to leave Peiping. If July 16, 1926, Wen was spending that summer in Hupeh with his family, or if he were back in Nanking, he would be most unsettled and could not be tending the lily pond and lawn in the garden as the letter says. Yü-ming Shaw, p. 33, quite appropriately points out how the "Red Beads" series depicts Wen's marital history from that of two strangers thrown together by parental dictate to that of mutual respect and affection. "The Drum Singer," *CW*, Section *ting*, pp. 7–9, also portrays the same marital process.

44. *CW*, Chronology, p. 39.

45. *CW*, Section *keng*, pp. 20, 26, 74. The essays in question are Hu Shih's critical comments written in September, 1922, on *Ts'ao-erh* (*The Grass*) by K'ang Pai-ch'ing, and *Tung-yeh* (*Winter Night*) by Yü P'ing-po. Hu objected to the vague philosophical ideas in the *Winter Night*, urging Yü to write more plainly in the common language. See *Hu Shih wen-ts'un* (*Collected Works of Hu Shih*) (Taipei, 1953), II, pp. 500–14.

46. In his essay on the *pai-hua* poems published in *THW*, Special Supplement No. 7 (June, 1921), p. 9, Wen quoted Pope's *An Essay on Criticism* (I, pp. 100–104):

> The generous critic fanned the poet's fire,
> And taught the world with reason to admire,
> Then criticism the muses' handmaid proved,
> To dress her charms, and make her more beloved.

47. Letter to Liang Shih-ch'iu, in *CW*, Chronology, p. 40.

48. *Ibid.*, p. 41.

49. *CW*, Section *keng*, p. 18.

50. While Wen's theory is generally defensible, his own illustration cited here is rather lame. The poem he cites contains thirty-six lines, in varied tercet stanzas with end rhymes in *a-b-a, a-c-a*, etc. The first line of each stanza ends on the same word "sunshine." Thus he has demonstrated no more than an ability to find twelve words to rhyme with "sunshine" in the entire Chinese vocabulary.

51. Chu Hsiang, "Comment on Wen," pp. 63–74.

52. "*Tung-yeh* p'ing-lun" ("Review of the *Winter Night*"), *CW*, Section *ting*, p. 143. The *Winter Night* was published in Shanghai in 1921.

53. *CW*, Section *ting*, pp. 144–46.

54. *Ibid.*, p. 149.

55. "*Nü-shen* chih ti-fang se-ts'ai" ("The Local Color of the *Goddesses*"); the essay was completed before the end of November, 1922,

in Chicago. *CW*, Section *ting*, pp. 105–21. Also *CW*, Section *keng*, p. 27.

56. More detailed concordances between Wen's images and those of Arnold, Tennyson, Keats, etc., have been compiled by Marc Michael Whitacre, "The English Influence in the Poetry of Wen I-to," unpublished M.A. thesis, University of Arizona, 1974.

57. Wen's statement is in *CW*, Section *ting*, p. 195. Taine's celebrated formula is, of course, stated and restated in most of his works. For a succinct summary, see his *Histoire de la littérature anglaise*, 12th ed. (Paris, 1905), Introduction, pp. xxv–xxxi.

58. "*Nü-shen* chih shih-tai ching-shen," ("The Spirit of the Time in the *Goddess*"), *CW*, Section *ting*, pp. 185–94. The essay was written shortly after Nov. 22, 1922.

59. Review of Kuo Mo-jo's translation of the Rubaiyat. *CW*, Section *ting*, p. 216.

60. *CW*, Chronology, p. 41.

61. *Ibid.*, p. 42.

62. *Ibid.*, p. 44.

63. According to a letter to me, dated Jan. 4, 1959, from Joan Shinew, librarian at Colorado College, the hall has been torn down to make way for a new student union building.

64. According to a letter to me, dated Jan. 25, 1959, from Mrs. Mary M. Lofland (Mary Merryman), Wen's classmate at Colorado College.

65. *CW*, Chronology, p. 43.

66. Letter to me from Mrs. Lamont R. Keller (Eva Clark) of Colorado Springs, dated January 26, 1959. She was in the same art class with Wen.

67. He had been much impressed by American art in his Tsing Hua days. See his discussion of magazine covers in America, *THW*, No. 192 (Oct. 1, 1920).

68. He never ceased to admire the fourteenth century Italian master. Even the religiosity of the Fra, something Wen could not readily share, found expression in the imagery of Wen's poetry, including his very last *pai-hua* poem, the "Miracle." Wen wanted to introduce Cézanne to China in an art and literary journal he planned to launch. *CW*, Section *keng*, pp. 29–30.

69. Liang, *About Wen I-to*, p. 31, also notes that Wen liked Velasquez at that time.

70. *Ibid.*, pp. 47–48.

71. The poem is erroneously referred to as "Sphinx" in *CW*, Chronology, p. 44.

72. Answers from Liang and Wen appeared in the same campus

paper on March 28, 1924, entitled "Reply from a Chinee," and "Another Chinee Answering" respectively.

73. First published in December, 1923; see *CW*, Section *ting*, pp. 275–79.

74. Wen's record at the Art Institute of Chicago was an "A" average; see *CW*, Section *keng*, p. 73. According to Joan Shinew's letter dated March 24, 1959, Wen's academic record at Colorado College was "A plus."

75. His letter dated 1922, *CW*, Section *keng*, pp. 68–69.

76. Hsiung and Yü both later became noted playwrights.

77. *CW*, Chronology, p. 45.

78. The poem, written in English, shows the clear influence of Housman. It was never published in Wen's lifetime. Liang Shih-ch'iu printed it in his *About Wen I-to*, pp. 54–55.

79. "Chung-hua hsi-chü kai-chin she," *CW*, Section *keng*, p. 28.

80. *CW*, Section *keng*, pp. 29–32.

81. *Ibid.*, p. 33.

82. These two societies are described as "patriotic youth organizations in America, active about the time of the May 30, 1925 incident." See the confidential pamphlet issued by the Nationalist Party, *Chung-kuo ko hsiao-tang hsien-k'uang* (*The Present Situation of the Various Minor Political Parties*) (n.p., August 1946), p. 36. Hereafter cited as *Minor Political Parties*. Also see Liang, *About Wen I-to*, pp. 49–51.

83. *CW*, Section *keng*, p. 36. Lo was already politically very active and had become a leader among the students. Recalling one such discussion, Ku I-ch'iao, later head of the electrical engineering department at the National Tsing Hua University, said that Wen threatened to shoot P'an Kuang-tan with a pistol if the latter in his study of eugenics found the Chinese race to be destined to decline. See Ku's "Huai ku-yu Wen I-to hsien-sheng" ("Reminiscence on My Old Friend Wen I-to"), *Wen-i fu-hsing* (*Renaissance*), III, 5 (July 1947), p. 535.

84. *CW*, Section *keng*, p. 36.

85. Hsiung Fo-hsi, "Tao Wen I-to hsien-sheng" (Mourning Mr. Wen I-to), *Wen-i fu-hsing* (*Renaissance*) II, 1 (August 1946), p. 7. Hereafter cited at Hsiung, "Wen I-to."

86. "In Hospital" by William Ernest Henley of England was a successful experiment in "unrhyming rhythms," as the author himself described it. Written in 1873–1875, it contains twenty-eight poems that vary in the number and length of stanzas, depicting his impressions and observations of the "Old Edinburgh Infirmary." See his *Poems* (New York, 1912), pp. 3–43.

87. This poem, first published in the *Ta-chiang Quarterly* (July 1925), p. 151, later was revised and included in his *Dead Water*.

The prefacing note of the poem was further revised before inclusion in *CW*, Section *ting*, pp. 28–30. Hsu, *Twentieth Century*, pp. 55–56.

88. I thought of Thomas Hood immediately at the very first reading of Wen's "Laundry Song" back in 1941. C. T. Hsia in his "Obsession with China: Moral Burden of Modern Chinese Literature" *China in Perspective* (Wellesley College, 1967), pp. 101–19, also suggests Thomas Hood. Liang Shih-ch'iu explained to me the background of his remark about Wen and Kipling (*About Wen I-to*, p. 40), on March 27, 1978, in Taipei. Prof. Daeler at Colorado, Liang said, stressed the rhythmic features of Kipling's works which impressed Wen.

89. "Nan-hai chih shen," ("The God from the South Seas"). *Ta-chiang Quarterly* I, 2 (November 1925), pp. 71–78.

90. *CW*, Section *keng*, p. 36.

91. *Ibid.*, p. 70; Chronology, p. 40.

92. Liang, *About Wen I-to*, p. 59.

93. Sukhorukov, V. T., "Wen I-to," *Dumy o Khrizanteme* (Thoughts on the *Chrysanthemum*), Perevod a Kitaiskogo Gennadiia Jaroslavtseva (translated from Chinese by Gennadii Jaroslastsev), (Moscow, 1973) pp. 7–8. Hereafter cited as Sukhorukov.

94. During his years of editing and writing for Tsing Hua publications, Wen never wrote or commented on specific stories about the suffering of the Chinese people as others did. See, for instance, the lengthy articles about banditry and disorder in the northeastern provinces, *THW*, No. 83 (Oct. 18, 1916), pp. 5–9; and in Szechwan, *THW*, No. 97 (Feb. 22, 1917), pp. 10–13. At that time Wen urged promotion of Chinese studies in the most general terms.

95. *CW*, Chronology, p. 47.

96. *Ibid.*, p. 48.

Chapter Four

1. *CW*, Section *ting*, p. 10.

2. Chu Hsiang, "Wen I-to yü Szu-shui" ("Wen I-to and the *Dead Water*"), *Wen-i fu-hsing (Renaissance)*, III, 5 (July 1947), p. 528. Hereafter cited as Chu, "Wen and the *Dead Water*."

3. Although never much concerned for money, Wen was always keenly aware of his family responsibility. See his letters to his family, *CW*, Section *keng*, pp. 70–71, 79.

4. The institution was known as Pei-ching Mei-shu Chuan-men Hsüeh-hsiao. *CW*, Chronology, p. 48, is in error. For this and the history of the school, see Chuang Shen, "Tui Pei-ching mei-shu chiao-yü ti k'ao-ch'a yü chien-t'ao: 1900–1945" (A Study of Art Education in Peking: 1900–1945) *Ming Pao Monthly*, 149 (May, 1978), pp. 35–41.

5. Chu Hsiang, "Wen and the *Dead Water*," p. 528.

6. Liu Hsia (Ch'en Shan-hsin), *Shih-pa-nien lai chih Chung-kuo ch'ing-nien-tang* (*The Eighteen Years of the Chinese Youth Party*) (Chengtu, 1941), pp. 37–38.

7. The four chapters of the "Ta-chiang Declaration" were first published by installment in four consecutive issues of *THW*: Nos. 354–357, all in October, 1925. They appeared together in the *Ta-chiang Quarterly*, November, 1925. The four chapter headings are: "Imperialistic Aggression and Nationalism"; "The Causes of Disorder in China Today"; "The Nationalism of the Ta-chiang Society"; and "The Purpose of the Ta-chiang Society."

8. *THW*, No. 355 (Oct. 16, 1925), pp. 434–35.

9. *THW*, No. 356 (Oct. 23, 1925), p. 500.

10. *Ibid.*, p. 504.

11. *THW*, No. 357 (Oct. 30, 1925), p. 555.

12. At the beginning, the Awakened Lion Society was a splinter group of the Shao-nien Chung-kuo hsüeh-hui (Young China Study Society), which included Marxists. In 1923, Tseng Ch'i and Li Huang organized this group into a political party in Paris without giving it a definite name. In 1925, the leaders returned to China and became active in Chinese politics. However, it was not until 1929 that this party officially adopted the name Chung-kuo ch'ing-nien tang (Chinese Youth Party). See Hsiao Wen-che, *Hsien-tai Chung-kuo cheng-tang yü cheng-chih* (*Political Parties and Politics in Contemporary China*) (Nanking, 1946), p. 2.

13. *CW*, Chronology, pp. 48–49; Section *keng*, p. 38.

14. The Chinese name was "Pei-ching kuo-chia chu-i t'uan-t'i lien-ho hui." *CW*, Section *keng*, p. 38.

15. *Ibid.*, p. 40. According to *Minor Political Parties*, p. 37, the meeting was called to "oppose Russia and aid the Overseas Chinese."

16. At that time, Wen seemed to regard the Chinese Communists and their sympathizers as merely imitating the Russian Communists, hence unworthy of the name. *CW*, Section *keng*, p. 40.

17. Yang Chia-lo, *Chia-wu i-lai Chung-Jih chün-shih wai-chiao ta-shih chi-yao* (*Important Sino-Japanese Military and Diplomatic Events Since 1894*) (Changsha, 1941), pp. 61–69.

18. Hosea B. Morse and Harley F. MacNair, *Far Eastern International Relations* (New York, 1931), p. 683.

19. *CW*, Chronology, p. 49.

20. Hsü Chih-mo said that the Crescent Group was first formed in 1923. *Compendium*, X, 124.

21. Hsü Chih-mo, "Shih-k'an p'ien-yen" ("Introducing the 'Poetry Journal,'"), *Compendium*, X, pp. 117–18.

22. In this Wen agreed with the views expressed in Gautier's *Emaux et Camées* (first published in 1852).

23. The important articles are, "Shih-ti ko-lü" ("The Form of Poetry"), first published on May 13, 1926, collected in *CW*, Section *ting*, pp. 245–53; and "Hsi-chü ti ch'i-t'u" ("Drama at the Crossroads"), first published on June 24, 1926, collected in *ibid.*, pp. 271–74.

24. *Ibid.*, p. 247. Wen quoted Bliss Perry's *A Study of Poetry*, p. 202, to support his argument. C. Tung, "The Search for Order and Form: The Crescent Moon Society and the Literary Movement of Modern China, 1928–1933" (unpublished doctoral dissertation, Claremont Graduate School, 1971, hereafter cited as C. Tung), p. 137, points out how Wen changed Perry's words slightly to strengthen his own argument.

25. "Lao ch'ü chien yü shih-lü hsi," *CW*, Section *ting*, p. 246.

26. *CW*, Chronology, p. 36.

27. Patricia Uberoi, "Rhythmic Techniques in the Poetry of Wen I-to." *United College Journal*, 6 (1967–1968), p. 4. In this admirable study of the prosody in Wen's poetry, Uberoi maintains that Wen did not discuss the element of "stress" in the Chinese language. While Wen did not specifically use the term "stress," throughout his treatise he emphasized the importance of *yin-chieh* (literally "sound unit") which, strictly speaking, in most cases is the Chinese "word." Thus *szu-shui* is one word, a spondee possibly, but trochaic in most natural Mandarin speech; *ch'ui-pu-ch'i* is definitely one word, and most commonly pronounced as a dactylic. The lack of a rigidly fixed stress pattern for multisyllabic words in *pai-hua* does not mean there is no natural stress pattern when the words are spoken in natural sentences. Wen (*CW*, Section *ting*, p. 249) also specifically referred to a study by Jao Meng-k'an, "Hsin-shih ti yin-chieh" ("Meter in New Poetry"), "Poetry Journal" in *Peking Morning News* (April 22, 1926), pp. 49–50. Jao considered the function of end rhymes as "locking in and fixing the *i-yang* pattern in a poem." (p. 49). *I-yang*, or unstressed-stressed, is a common notion about poetic prosody that no traditional Chinese poet could afford to overlook. Nor did Wen I-to ignore it. There is a problem in introducing the "stress" idea into the prosodic analysis of *pai-hua* poetry. Uberoi recognizes this fact; and a study like the one by Lo Nien-sheng, "Shih-ti chieh tsou' ("The Rhythm of Poetry"), *Wen-hsüeh p'i-p'ing* (*Literary Criticism*), 3 (June 25, 1959), pp. 18–24, fully demonstrates how clumsy it can be.

28. The emphasis on form by the Crescent poets invited much criticism. Some critics spoke disparagingly of the neat tou-fu-kan (bean-cake square) pattern of Wen's poems. See Ch'ü I, "Hsin-shih ti

tsung-chi yü ch'i ch'u-lu" ("The Footprints and Future Prospects of Modern Poetry"), *Wen-hsüeh* (*Literature*), VIII, 1 (January 1937), p. 17; Mao Tun (Shen Yen-ping), "Lun Ch'u-ch'i pai-hua shih" ("On the Early pai-hua Poetry"), *Wen-hsüeh* (*Literature*), VIII, 1 (January 1937) p. 108; and Shih Ling, "Hsin-yüeh shih p'ai" ("The Crescent School of Poetry"), *Wen-hsüeh* (*Literature*), VIII, 1 (January 1937), p. 127. Most critics, however, noted Hsü Chih-mo's admission of the danger of over-emphasis on "form" in his article, "Shih-k'an fang-chia" ("A Holiday for the 'Poetry Journal'"), in *Compendium*, X, pp. 119–122.

29. 'Hsien-la-fei chu-i' ("The Pre-Raphaelite Doctrine"), first published on May 26, 1928, collected in *CW*, Section *ting*, pp. 255–269.

30. Chu Hsiang, "Wen and the *Dead Water*," p. 528.

31. *CW*, Section *ting*, p. 250.

32. Tung Ch'u-p'ing "Ts'ung Wen I-to ti *Szu-shui* t'an tao ko-lü-shih ti wen-t'i" ("Wen I-to's *Dead Water* and the Question of Formalist Poetry"), *Wen-hsüeh p'ing-lun* (*Literary Criticism*), 6 (August 1961), p. 84.

33. See works by Uberoi and Tung Ch'u-p'ing (footnotes 27 and 32 above); their works are dated 1968 and 1961 respectively.

34. *CW*, Section *ting*, p. 28.

35. C. Tung, pp. 144–47.

36. *CW*, Section *ting*, p. 248.

37. "Ta chuan-pien shih-ch'i ho-shih lai ni?" ("When Will the Great Turning Point Arrive?"), quoted in Li Ho-lin, *Chin erh-shih-nien Chung-kuo wen-i szu-ch'ao lun* (*Chinese Literary Thought in the Past Twenty Years*) (Shanghai, 1948), p. 86.

38. "Hsin wen-hsüeh yen-chiu che ti tse-jen yü nu-li" ("The Responsibility and Effort of the Students of the New Literature"), first published in Feb. 1921, collected in Chang Jo-ying (Ch'ien Hsing-ts'un), *Hsin-wen-hsüeh yün-tung shih-liao* (*Historical Documents of the New Literary Movement*) (Shanghai, 1936), p. 297. Hereafter cited as Chang Jo-ying.

39. "Hsin wen-hsüeh chih shih-ming" ("The Mission of the New Literature"), first published in May 1923, in *Compendium*, II, p. 180.

40. "Wen-hsüeh chih she-hui ti shih-ming" ("The Social Mission of Literature"), in Chang Jo-ying, p. 340.

41. There are written accounts of political pressure on writers and their activities around 1924. See Hsüan Chu (Shen Yen-ping), in *Compendium*, II, p. 135; Juan Wu-ming (Ch'ien Hsing-ts'un) in *ibid.*, X, pp. 260–63.

42. The leader of this group, Chiang Kuang-ch'ih (also Chiang Kuang-tz'u), joined the Communist Party about 1927. See Joseph

Schyns, *One Thousand and Five Hundred Modern Chinese Novels and Plays* (Peiping, 1948), p. 18.

43. "Wen-i-chia ti chüeh-wu" ("The Awakening of the Men of Letters"), in Chang Jo-ying, pp. 361–62.

44. *Ibid.*, p. 375.

45. *Ibid.*, p. 387.

46. For a brief summary of these literary movements, see Wang Yao, *Chung-kuo hsin-wen-hsüeh shih-kao* (A Draft History of Modern Chinese Literature) (Shanghai, 1954), I, pp. 41–58; Liu Shou-sung, *Chung-kuo hsin-wen hsüeh shih ch'u-kuo* (A Preliminary Draft History of Modern Chinese Literature) (Peking, 1957), I, pp. 127–146.

47. *CW*, Section *ting*, p. 253.

48. *Ibid.*, p. 272.

49. *Ibid.*, p. 273; and "Shih yü li-shih t'i-chi" ("A Note to 'Poetry and History' "), *ibid.*, p. 242.

50. *Ibid.*, p. 274. In 1923, Kuo Mo-jo dramatized the story of Cho Wen-chün who eloped with the poet Szu-ma Hsiang-ju of the second century B.C. See *Compendium*, X, p. 472.

51. Letter to Tso Ming, *CW* Section *keng*, p. 44.

52. "Shih-jen ti hun-man" ("The Dogmatism of the Poets"), *CW*, Section *ting*, pp. 243–44.

53. Hsü Chih-mo, *Meng-hu chi* (*The Tiger*) (Shanghai, 1931), p. 8.

54. Shen Ts'ung-wen, "Lun Wen I-to ti *Szu-shui*" ("On the *Dead Water* by Wen I-to"). *Hsin-yüeh* (*Crescent*), III, 2 (September 1931), p. 96. Hereafter cited as Shen, "On *Dead Water*."

55. First published in March, 1927. See *Dead Water*, pp. 76–79.

56. "Fa-hsien," *Dead Water*, pp. 58–59. Hsu, *Twentieth Century*, p. 58.

57. "Wen-i yü ai-kuo–chi-nien san i-pa" (Literature and Patriotism—Commemorating the March Eighteenth Incident), *CW*, Section *ting*, pp. 239-40.

58. *CW*, Section *keng*, p. 41. In April, 1926, the Fengtien and Chihli armies were still fighting the Nationalist armies.

59. *Dead Water*, pp. 39–41. Hsu, *Twentieth Century*, pp. 65–66.

60. The poem was first published in the "Poetry Journal," 3 (April 15, 1926), in the *Peking Morning News*. Liang, *About Wen I-to*, p. 36, states that the poem "Dead Water" was written when Wen and Liang were studying Browning's "The Ring and the Book" together, presumably at Colorado Springs in 1923–1924. However, Jao Meng-k'an, one of Wen's four closest poet-friends upon his return to China, said that the poem was touched off by the sight of a ditch of putrid water, an open sewer, in the Hsi-tan district of Peking (see Envoi).

While it is entirely possible that the poem is nothing more than an exercise of Wen's imagination, the strength of imagery in the poem tends to support Jao's explanation that Wen had been deeply affected by what he had seen in China and was later inspired by an actual sight in Peking.

61. *CW*, Chronology, p. 49; Section *keng*, p. 38.

62. Hsü Chih-mo said that toward the end of Sept., 1926, Wen "was somewhere in the war-ravaged area. Nobody knew his exact location." See *Compendium*, X, p. 124. The Northern Expedition started from Canton in July, 1926; some troops reached the Wuhan area around the end of that month.

63. "Yeh-hsü – tsang ko" ("Perhaps – A Dirge"); other poems inspired by his daughter's death were "Wang-tiao t'a" ("Forget Her"), and "Wo yao hui-lai" ("I Want to Come Home"), all collected in *Dead Water*.

64. The Ta-chiang Society never won any recognition as an effective political group in China. Its name is mentioned only in the historical accounts of the Chinese Youth Party as one of the two organizations in America that gave support to the Chinese Youth Party around 1925. The Chinese Youth Party itself was suppressed by the Kuomintang after April, 1927, in Shanghai and Nanking. Its leaders fled north to seek shelter under the warlord Chang Tso-lin, and thereafter the party existed only in name until the 1940s when it became somewhat more active in Chungking and later Nanking.

65. Shen Ts'ung-wen, 'On *Dead Water*," p. 95.

66. Chu Hsiang, "Wen and *Dead Water*," p. 528. Chu and Wen had an unusual friendship which, in spite of strong differences in their theories of poetics, managed to survive until Chu's suicide. Ku I-ch'iao bore witness to their quarrels and their close association. My interview with Ku, Feb. 5, 1978, in Philadelphia. See also *CW*, Section *keng*, p. 52.

67. Chu Tzu-ch'ing made a full study of Wen's patriotic poems in 1943; see his *Selected Works*, pp. 137–41. In 1946, he again wrote on this subject, see *ibid.*, p. 159. For his earlier comments on Wen's poetry, see *Compendium*, VIII, Preface.

68. See works by Yokoyama Eizo, Horita Natsu, Sato Tamotsu, Okiyoshi Kukio, Nagano Shigeji, Imamura Yoshio, Takeuchi Minoru, and Ogawa Tamaki. For representative Russian views, see the works by Fedorenko (pp. 360–62) and Sukhorukov (pp. 17–18). Full citations of these works are in the bibliography at the end of this book.

69. *CW*, Section *ting*, p. 5. Hsu, *Twentieth Century*, pp. 57–58.

70. "Ni chih-che t'ai-yang ch'i-shih," *Dead Water*, pp. 5–6. Hsu, *Twentieth Century*, p. 59.

71. "Ni k'an," *Dead Water*, pp. 24–26.

72. "Ta ku shih," *CW*, Section *ting*, pp. 7–9.

73. "Shen-mo meng" and "Ni mo yuan wo," *CW*, Section *ting*, pp. 7, 10–11.

74. Hsu, *Twentieth Century*, pp. 55, 66.

75. *Dead Water*, pp. 3–33. Hsu, *Twentieth Century*, pp. 56–57.

76. *Dead Water*, pp. 27–29. In translating this poem, I have considered Wen's revision in *CW*, Section *ting*, pp. 12–13. The Chinese expression for "paper ashes" in the last line is *chih-ch'ien* (paper money, burnt for the dead), almost untranslatable in a poem. Hsu, *Twentieth Century*, p. 65.

77. *CW*, Section *ting*, pp. 18–19. Hsu, *Twentieth Century*, pp. 59–60.

78. *CW*, Section *ting*, pp. 5–6.

79. *Dead Water*, pp. 80–81.

80. "Tsui-kuo," *ibid.*, pp. 73–75.

81. "Huang-ts'un," *ibid.*, pp. 66–67. Hsu, *Twentieth Century*, 60–61. Accounts of human suffering were legion in Chinese writing during those years, and they kept reappearing as disasters of various kinds recurred year after year. In 1947, Mu Tan (Cha Liang-cheng), a younger poet whose works were valued by Wen I-to as much as Hsü Chih-mo's (see *CW*, Section *hsin*, pp. 516ff), echoed Wen's "Deserted Village" with his own "Deserted Village":

> Dried weeds, fallen walls, gaping huts,
> Speechless toppled trees, a jumble of dead silence....
> Even clouds high in the sky had no heart to linger, as crows
>   returning for the spring
> Forced themselves to caw, circling above the deserted yard,
> As though they've discovered and were pleased with the clinging
> Uncomplaining defeat of man. The abandoned earth
> Was the only statement, addressed to
> Spring breeze and sunset—
> . . . .

See *Wen-hsüeh tsa-chih* (*Literature Magazine*), II, 3 (August 1947), p. 58ff. A third poem of the same title, by Yao P'eng-tzu, is in *Compendium*, VIII, p. 369.

82. "Hsin-t'iao," *Dead Water*, pp. 52–53. Title changed to "Ching-yeh," *CW*, Section *ting*, pp. 20–21. Hsu, *Twentieth Century*, p. 62.

83. "Ch'i-tao," *Dead Water*, p. 60. Hsu, *Twentieth Century*, pp. 63–64.

84. "I-chü-hua," *Dead Water*, pp. 64–65. Hsu, *Twentieth Century*, p. 64.

85. "I-ko kuan-nien," *Dead Water*, pp. 56–57. Hsu, *Twentieth Century*, p. 58.
86. "Wen I-to hsien-sheng ti shu-cho" ("Mr. Wen I-to's Desk"), *Dead Water*, pp. 90–91. This poem was first published in the *Ta-chiang Quarterly*, Nov., 1925. Though it antedated some other poems in *Dead Water*, Wen's own use of it as an epilogue to the anthology was far from accidental.
87. *Crescent*, I, 1 (March 1928), pp. 6–10.
88. Li Ho-lin, *Chung-kuo wen-i lun-chan* (*The Literary Controversies in China*), (Shanghai, 1940), pp. 292–93. Hereafter cited as Li, *Literary Controversies*.
89. Liang Shih-ch'iu published his "Wen-hsüeh yü ko-ming" ("Literature and Revolution") in *Crescent*, I, 4 (June 10, 1928), pp. 35–45. The Leftist writer Feng Nai-ch'ao wrote a lengthy critique, collected in Li, *Literary Controversies*, pp. 255–81. Liang joined the editorial board of *Crescent* in April, 1929. His quarrel with Lu Hsün was recorded in subsequent issues of that monthly.
90. "Ta-pien," *Crescent*, I, 2 (April 10, 1928), p. 65.
91. Wen gave it a title, "Ch'ing-yüan" ("Willing"), and published it in *Crescent*, I, 4 (June 10, 1928), p. 123.
92. First published in *Crescent*, I, 6 (August 10, 1928), pp. 1–15; collected in *CW*, Section *ping*, pp. 143–156, especially p. 143.
93. *Ibid.*

Chapter Five

1. *Crescent*, I, 2 (April 10, 1928), various paging.
2. There were people who spoke disparagingly of Wen's preparation and qualification for a professorship in the Chinese classics. See the editorial note to an article by Wen on the *Book of Poetry* in *Ta-hsüeh* (*The Great Learning*), VI, 2 (July 1947), p. 105.
3. "Shao-ling hsien-sheng nien-p'u hui-ch'ien" ("Collated Notes on the Chronology of Tu Fu"), first published April, 1930–Jan., 1931; collected in *CW*, Section *ping*, pp. 45–100. William Hung, *Tu Fu, China's Greatest Poet* (Harvard University Press, 1952), p. 4. Hung is quite critical of Wen's work, but Chu Tzu-ch'ing, in his *Piao-chun yü ch'ih-tu* (*Standard and Measure*) (Shanghai, 1949), p. 8, regards Wen's achievement as even greater than that of the famous Ch'ing philologist Wang Nien-sun (1744–1832). Professor Mitsuo Kondo compared Wen's research with that of Tai Chen (1724–1777) and pointed out their similar merits. See *Mon Itta: Uta to shi* (*Wen I-to: The Song and Poetry*) (Tokyo, 1956), p. 58.
4. First published in *Crescent*, II, 9 (Nov. 10, 1929); collected in *CW*, Section *i*, pp. 275–90.

5. *CW*, Section *i*, p. 281.

6. *Ibid.*, p. 289.

7. *CW*, Chronology, p. 54.

8. *Ibid.*

9. Tsang K'o-chia, "Hai" ("The Sea"), *Wen-i fu-hsing* (*Renaissance*) III, 5 (July 1947), p. 537.

10. In 1931 Shen Ts'ung-wen said that Wen's poetry reflected too much cool wisdom, and was "too quiet and sophisticated" for youth to appreciate. According to Shen, Chinese youth at that time was interested in two types of poetry; the first embodying a strong note of social protest as typified by Kuo Mo-jo's poems, and the other praising romantic love as exemplified by Hsü Chih-mo's works. See Shen's article in *Crescent*, III, 2 (Sept. 1931), pp. 95–101.

11. Liang, *About Wen I-to*, p. 87.

12. See footnote 78, Chapter 3, *supra*.

13. *Wen I-to hsüan-chi* (*Selected Works of Wen I-to*), (Shanghai, 1951), pp. 89–92. Hereafter cited as Wen, *Selected Works*. Hsu, *Twentieth Century*, pp. 67–68.

14. The revived journal is a separate publication, not a section of another publication as its predecessor had been. Hsü's effort to get Wen to write poetry again is described in Liang, *About Wen I-to*, pp. 86–87.

15. I originally thought the reason was that his wife was expecting their sixth child. Since only two had survived among the five born thus far, they had to weigh the advantage of having somewhat better care among the big family in Hupeh. But Liang Shih-ch'iu's letter to me, dated August 19, 1978, says this was not the case.

16. These two short critical essays are, "Lun *Hui yü hui*" ("On *Regret and Return*"), in the form of a letter addressed to Ch'en Meng-chia, who co-authored the volume of poems reviewed, collected in *CW*, Section *ting*, pp. 283–84; and "T'an shang-lai t'i" ("On the Sonnet Style"), written on Feb. 19, 1931, collected in *ibid.*, pp. 281-82.

17. Feng I, "Hun-che hsüeh-szu ti chi-i" ("Blood-stained Memory"), *Wen-i fu-hsing* (*Renaissance*), II, 4 (November 1946), p. 392. Hereafter cited as Feng, "Memory."

18. Tsang K'o-chia, "Wo-ti hsien-shen Wen I-to" ("My Teacher Wen I-to"), quoted in *CW*, Chronology, p. 56.

19. Liang, *About Wen I-to*, pp. 98–100. Yü-ming Shaw, p. 63, has a somewhat different interpretation, which attributes Wen's trouble to his conservative politics at the moment.

20. Feng, "Memory," pp. 393–94.

21. Hsiung, "Wen I-to," p. 8. Cf. footnote 85, Chapter 3, *supra*.

22. *CW*, Section *keng*, pp. 51–52.

23. When his youngest daughter was born in Feb., 1936, he had already lost three of his eight children.

24. Professor Chi-chen Wang's letter to me, dated April 2, 1959.

25. *Tsing Hua University Yearbook* (1933), Literary Section, p. 8.

26. Ku, "Reminiscence on My Old Friend Wen I-to," p. 535. Cf. footnote 83, Chapter 3, *supra*. Ku was then vice-minister of education.

27. The three studies of the *Songs of Ch'u* completed in the 1930's are: "T'ien-wen shih t'ien" ("On the word 'Heaven' in the Chapter 'Heavenly Questions' in the *Songs of Ch'u*"), 1934; "Li Sao chieh ku" ("Exigesis of the 'Li Sao'"), 1936; and *Ch'u-tz'u chiao-pu* (Supplement to Liu Shih-p'ei's *Collated Notes on the Songs of Ch'u*) first published by installment in 1935–1936, separate volume in 1942. Professor James R. Hightower said that Wen's studies, along with those of Lin Keng, "are the most important contribution to an understanding of the *Songs of Ch'u*." See his "Ch'ü Yüan Studies," in *Silver Jubilee Volume of the Zinbun-Kagaku-Kenkyusyo* (Kyoto University, 1954), p. 212. The three studies of the *Book of Poetry* are "K'uang-chai ch'ih-tu" ("Correspondence from the K'uang Studio"), 1934; "Shih Hsin-t'ai 'hung' tzu shuo" ("On the Word 'Hung' in the 'Hsin-t'ai' Poem"), 1935; and "Shih-ching hsin-i" ("New Interpretation of the *Book of Poetry*"), 1937. All these and the articles on the *Erh-ya* are collected in *CW*. See its Table of Contents, p. ii. Some minor flaws in Wen's research, such as neglecting to note at certain places where he arbitrarily altered the wording of a text, even though not in a direct quotation, are pointed out in Mitsuo, *Uta*, p. 59.

28. Arthur Waley, *The Book of Songs* (London, 1954), p. 72.

29. *CW*, Section *i*, pp. 201–08. This study was first published in July, 1935. In 1944, he revised the organization of the study and incorporated it in his "Shih-ching t'ung-i" ("A Thorough Exploration of the Meaning in the *Book of Poetry*"), *CW*, Section *i*, pp. 103–201.

30. In 1957, Sun Tso-yün used Wen's approach to study the *Book of Poetry*, and acknowledged his indebtedness to Wen. See his "Shih-ching lien-ko fa-wei" ("Interpretations of the Love Songs in the *Book of Poetry*.") *Wen-hsüeh i-ch'an tseng-k'an* (*Additional Studies in our Literary Heritage*) (Peking, 1957), V, pp. 1–24. Li Ch'ang-chih, who did not quite agree with Wen, complained that scholars interested in the *Book of Poetry* used to follow the interpretations of Mao, Cheng, or Chu Hsi, but "nowadays most of them quote Lin I-kuang and Wen I-to." See Li's *Shih-ching shih-i* (*An Attempt at Translating the* Book of Poetry *into Pai-hua*) (Shanghai, 1956), p. 175. Yü Kuan-ying, Professor of Chinese, Peking University, follows Wen's interpretations of "*hung*" as "toad" in his *Shih-ching hsüan i*

(*Pai-hua Translation of Selected Poems from the* Book of Poetry) (Peking, 1956), p. 39.

31. Kuo Mo-jo, "Lun Wen I-to tso hsüeh-wen ti t'ai-tu" ("On Wen's Attitude toward Scholarship"), *Li-shih jen-wu (Historical Personages)* (Shanghai, 1949), p. 186; also see *CW*, Preface by Kuo, p. 2. Wen himself had a second thought on this subject and stated that it is possible to interpret *hung* as "wild goose" elsewhere in the *Book of Poetry*. See *CW*, Section *chia*, p. 126.

32. "Kao-t'ang Shen-nü ch'uan-shuo chih fen-hsi" ("An Analysis of the Legend of the Goddess of Kao-t'ang"), *CW*, Section *chia*, pp. 81–116.

33. *CW*, Section *chia*, pp. 343–56.

34. *Ibid.*, pp. 356–367.

35. My interview with Ku I-ch'iao, February 6, 1978, in Philadelphia.

36. Shih, *The Path*, pp. 59–60.

37. In Sept., 1933, Wen had spoken of his desire to visit Loyang because Tu Fu had lived there. *CW*, Section *keng*, p. 52.

38. *CW*, Chronology, p. 59.

39. *Ibid.*, p. 60.

40. *Ibid.*, pp. 60–61.

41. Wen's speech, "Pa-nien ti hui-i yü kan-hsiang" ("Reminiscence and Reflections on the Past Eight Years"), in *Lien-ta pa-nien (Eight Years of Lienta)*, pp. 3–4. After their removal to Changsha, Tsing Hua, Nan-k'ai, and Peking universities operated under the joint name National Temporary University of Changsha. The name was further changed to National Southwest Associate University (official English translation of the name), or Lienta for short, upon their arrival in Kunming.

Chapter Six

1. During a lunch break I walked out of the library with P'an Kuang-tan on my way home via the main drive on the Tsing Hua campus. We talked about the poet, Wen I-to. Then I put together my two impressions of him, one on the riverside at Ch'en-chia-ying in the winter of 1940, and the other in the Research Institute for the Humanities in the winter of 1943, and developed them into these few lines to mark my sorrowful thought of him who had left us for over six months already.   —M.C.C.

2. *Wen-i fu-hsing (Renaissance)*, III, 5 (July 1, 1947), p. 540.

3. "Ch'ang-cheng jih-chi" ("Diary on the Long Journey"), *Eight Years of Lienta*, pp. 8–17. *CW*, Chronology, pp. 63–64. Ch'ien Neng-

hsin, *Hsi-nan san-ch'ien wu-pai-li* (*3500-li Southwestward*). Thirty-nine photographs and comments on the march of Lienta students, obtained from Professor John Israel of the University of North Carolina, who found them in 1974 through the International Student Service of Geneva.

4. Shih, *The Path*, p. 71. Also see *Eight Years of Lienta*, p. 10.

5. Feng Tzu, "Hsieh tsai I-to hsien-sheng ti chou-nien chi" ("Written on the First Anniversary of Mr. Wen I-to's Death"), *Memorial Issue, THW*, p. 38.

6. In 1926, Wen bemoaned the loss of the tradition of "tenderness and gentility" among contemporary poets. Cf. footnote 52, Chapter 4, *supra.*

7. Liu Chao-chi, *Hsi-nan ts'ai-feng lu* (*Lyrics from Southwest China*) (Shanghai, 1946), preface. Also see *CW*, Section *ting*, p. 229.

8. "Kung-t'i shih ti tzu-shu" ("The Self-redemption of the 'Palace-style' Poetry"), completed on Aug. 22, 1941, collected in *CW*, Section *ping*, pp. 11–22.

9. See Sato Tamotsu's work.

10. *CW*, Chronology, p. 64. Also see *Eight Years of Lienta*, p. 6.

11. *CW*, Chronology, p. 64.

12. Lienta, short for Kuo-li Hsi-nan Lien-ho Ta-hsüeh.

13. He received a head injury in an air raid on Sept. 28, 1938. In Oct. 1940, a bomb fell in the courtyard of his house. It could have wiped out his entire family had it exploded. *CW*, Chronology, pp. 65, 67.

14. He discusses the difficulty of raising travel funds for his wife and children, and the problem of renting a place to live, in his letters collected in *CW*, Section *keng*, pp. 60–67. For his life and poverty in Kunming. see Shih, *The Path*, pp. 86–89. For the life of university people in Kunming in the early 1940's, see an article by Fei Hsiao-t'ung, in *Eight Years of Lienta*, pp. 55–60, and another article by a student in the same work, pp. 62–79. As a student there at the time, I also draw on my own memories of the situation. Parts of Robert Payne's diary kept in Kunming, as reflected in his *Forever China* (New York, 1945), pp. 566–68, are realistic descriptions.

15. In June, 1937, drinking tea was an event worthy of his reporting to his wife in a letter. *CW*, Section *keng*, p. 63.

16. Su Hsüeh-lin, "Wen I-to szu yü chih shou" ("Wen I-to Died at the Hands of His Nephew"). *Wen-t'an hua-chiu* (*Reminiscences About the Literary Scene*) (Hong Kong, 1968) p. 148. Hereafter cited as Su Hsüeh-lin, *Reminiscences.*

17. Wen did this in two studies of the "Nine Songs": "Tsen-yang tu 'Chiu-ko'" ("How to Read the 'Nine Songs'"), published in Jan.,

1941, and collected in *CW*, Section *chia*, pp. 279–303; and "Shen-mo shih 'Chiu-ko' " ("What Are the 'Nine Songs'?"), completed in Nov., 1941, collected in *ibid.*, pp. 263–78. Wen said, "Chiu-ko" does not mean "Nine Songs" since there are actually eleven songs. The "Chiu" refers to the nine stanzaic pauses in many ancient Chinese verses and songs. Hence, "Chiu-ko" is a style name similar to such later style names as "ch'i-lü" and "wu-ku," or seven-syllable and five-syllable lines. See *ibid.*, pp. 264–66.

18. *CW*, Section *chia*, p. 272. *Ch'ien Han shu* (*History of the Former Han Dynasty*) (Po-na edition), "Li-yüeh chih," 2.13a-b.

19. " 'Chiu-ko' ku ko-wu chü hsüan-chieh," *CW*, Section *chia*, pp. 328–29. According to *CW*, Chronology, p. 84, it was written in June, 1946, about a month before his death. But *Eight Years of Lienta*, p. 166, tells us that shortly before Wen's death he was working on a vernacular translation of the "Chiu-ko" for which he had asked the composer Chao Feng to compose a musical accompaniment. Judging by the development of Wen's interest in the "Chiu-ko," it seems that he must have conceived of this rearrangement around 1942 or 1943, and afterwards continued to work on the vernacular version. The translation of the first line of the poem is from Arthur Waley, *The Nine Songs*, p. 53. A comparison of the translations of Waley and Hawkes and Wen's rearrangement of the "Nine Songs" is particularly rewarding. In preparing his translation, Waley consulted Wen's studies. Waley amassed a wealth of notes on the cultural and historical background of these songs, but he did not attempt to recreate them as an integrated whole. Due to the difficulties of the ancient text, he left many points admittedly vague. Hawkes acknowledges his great debt to Wen, and indeed Hawkes' interpretation of how the songs were put together reflects much of Wen's analysis. But he also made no attempt at recreating the sequence as a stage piece. Both Waley and Hawkes treated the third and fourth songs as addressed to two female deities, but Wen held a different view. In textual elucidation and emendation Hawkes follows, in most cases, Wen's earlier study of the *Songs of Ch'u*. Waley regarded the *hsi* syllables in these songs as meaningless syllables, but Wen offered an ingenious way to explain the function of this word; he suggested that the reader replace *hsi* with various "particles," prepositions or connectives, and then the meaning of the line would clearly emerge. It would be another boon to the study of this classic if some day Wen's vernacular translation could become available.

20. Kuo Mo-jo, *Ch'ü Yüan yen-chiu* (*Studies on Ch'ü Yüan*) (Shanghai, 1950), pp. 125–26. This work was first published in 1942. In "Ch'ü Yüan Studies," p. 205, Hightower states that the evidence for

Kuo's theory "is ingenious but specious and sometimes perverse," and that in interpreting the "Li Sao," Kuo made several brilliant suggestions, "not all of them acceptable."

21. Lin Keng, *Shih-jen Ch'ü Yüan chi ch'i tso-p'in yen-chiu* (*A Study on the Poet Ch'ü Yüan and His Works*) (Shanghai, 1953), pp. 42–51. This section of the work was written in the early 1940's.

22. "Tuan-chieh ti li-shih chiao-yü" ("The Historical Lesson of the Dragonboat Festival"), written in July, 1943, collected in *CW*, Section *chia*, pp. 239–43.

23. The several studies of the *Book of Poetry* included in *CW* are but a part of the result of Wen's philological work. Chu Tzu-ch'ing, editor of *CW*, said a number of voluminous manuscripts by Wen remained to be edited. See his postscript in *CW*, p. 7. The 8,841 pages of handwritten manuscripts are now kept at the Peking library. See *The People's Daily* (Peking), July 20, 1956, p . 8.

24. See the preface to his 'Feng-shih lei-ch'ao" ("The *Feng* Poems Arranged by Themes"), *CW*, Section *hsin*, pp. 5–8. This work was not published until after Wen's death, but it must have been drafted between 1940 and 1943 when he was developing his new views on the classics and teaching a course on the *Book of Poetry*. There is a good discussion of Wen's contribution to the study of the *Book of Poetry* in Hsia Tsung-yü, "Wen I-to hsien-sheng ho *Shih-ching*" ("Wen I-to and the *Book of Poetry*"), *Hsin Chien-she* (*Reconstruction*), 121 (October, 1958), pp. 63–66.

25. Marcel Granet, *Festivals and Songs of Ancient China*, (London, 1932), pp. 207–08.

26. Wen was always careful in acknowledging his intellectual debts, yet in these studies on the *Book of Poetry* he makes no mention of any Western work. The only exception is the mention of Karlgren's phonological system, which Wen adopted to arrive at the approximate ancient sounds of the words in the "Fou-i" poem. See *CW*, Section *chia*, p. 348. Waley's translation of the *Book of Songs*, first published in England in 1937, was perhaps not readily obtainable in wartime China.

27. Legge James, trans. *Chinese Classics.* (London, 1895), Vol. IV. pt. 1, pp. 17–18.

28. Po-na edition, 29.19b-20a.

29. Arthur Waley, trans. *Book of Songs*, (London, 1954), p. 152.

30. The translation of this stanza is mine, based entirely on Wen's explication. In the above comparative study of one stanza, one could also cite Ezra Pound's version (*Classic Anthology Defined by Confucius*, p. 6), but it does not contribute much to the solution of the textual problems.

31. "Yin-yü," *CW*, Section *chia*, pp. 117–19.

32. "Shuo yü" ("On Fish"), *CW*, Section *chia*, pp. 117–38. Although this essay was not published until the summer of 1945, the main research must have been done about 1943. The conclusion of this study, however, seems to have been written after the summer of 1943.

33. *CW*, Section *chia*, p. 12.

34. "Chiang-yüan lü ta-jen chi k'ao" ("An Investigation of the Legend of Lady Chiang's Treading in the Footprint of the Giant"), *CW*, Section *chia*, pp. 73–80.

35. "Fu Hsi k'ao" ("An Inquiry on Fu Hsi"), *ibid.*, pp. 3–68.

36. Maspero in "Legendes mythologiques dans le *Chou King*," *Journal Asiatique*, CCIV (1924), pp. 44–45, criticized Chinese scholars for their euhemerism. His observation that the flood legend had no necessary connection with any actual inundation of China (*ibid.*, p. 67), and that it is a legend about the origin of man and civilization (*ibid.*, p. 70), is in agreement with Wen's thesis.

37. Hsü Liang-chih, *Chung-kuo shih-ch'ien shih-hua* (*A Historical Treatise on Pre-historic China*) (Hong Kong, 1956), pp. 112, 152. The author of this work acknowledges his indebtedness to Wen and expands Wen's investigation into a substantial part of this book. Other scholars in favor of the theory about the totemic character of ancient Chinese culture include Li Chi, *The Beginnings of Chinese Civilization* (University of Washington, 1957), p. 20; Fu Szu-nien, *Fu Men-chen wen-chi* (*Collected Works of Fu Szu-nien*) (Taipei, 1952), pp. 236–240; and Lü Chen-yü, *Chung-kuo min-tsu chien-shih* (*A Short History of the Chinese People*) (Harbin, 1948), pp. 14–15.

38. "*I-lin* ch'iung chih" ("The Gems from the *I-lin*"), *CW*, Section *hsin*, pp. 141–52. In this work Wen selected excerpts from the *I-lin*, a st dy of the *Book of Changes* by the Han Dynasty scholar Chiao Yen shou.

39. "*Chou I* i-cheng lei ts'uan" (Selections from the *Book of Changes* Annotated and Grouped by Subject-matter), *CW*, Section *i*, pp. 5–65.

40. *CW*, Preface by Kuo Mo-jo, p. 5; Chronology, p. 68.

41. Wen I-to, "K'uang-chai t'an-i" ("Talks on Art at the K'uang Studio"). *Wen-shüeh tsa-chih* (*Literature Magazine*), III, 4 (September 1937), pp. 15–16.

42. "Song and Poetry," *CW*, Section *chia*, pp. 181–91. It was first published in June, 1939.

43. Wen's assumptions about the development of poetry and songs among primitive peoples touch upon one widely accepted hypothesis on the origin of language. See, for instance, Susanne K. Langer,

Philosophy in a New Key (New York: Mentor, 1955), pp. 83ff; and Ernst Cassirer, *Language and Myth* (New York: Dover, 1953), pp. 38ff.

44. Wen's discussion on this ancient definition of poetry appears in *CW*, Section *chia*, pp. 184–89. The definition is attributed to Cheng Hsüan, who wrote the noted commentary on the *Yao-tien*.

Chapter Seven

1. *Wen-i fu-hsing* (*Renaissance*), III, 5 (July 1, 1947), p. 539.

2. *Heroes and Martyrs*, p. 247. Chao Ch'en, "I Wen I-to shih" ("Remembering My Teacher Wen I-to"), *Memorial Issue, THW*, p. 31. Cf. footnote 4, Chapter 6, *supra*.

3. Wang I, "K'u Wen I-to hsien-sheng" ("Mourning Wen I-to"), *Heroes and Martyrs*, pp. 307–08.

4. For military developments, see F. F. Liu, *A Military History of Modern China* (Princeton University Press, 1956), pp. 208–25; *China Handbook* 1954-55 (Taipei, 1954), pp. 587ff.

5. U.S. Department of State, *U. S. Relations with China* (Washington D.C., 1949), pp. 65–71; Liu, *Military History*, pp. 174–91; Herbert Feis, *The China Tangle* (Princeton University Press, 1953), pp. 14–19, 185–99.

6. For the Communist side of the story, see Liao Kai-lung, *From Yenan to Peking* (Peking, 1954), pp. 1–28; and his *Hsin Chung-kuo shih tsen-yang tan-sheng ti* (*How the New China Was Born*) (Shanghai, 1950), pp. 25–29. For the Kuomintang side of the story, see Chiang Kai-shek, *Su-o tsai Chung-kuo* (*Soviet Russia in China*) (Taipei, 1957), pp. 116–18, 121–26.

7. Ch'ien Tuan-sheng, *The Government and Politics of China* (Harvard University Press, 1950), pp. 371–75.

8. *Chung-kuo hsin min-chu yün-tung chung ti tang-p'ai* (*Political Parties in the New Democratic Movement in China*) (Shanghai, 1946, pp. 28–61; *Minor Political Parties, passim*; Melville T. Kennedy, Jr., "The Chinese Democratic League," *Harvard University Regional Studies on China* (mimeographed), 7 (1953), pp. 136–75; Anthony J. Shaheen, *The China Democratic League and Chinese Politics*, 1939–1947, unpublished doctoral dissertation (University of Michigan, 1977), pp. 208–61.

9. Graham Peck, *Two Kinds of Time* (Boston, 1950), pp. 470–71.

10. For the situation in Yunnan around 1945, see Chang Wen-shih, *Yün-nan nei-mu* (*Inside Yunnan*) (Kunming, 1949); Peck, pp. 437–59. Wen himself wrote a report on the December 1, 1945, incident in *CW*, Section *wu*, pp. 73–76.

11. Frank Tao, "Student Life in China," *China After Seven Years of War*, ed. Hollington K. Tong (Chungking, 1944), pp. 94–111; *Eight Years of Lienta*, pp. 65–79. And my own experience there, 1941-1944.

12. *Eight Years of Lienta*, pp. 71–72; Shih, *The Path*, p. 86.

13. The K'un-hua Middle School, see *CW*, Chronology, pp. 73, 75–76.

14. Graham Peck also describes the death of a sick and abandoned soldier in *Two Kinds of Time*, pp. 475–76.

15. *CW*, Chronology, p. 72.

16. Shih, *The Path*, p. 112.

17. *CW*, Chronology, p. 74, places the date of this event in the summer of 1944. Two other writers prefer the summer of 1943; see *Heroes and Martyrs*, pp. 38, 161. My recollection, and the development of Wen's ideas and attitudes in those years, support the date in the Chronology. The undated article, "Wei-ta ti shih-shih, pu hsiu ti i-i" ("A Thing of Greatness with Undying Significance"), *CW*, Section *wu*, pp. 49–53, must have been written immediately after his meeting with his nephew. Su Hsüeh-lin, *Reminiscences*, pp. 143–50, asserts that the nephew must have been a Communist agent sent to win Wen over to the Yenan side.

18. *CW*, Chronology, p. 74.

19. *Ibid.*, p. 75.

20. "Tsu-chih min-chung yü pao-wei ta Hsi-nan" ("Organize the People and Defend the Great Southwest"), in *CW*, Section *chi*, p. 306.

21. *Memorial Issue, THW*, p. 31; Wen Shan, "Chiao wo hsüeh-pu ti jen" ("He Who Taught Me to Walk"), *The People's Daily* (Peking), July 14, 1956, p. 8; K'ang Ch'ien, "I Wen I-to hsien-sheng" ("Remembering My Teacher Wen I-to"), *The People's Daily* (Peking), July 15, 1956, p. 7.

22. Shih, *The Path*, p. 112.

23. For a brief biography of Ch'u T'u-nan, see Human Relation Area Files, *Southwest China* (New Haven, 1956), II, pp. 719–20.

24. For a brief biography of Li Kung-p'u, see *Heroes and Martyrs*, pp. 3–6.

25. *CW*, Chronology, p. 76. Shih, *Wen I-to*, pp. 22–23, describes the books that interested Wen in 1943-1944. Also see Mien, *Wen I-to*, pp. 62–63. *CW*, Postscript by Wu Han, p. 3, mentions Kuo Mo-jo's *Ch'ing-t'ung shih-tai* (*The Bronze Age*) and *Shih p'i-p'an shu* (*Ten Critical Essays*) as Wen's favorite books. These works by Kuo study the nature and characteristics of Chinese culture and society. Wen accepted Gorky's criterion for evaluating a writer. See *CW*, Section

chia, p. 258. On the question of how much Communist influence was exerted on Wen to cause his last change in attitudes, no post mortem in a politically divided world could yield a completely reliable answer. It was easy for Rightist writers to claim that Wen was being used by the Communists, with a convenient reference to a statement by Wu Han, quoting Wen as saying, ". . . Why can't we (the Democratic League) be the Communist Party's tail? The Communist Party is doing the right things!" Wu Han, *Ch'un-t'ien chi* (*Spring Days*) (Peking, 1961), p. 29. It is equally easy for the Communists to claim credit for having converted Wen, though not to Party membership. Wang I, the junior instructor who went to warn Wen just before the assassination, later insisted on his being sent by the Communist Party, as he did in the *Enlightenment Daily* on July 15, 1958; so did Wen's son, Wen Li-ho, in *Tien-ying wen-hsüeh* (*Literature for the Movie Screen*), No. 5 (1959), p. 82. Wen Li-ho states that Communist agents were specifically assigned to work on his father to win him over to the Yenan side.

26. His letter to Tsang K'o-chia, *CW*, Section *keng*, p. 56. In August, 1945, Ku I-ch'iao, his old friend since Tsing Hua School days, now prominent in the Nationalist government, passed through Kunming. He spoke privately with Wen for hours, urging him to be cautious, but Wen dismissed all cautions. My interview with Ku, February 5, 1978, in Philadelphia.

27. This is how Wen described himself in his letter to Tsang, *ibid.,* p. 54.

28. Wen praised T'ien Chien and Mayakovsky in the same breath. See Shih, *The Path,* p. 99. In 1945 Wen asked Kuo Mo-jo, who was going to Moscow, to buy a set of Mayakovsky's works for him. See *Heroes and Martyrs,* p. 251. Almost every history of modern Chinese literature published after World War II discusses Mayakovsky's influence on modern Chinese poetry. For instance, Liu Shou-sung, *Wen-i san-lun* (*Random Treatises on Literature*) (Wuhan, 1955), p. 95. Wen's commentary on T'ien Chien has become a widely quoted appraisal of that younger poet. Liu, *A Preliminary Draft History of Modern Chinese Literature,* II, p. 92. Robert Payne discusses Mayakovsky's influence on T'ien in *Contemporary Chinese Poetry* (London, 1947), p. 27. The Russian sinologist Fedorenko also stresses the same point in his *Chinese Literature* (Moscow, 1956), pp. 344, 448, 639, and 648–49.

29. Tsang K'o-chia, "Wo-ti hsien-sheng Wen I-to" ("My Teacher Wen I-to"), *Heroes and Martyrs,* p. 142. *CW*, Chronology, p. 70.

30. *CW*, Section *ting,* p. 236. On Poet's Day (fifth day of the fifth lunar month), 1945, he lectured on T'ien Chien, referring to him

as a "fighting poet." *CW*, Section *chi*, pp. 51–52.

31. "Shih-tai ti ku-shou," *CW*, Section *ting*, pp. 233–38.

32. Sixty articles and documents on this debate by Lu Hsün, Kuo Mo-jo, and others are collected in *Kuo-fang wen-hsüeh lun-chan* (*Debate on the Literature of National Defense*) (Shanghai, 1936).

33. *CW*, Section *keng*, p. 54.

34. The essay is "The Direction of the Historical Development of Literature," first published in April, 1943, and collected in *CW*, Section *chia*, pp. 201–06. The outline is given in Chu Tzu-ch'ing's Preface in *CW*, pp. 20–21. Chu was then editing Wen's manuscript of "A History of Chinese Literature."

35. Wen's thesis is in general agreement with that of Professor Ch'en Shih-hsiang (d. 1971) of the University of California at Berkeley. See the latter's essay "The Cultural Essence of Chinese Literature," in *Interrelations of Culture* (UNESCO, 1953), pp. 43–85.

36. He stresses this point in various articles. For instance, see *CW*, Section *chi*, p. 42.

37. "Chan-hou wen-i ti tao-lu" ("The Path for Post-war Literature") *CW*, Section *chi*, pp. 31–38. This undated speech was possibly made around the end of World War II.

38. "Shih yü p'i-p'ing" ("Poetry and Criticism"), written in the winter of 1943, collected in *CW*, Section *chi*, pp. 43–49. See particularly pp. 45–46.

39. "Lun wen-i ti min-chu wen-t'i" (The Question of Democracy in Literature), *ibid.*, pp. 39–42, a speech made shortly before his death.

40. "Hua-chan" ("Exhibits of Paintings"), *CW*, Section *wu*, pp. 67–70.

41. Sun Tz'u-chou, a specialist in the *Songs of Ch'u*, published this iconoclastic study after he had given the gist of his views in a lecture on Poet's Day, 1944, in Chengtu. Wen described this controversy in *CW*, Section *chia*, pp. 248–49.

42. Wen's last views on Ch'ü Yüan are expressed in two articles, "Ch'ü Yüan wen-t'i" ("The Question on Ch'ü Yüan"), written in December, 1944, *CW*, Section *chia*, pp. 245–58; and "Jen-min ti shih-jen—Ch'ü Yüan" ("People's Poet—Ch'ü Yüan"), written in June, 1945, *ibid.*. pp. 259–61.

43. "San-yüeh wu-chün, tse huang-huang, ju yeh," *ibid.*, p. 253.

44. Cf. footnotes 20, 21, Chapter 6, *supra*.

45. See, for example, most of the articles in *Ch'u-tz'u yen-chiu lun-wen chi* (*Collected Essays on the Songs of Ch'u*) (Peking, 1957).

46. "Ts'ung tsung-chiao lun Chung-Hsi feng-ko" ("An Exposition of Chinese and Western Characters on the Basis of Religion"), writ-

ten in April, 1944, collected in *CW*, Section *wu*, pp. 25–30.

47. "I K'ung-chiao wei kuo-chiao p'ei-t'ien i" ("On Worshipping Confucianism as Our National Religion"), in *K'ang Nan-hai wen-chi (Collected Works of Kang Yu-wei)* (n.p., n.d.), 5.2a-5b.

48. Liang Ch'i-ch'ao, *Yin-ping-shih ho chi (Collected Works of the Ice-drinker's Studio)*, 2nd. ed. 16 vols. (Shanghai, 1941), 3.9–11; 6.67–70.

49. *Ibid.*, 9.50, 58; also see Joseph R. Levenson, *Liang ch'i-ch'ao and the Mind of Modern China* (Harvard University Press, 1953), pp. 92–101.

50. Cf. footnotes 48–50, *supra;* also see C. K. Yang, "The Functional Relationship between Confucian Thought and Chinese Religion," *Chinese Thought and Institutions*, ed. John K. Fairbank (University of Chicago Press, 1957), pp. 269–72.

51. "Chia-tsu chu-i yü min-tsu chu-i" ("Familism and Nationalism"), written in April, 1944, in *CW*, Section *wu*, pp. 3–6.

52. "Fu-ku ti k'ung-ch'i" ("The Atmosphere of the 'Revival of Ancient Learning'"), also written in April, 1944, *ibid.*, pp. 7–12.

53. "Shen-mo shih Ju-chia" ("What Is A Confucian?"), written in Jan., 1945, *ibid.*, pp. 13–18.

54. "Kuan-yü Ju, Tao, t'u-fei" ("About Confucians, Taoists, and Bandits"), written in April, 1944, *ibid.*, pp. 19–24.

55. "K'o-p'a ti leng-ching," written in July, 1944, *CW*, Section *wu*, pp. 55–58.

56. "Yü chan yü ch'iang" ("The Longer We Fight, The Stronger We Become"), also written in July, 1944, *ibid.*, pp. 59–62.

57. "I-ko pai-jih meng" ("A Nightmare in Daytime"), written in Dec., 1944. *ibid.*, pp. 63–66.

58. *CW*, Section *chi*, pp. 11–14.

59. *CW*, Section *wu*, p. 6.

60. He hinted at this in a letter to Tsang Ko'-chia, dated Oct. 12, 1944; *CW*, Section *keng*, p. 57. In the same month, he addressed a mass rally in Kunming. He accused the Nationalists of tying the hands of the Communist army which was fighting the Japanese. *CW*, Section *chi*, p. 3. His impression of Yenan was largely based on reports he received from former students who had gone there. See his letter to Feng I, in *Renaissance*, II, 4 (November 1946), p. 395.

61. *Heroes and Martyrs*, p. 245.

62. *CW*, Section *chi*, pp. 27–28. Among the numerous descriptions of Wen's oratorical art, that of Hsia K'ang-nung is probably most striking. Hsia said that when Wen spoke, "his simple words warm the hearts of the audience; even the four walls of the auditorium begin to heat up." See Hsia, "Hua shih-tai ti szu-che" ("He Died

Making An Epoch"), *Ta-hsüeh* (*The Great Learning*), VI, 3–4 (August 1947), pp. 17–19.

63. *Heroes and Martyrs*, p. 306. Later, Wang I claimed that he was sent by the Communist Party to warn Wen to be careful. See *The Enlightenment Daily*, July 15, 1958, p. 3.

64. *Ibid.*, p. 196.

65. *CW*, Chronology, pp. 80–81.

66. The price was reported to be 400,000 Chinese dollars, about $200 in American money at that time. There are many sources which give varying versions of this story. The most believable one seems to be in Liang Shu-ming and Chou Hsin-min, *Li-Wen an tiao-ch'a pao-kao shu* (*Report on the Investigation of the Li-Wen Case*) (Headquarters, Chinese Democratic League, September 30, 1946), p. 20.

67. *CW*, Chronology, p. 83. Shortly before the assassination, Nationalist agents, or some other extreme Rightist elements, issued posters identifying Wen as a Communist terrorist. Immediately after the murder, they charged the Communists with murdering Wen. However, the Kuomintang confidential pamphlet, *Minor Political Parties* (p. 13), issued in Aug., 1946, still groups Wen with those "without party affiliation or whose political background is unclear." Also see Shaheen, pp. 371–74.

68. *Heroes and Martyrs*, p. 254.

69. Professor Ch'en Shih-hsiang of the University of California at Berkeley confirmed the invitation.

70. Wen's wife had been suffering from a heart condition for quite some time. *Heroes and Martyrs*, p. 246.

71. The details of these two assassinations are probably best researched in the report by Liang and Chou, and the eye-witness account by Wen's son, Li-ho, who was gravely wounded at the same time, in *Memorial Issue, THW*, pp. 10–12. A student in Kunming at the time wrote another report in *ibid.*, pp. 13–16. Also see *Heroes and Martyrs*, pp. 15–26, 323–53, 378–79. For a few days after the murders, eleven professors and friends of Wen obtained refuge in the American Consulate compound. A report on this incident by James G. Endicott, American missionary, is quoted in Jack Belden, pp. 7–8. There is also a confidential report filed by the American Consulate.

72. *CW*, Chronology, p. 85.

73. The most complete version of Wen's last speech is in Wen, *Selected Works*, pp. 204–07.

Chapter Eight

1. *China Daily News* (*Hua-ch'iao jih-pao*, New York), July 30, 1977, p. 5.

2. Conflicting reports, mostly very brief, were released by Kuomintang and pro-Kuomintang papers on the results of the supposedly official investigation. They tended to blame a couple of uniformed soldiers for taking the law into their own hands because they had become irate over Wen's criticism of the government. The authorities in Chungking did allow two League leaders, Liang Shu-ming and Chou Hsin-min, to spend some days in Kunming interviewing the murder suspects and conducting their own investigation. Their report was later printed. Considering the explosive political atmosphere of the time, the Liang-Chou report was perhaps as factual as possible. Rightist writers have charged that it was all a Communist plot, sacrificing a vociferous fellow-traveler, Wen I-to, to create an incident with repercussions hopefully favorable to the Communist cause. Su Hsüeh-lin's article in *Reminiscences* belongs to this group, but it lacks documentation and the author was not at the scene of the incident. Also see Shaheen, pp. 372–74.

3. *The Wen-hui Daily* (Shanghai), October 20, 1946.

4. The epigram is: "With my eyebrows raised I can calmly face the challenge of a thousand men; but with my head bowed, I am a willing beast of burden serving the weak and the young." See Liu Shou-sung, *Chung-kuo hsin-wen-hsüeh shih ch'u-kao* (*A Preliminary Draft History of Modern Chinese Literature*) 2 Vols. (Peking, 1956) I, p. 280.

5. Mao Tse-tung, *Mao Tse-tung hsüan-chi* (*Selected Works of Mao Tse-tung*) 4 Vols. (Peking, 1951-1953) IV, p. 1499.

6. For these services, see *Kuan-ch'a* (*Observation*), II, 23 (Aug. 2, 1947), pp. 17–19; *The People's Daily*, July 16, 1956, p. 1.

7. *Tien-ying wen-hsüeh* (*Literature for the Movie Screen*), 2 (1959), pp. 30–58. The responses are in *ibid.*, 5 (1959), pp. 82–94.

8. A *China News Service* release dated June 27, 1978, says that the famed actor Chao Tan has been assigned to portray the hero Wen I-to. There is no mention of the name of the scriptwriter.

9. See Chu Kuang-ch'ien, "Shih-ti i-hsiang yü ch'ing-ch'ü" ("Poetic Imagery and Feeling"), *Wen-hsüeh tsa-chih* (*Literature Magazine*), II, 10 (March 1948), pp. 1–4; Tung Ch'u-p'ing's articles cited in footnote 32, Chapter 4 above; Wang Li, "Chung-kuo ko-lü shih ti ch'uan-t'ung ho hsien-tai ko-lü shih ti wen-t'i" ("The Tradition of Chinese Poetic Forms and Modern Poetic Forms"), *Wen-*

hsüeh p'ing-lun (*Literary Criticism*), 3 (June 25, 1959), pp. 1–12; Pien Chih-lin, "Kuan-yü shih-ko ti fa-chan wen-t'i" ("On the Development of Poetry"), *People's Daily*, January 13, 1959; and Ho Ch'i-fang, "Kuan-yü hsien-tai ko-lü shih" ("On Modern Formalist Poetry"), *Chung-kuo ch'ing-nien* (*Chinese Youth*), 10 (1954), pp. 14–19; Ho Ch'i-fang, "Kuan-yü shih-ko hsing-shih wen-t'i ti cheng-lun" ("Debate on the Form of Poetry"), *Wen-hsüeh p'ing-lun* (*Literary Criticism*), 1 (1959), pp. 1–22; and Ho Ch'i-fang, "Tsai-t'an shih-ko hsing-shih wen-t'i" ("Further Discussion on the Form of Poetry"), *ibid.*, 2 (1959), pp. 55–75.

10. See Chao Li-sheng (Feng I), "Chin-p'ing Wen I-to hsien-sheng ti hsüeh-shu ch'eng-chiu—chien lun Chung-kuo wen-hsien hsüeh ti hsin shui-p'ing" ("An Attempt at Commenting on Wen I-to's Scholarly Accomplishment. Also on the New Standard for Chinese Classical Research"). *Hsin chien-she* (*Reconstruction*), I, 8 (December 1949), pp. 15–16.

11. See, for example, Li I-chih, *Shih san-pai-p'ien chin-i* (*The Book of Poetry Translated into Present-day Language*) (Taipei, 1964); Wen Huai-sha, *Ch'ü Yüan "Chiu-ko" chin-i* (*Ch'ü Yüan's "Nine Songs" Translated into Present-day Language*) (Hong Kong. 1974).

12. For his earlier expressions on *ling*, see the two epitaphs he wrote for his schoolmates in *THJ*, IV, 6 (May 1919), pp. 49–50; and IV, 8 (July, 1919), pp. 78–79. For later uses of the term, see his discussion of the nobility of maternal instinct in *CW*, Section *chia*, p. 347.

13. Shih, *The Path*, p. 6.

14. *CW*, Section *ting*, pp. 241–42.

15. Lu Hsün said this in 1918. See Wen Chi-tse, *Lu Hsün he t'a chiao-tao ch'ing-nien ti hua* (*Lu Hsün and What He Taught to Youth*) (Peking, 1956), pp. 44–47; Sung Yün-pin, *Lu Hsun yü lu* (*Lu Hsün's Epigrams*) (Shanghai, 1950), p. 131. The lines "Your minister will exert and exhaust himself [to serve you] until his death," which Wen quoted in his poem on Keats, were also quoted by Mao Tse-tung to describe Lu Hsün's dedication to the cause of the common people. See *Selected Works of Mao Tse-tung*, III, pp. 898–99.

16. "Dead Water" was inspired by the sight of the stenchy, polluted ditch, called Dragon Hollow, in the Hsi-tan district of Peking. The place has been built up, and the ditch has been covered by highrise buildings, including the Palace of the Nationalities.—J.M.K.

17. *People's Literature*, 7 (Peking, 1962), p. 44.

18. One wonders how this accomplice was connected to the other three executed soon after the assassination: Hsiung Kuang-fu, Wang Chieh-min, and Ch'in Yung-ho. See *Enlightenment Daily* (Peking), June 29, 1957, p. 2.

Selected Bibliography

PRIMARY SOURCES*

*I am indebted to my able graduate student, Ping-wai Huang, for locating the poem, "The Song of Yü-yang," and to Professor Mary Fung of Hong Kong University, for discovering Wen's letter to Chang Hsi-jo. — K.Y.H.

1. Works by Wen I-to

"Ch'ang-ch'eng-hsia chih ai-ko" ("A Lament under the Great Wall"). *Ta-chiang Quarterly* (July 1925), pp. 24–32.

"Cheng-ch'iu i-shu chuan-meng-che ti hu-sheng" ("Calling for Professional Artists"). *Ch'ing-hua chou-k'an* (*Tsing Hua Weekly*, or *THW*), 192 (October 1, 1920), pp. 1–6.

"Ch'i-fu-che-le" ("The Wronged"). *Shih-k'an* (*Poetry Journal*, supplement to *Peking Morning News*), No. 1 (April 1, 1926), p. 3.

"Ch'i-tzu chih ko" ("The Song of Seven Offsprings"). *Ta-chiang Quarterly* (November 1925), pp. 29–32.

"Chih yu-jen shu" ("Letter to Friends"), *THW*, 97 (February 22, 1917), pp. 9–10.

"Chin-kung-che" ("The Tribute Bearer"), *THW*, Double-four Special Supplement (April 4, 1922), p. 71.

"Ch'in-shih huang-ti" ("The First Emperor of Ch'in"). *Ch'en-pao ch'i-chou-nien chi-nien tseng-kan* (*The Seventh Anniversary Supplement to Peking Morning News*), pp. 400–01. Peking, December 1, 1925.

"Ch'ing-hua ch'u-pan-wu yü yen-lun-chia" ("Tsing Hua's Publications and Spokesmen"). *THW*, 192 (October 1, 1920), pp. 16–19.

"Ch'ing-hua hsüeh-sheng tai-piao-t'uan chi Hsü chün Yüeh-che wen" ("A Eulogy for Mr. Hsü Yüeh-che in Behalf of the Delegation of the Tsing Hua Student Body"). *Ch'ing-hua hsüeh-pao* (*Tsing Hua Journal*, or *THJ*), IV, 8 (1919), pp. 78–79.

"Ch'ing-hua t'i-yü" ("Physical Education at Tsing Hua"). *THJ*, IV, 8 (1919), p. 79.

"Ch'ing-hua t'u-shu-kuan" ("Tsing Hua's Library"). *THJ*, IV, 8 (1919), p. 80.

"Ch'ing-yüan" ("Willing"—Translated from A.E. Housman's poem). *Crescent*, I, 4 (June 10, 1928), various paging.

"Ch'u-pan-wu ti feng-mien" ("The Cover-designs of Current Publications"). *THW*, 187 (April 24, 1920), pp. 19–25.

Ch'üan-chi (*Complete Works*). Edited by Chu Tzu-ch'ing and others. 4 vols. Shanghai, 1948.

"Ch'üan T'ang-shih chiao-tu fa chü-li" ("An Example of Exegetical Study of the *Complete T'ang Poems*") *Wen-che Yüeh-k'an* (*Literature and Philosophy Monthly*), I, 5 (February 1936), pp. 16–24.

"Chung-wen k'o-t'ang ti chih-hsü i-pan" ("The General Situation of Order in the Chinese Classes"). *THW*, 214 (April 1, 1921), p. 21.

"Erh-yüeh-lu man-chi" ("Random Notes from the Two-month Hut"). *THW*, 81 (October 4, 1916), 14; 88 (November 23, 1916). pp. 13–14.

"Hsin chün-tzu kuang-i" ("The Expanded Definition of the New Chün-tzu"). *THW*, 92 (December 21, 1916), pp. 1–2.

"Hsin-shih ti ch'ien-t'u" ("The Future of New Poetry"). *T'ien-hsia wen-chang* (*World Literature*), II, 4 (November 1944), p. 12.

Hsüan-chi (*Selected Works of Wen I-to*). Shanghai, 1951.

Hsüan-chi (*Selected Works of Wen I-to*). Peking, 1952.

"Huang-chih t'iao-kao" ("Bulletins on Yellow Paper"). *THW*, 198 (November 12, 1920), p. 18.

"Hui-fu ho-p'ing" ("Restoration of the Peace"). *THW*, 226 (November 19, 1921), p. 16.

"Hui-fu lun-li yen-chiang" ("Restore the Lectures on Ethics"). *THW*, 218 (April 29, 1921), pp. 18–21.

"Hui-lai" ("Return"). *Crescent*, I, 3 (May 10, 1928), various paging.

Hung-chu (*Red Candle*). Shanghai, 1923.

"K'uang-chai t'an-i" ("Talks on Art at the K'uang Studio"). *Wen-hsüeh tsa-chih* (*Literature Magazine*), III, 4 (September 1937), pp. 15–16.

"Kung-kung chi-kuan ti-wei-hsin" ("The Dignity of a Public Office"). *THW*, 218 (April 29, 1921), p. 28.

"Liu Mei t'ung-hsin" ("Letters from America"). *THW*, 251 (September 23, 1922), pp. 26–32.

"Lü-k'o shih ti hsüeh-sheng" ("The Hotel-guest-like Students"). *THW*, 185 (April 24, 1920), pp. 22–23.

"Lun chen-hsing kuo-hsüeh" ("On Reviving Chinese Studies"). *THW*, 77 (May 17, 1916), pp. 1–2.

"Mei-kuo-hua ti Ch'ing-hua" ("The Americanized Tsing Hua"). *THW*, 247 (May 12, 1922), pp. 3–4.

"Nan-hai chih shen" ("The God from the South Seas"). *Ta-chiang Quarterly*, I, 2 (November 1925), pp. 71–78.

"Niao Yü" ("The Song of the Bird"). Shih-k'an (*Poetry Journal*, supplement to *Peking Morning News*), No. 6 (May 6, 1926), p. 14.

"Pai" ("Defeat"). *Kuo-li Ch'ing-hua ta-hsüeh nien-k'an*, 1933 (*National Tsing Hua University Yearbook*, 1933). (no pagination).

"Pi-chiao" ("Compare"). Shih-k'an (*Poetry Journal*, supplement to *Peking Morning News*), No. 2 (April 8, 1926), p. 20.

"Pien chih" ("On Temperament"). *THW*, 101 (March 22, 1917), pp. 1–2.

"P'ing pen hsüeh-nien chou-k'an li ti hsin-shih" ("A Critique of the Modern Poems Published in the *Weekly* during this School Year"). *THW*, Special Supplement 7 (June 1921), pp. 8–25.

"Shen-yeh ti lei" ("Tears Late at Night"). *THW*, Double-four Special Supplement (April 4, 1922), pp. 72–73.

Shih-wen hsüan-chi (*Selected Essays and Poems of Wen I-to*). Peking, 1955.

Szu-shui (*Dead Water*). Shanghai, 1928.

"Ta-pien" ("Rebuttal"). *Crescent*, I, 2 (April 10, 1928), various paging.

"Tai Ch'ing-hua ch'üan-t'i t'ung-hsüeh chi Sun Tso-chou wen" ("Eulogy for Sun Tso-chou on Behalf of the Entire Tsing Hua Student Body"). *THJ*, IV, 6 (1919), pp. 49–50.

"T'i-teng-hui" ("Lantern Parade"). *THJ*, IV, 6 (1919), pp. 52–53.

"Tien-ying pu-shih i-shu" ("The Motion Picture is Not Art"). *THW*, 203 (December 17, 1920), pp. 14–24.

'Ts'ung shih-erh-fang feng-hsüeh li" ("From the Twelve-sided Cave of Winds," translation of Housman's poem No. 32 in *Shropshire Lad*). *Crescent*, I, 7 (September 10, 1928), various paging.

"Tu-fei-chi" ("Dover Beach," translation of Mathew Arnold's poem). *THJ*, IV, 6 (1919), p. 53.

"Tui-yü Shuang-shih-chieh chu-tien ti kan-hsiang" ("Thoughts on the Double-ten Celebration"). *THW*, 195 (October 22, 1920), pp. 15–17.

"T'ung-hsin ti hua" ("Painful Words"). *THW*, 219 (May 6, 1921), pp. 23–24.

"Tzu-chih yü pei-chih" ("To Govern Oneself and to be Governed"). *THW*, 223 (September 15, 1921), p. 4.

"Tsui-hou i-tz'u yen-chiang" ("The Last Speech"). *Wen-ts'ui* (*Literary Gems*), No. 41 (August 1, 1946), p. 19.

"Wo-shih Chung-kuo jen" ("I Am Chinese"). *Ta-chiang Quarterly* (July 1925), pp. 97–99.

"Yü Chang Hsi-jo ti i-feng hsin" ("A Letter to Chang Hsi-jo, dated

July 1, 1944"). *Pei-ta pan-yüeh-k'an* (*Peking University Semi-monthly*), No. 8 (July 20, 1948), p. 5.

"Yu-she ti mi-lu" ("The Deer at A Sequestered House," translated from a poem by Thomas Hardy). *Crescent*, I, 2 (April 10, 1928), various paging.

"Yü-yang ch'ü" ("The Song of Yü-yang"). *Hsiao-shuo yüeh-pao* (*The Short Story Monthly*), XVI, 3 (March 1925), various paging.

"Yuan nei" ("In the Garden"). Ch'ing-hua sheng-huo chuan-hao (Special Issue: Life at Tsing Hua), *THW* (April 28, 1923), pp. 1–16.

WEN I-TO, KUO MO-JO and HSU WEI-YÜ. *Kuan-tzu chi-chiao* (*Collated Annotations to the* Kuan-tzu). Peking, 1956.

SECONDARY SOURCES

1. Works on Wen I-to's Writings—in Chinese

CHAO, LI-SHENG (Feng I). "Chin-p'ing Wen I-to hsien-sheng ti hsüeh-shu ch'eng-chiu—chien lun Chung-kuo wen-hsien hsüeh ti hsin shui-p'ing" ("An Attempt at Commenting on Wen I-to's Scholarly Accomplishment—also on the New Standard for Chinese Classical Studies"). *Hsin chien-she* (*Reconstruction*), I, 8 (Dec. 1949), pp. 15–16.

CHAO, TS'UNG. "Wen-t'an kuai-chieh Wen I-to" ("Wen I-to, An Unusual Figure on the Literary Scene"). *Hsien-tai Chung-kuo tso-chia lieh-chuan* (*Biographies of Contemporary Chinese Writers*), pp. 207–17. Hong Kong, 1970.

CH'EN, NING. *Wen I-to chuan* (*Biography of Wen I-to*). (n.p.), 1947.

CHU, HSIANG. "P'ing Wen chün I-to ti shih" ("Comments on the Poetry of Wen I-to"). *Hsiao-shuo yüeh-pao* (*The Short Story Monthly*), XVII, 5 (May 10, 1926), pp. 63–74.

———. "Wen I-to yü *Szu-shui*" ("Wen I-to and *Dead Water*"). *Wen-i fu-hsing* (*Renaissance*), III, 5 (July 1947), pp. 527–31.

CH'Ü, I. "Hsin-shih ti tsung-chi yü ch'i ch'u-lu" ("The Footprints and Future Prospects of Modern Poetry"). *Wen-hsüeh* (*Literature*), VIII, 1 (January 1937), pp. 7–25.

CHU, SHUN. "Chieh-shao Wen I-to hsien-sheng ti '*Ch'u-tz'u* chiao-pu'" ("Introducing Wen I-to's 'Exegetical Study of the *Songs of Ch'u*'"). *Kuo-wen tsa-chih* (*Chinese Literature Magazine*), II, 1 (July 1943), pp. 30–33.

CHU, TZU-CH'ING. "Chung-kuo hsüeh-shu chieh ti ta sun-shih" ("A Great Loss to the Chinese Scholarly World"). *Piao-chun yü ch'ih-tu* (*Standard and Measurement*), pp. 6–12. Shanghai, 1949.

———. "Wen I-to hsien-sheng tsen-yang tsou-che Chung-kuo wen-hsüeh ti tao-lu" ("How Wen I-to walked on his Path of Chinese Literature"). *Wen-hsüeh tsa-chih* (*Literature Magazine*), II, 5 (October 1947), pp. 6–15.

————. "Wen I-to hsien-sheng yü Chung-kuo wen-hsüeh ("Wen I-to and Chinese Literature"). *Kuo-wen yüeh-k'an* (*Chinese Literature Monthly*), 46 (August 20, 1946), p. 1.

HSIA, TSUNG-YÜ. "Wen I-to hsien-sheng ho *Shih-ching*" ("Wen I-to and the *Book of Poetry*"). *Hsin chien-she* (*Reconstruction*), 121 (October 1958), pp. 63–66.

HSIUNG, FO-HSI. "Tao Wen I-to hsien-sheng" ("Mourning Wen I-to"). *Wen-i fu-hsing* (*Renaissance*), II, 1 (August 1946), pp. 6–9.

HSU, CHIH-MO. "Shih-k'an fang-chia" ("A Holiday for the 'Poetry Journal' "). Chao Chia-pi, ed., *Chung-kuo hsin-wen-hsüeh ta-hsi* (*A Compendium of Modern Chinese Literature*), X, pp. 119–22. Shanghai, 1935–1941.

————. "Shih-k'an pien-yen" ("Introduction to the 'Poetry Journal' "). *Compendium*, X, pp. 117–19.

HUANG, YAO-MIEN. "Lun Wen I-to ti shih" ("On Wen I-to's Poetry"). *Wen-i ts'ung-k'an* (*Literature Magazine*), 1 (September 20, 1946), pp. 4–10.

HUANG, YANG-LIANG. "Wen I-to ti hsin-shih lun" ("Wen I-to's Treatise on New Poetry"). *Lun Ma-hua wen-i ti tu-t'e hsing* (*The Individuality of Malaysian Chinese Literature*), pp. 21–33. Singapore, 1960.

JAO, MENG-K'AN. "Hsia-yeh i wang-yu Wen I-to" ("Remembering my Late Friend Wen I-to on a Summer Night"). *Jen-min wen-hsüeh* (*People's Literature*) (July 1962), pp. 44.

————. "P'ing I-to ti 'Yüan Nei' " ("On Wen I-to's 'In the Garden' "). Ch'ing-hua sheng-huo p'i-p'ing hao (Special Issue: Comments on the Life at Tsing Hua), THW, 284 (June 1, 1923), pp. 7–14.

K'O, CHUNG-P'ING. "Ai shih-jen Wen I-to" ("Mourning the Poet Wen I-to"). *Ts'ung Yen-an tao Pei-ching* (*From Yenan to Peking*), pp. 26–32. Peking, 1950.

KUO, MO-JO. "Lun Wen I-to tso hsüeh-wen ti t'ai-tu" ("On Wen I-to's Attitude toward Scholarship"). *Li shih jen-wu* (*Historical Personages*), pp. 185–96. Shanghai, 1949.

LAO, HSIN. "Wen I-to ti tao-lu" ("Wen I-to's Path"). *Shih-ti li-lun yü p'i-p'ing* (*Theory and Criticism on Poetry*), pp. 15–20. Shanghai, 1950.

LIANG, HUI-JU. "Wen I-to lun shih p'i Hu Shih" ("Wen I-to Downgrades Hu Shih in Discussing Poetry"). *Ku-chin man-hua* (*Random Talks on Things Ancient and Modern*), pp. 105–109. Hong Kong, 1969.

————. "Wen I-to ti chiu-t'i-shih ho fang-yen-shih" ("The Classical-style Poems and Vernacular Poems of Wen I-to"). *Ku-chin man-hua (Random Talks on Things Ancient and Modern)*, pp. 110–14. Hong Kong, 1969.

LIANG, SHIH-CH'IU. *Ch'iu-shih tsa-i (Miscellaneous Reminiscences in the Autumnal Studio)*. Taipei, 1971.

————. "P'ing I-to ti shih liu shou" ("On Six Poems by Wen I-to"). Literary Supplement, No. 4, in *THW*, 269 (February 15, 1923), pp. 22–24.

————. *T'an Wen I-to (About Wen I-to)*. Taipei, 1967.

LIN, MAN-SHU. *Wen I-to yen-chiu (On Wen I-to)*. Hong Kong. 1974.

LIU, YA-TZU. "I-to hsien-sheng ch'eng-jen i chou-nien chi-nien" ("On the First Anniverary of Wen I-to's Death"). Wen I-to hsien-sheng szu-nan chou-nien chi-nien t'e-k'an (Memorial Issue: on the First Anniversay of Wen I-to's Death). *THW*, (1947), p. 25.

MA, CHÜN-CHIEH, "Chi shih-jen Wen I-to" ("About the Poet Wen I-to"). *Wen-i fu-hsing (Renaissance)*, III, 5 (July 1, 1947), p. 540.

MING, HSING-LI (J. Monsterleet, trans. by CHU, YÜ-JEN). "Wen I-to—chu-chung kuei-lü ti shih-jen" ("Wen I-to, a Poet Who Stresses Form"). *Hsin-wen-hsüeh chien-shih (Short History of New Literature)*, pp. 82–87. Hong Kong, 1957.

PAI, CHIEN. "Wen I-to yü Chung-kuo shih ti tao-lu" ("Wen I-to and the Direction for Chinese Poetry"). *Chung-kuo chien-she (China's Reconstruction)*, VI, 4 (July 1948), pp. 50–51.

SHEN, TS'UNG-WEN. "Lun Wen I-to ti *Szu-shui*" ("On *Dead Water* by Wen I-to"). *Hsin-yüeh (Crescent)*, III, 2 (September 1931), pp. 95–101.

SHIH, LING. "Hsin-yüeh shih p'ai" ("The Crescent School of Poetry"). *Wen-hsüeh (Literature)*, VIII, 1 (January 1937), pp. 125–37.

T'IEN, CHIEN. "Ai-tao Wen hsien-sheng" ("Mourning Mr. Wen"). *K'ang-chan shih-ch'ao (Poems of the War of Resistance)*, pp. 126–31. Peking, 1950.

TSANG, K'O-CHIA. "Hai" ("The Sea"). *Wen-i fu-hsing (Renaissance)*, III, 5 (July 1947), pp. 536–39.

————. "Wen I-to hsien-sheng ti i-shu ch'uang-tso" ("Wen I-to's Artistic Creations"). *Mei-shu (Fine Arts)* (April 1978), pp. 9–11.

————. "Wen I-to ti shih" ("Wen I-to's Poetry"). *People's Literature* (July 1956), pp. 119–25. The same essay also appears in *Hsin-hua pan-yüeh-k'an (New China Semi-monthly)*, XCI (September 21, 1956), pp. 145–50.

TUNG, CH'U-P'ING. "Ts'ung Wen I-to ti *Szu-shui* t'an tao ko-lü-shih ti wen-t'i" ("Wen I-to's *Dead Water* and the Question of Formalist

Poetry"). *Wen-hsüeh p'ing-lun* (*Literary Criticism*), 6 (August 1961), pp. 74–84.

WEI FA. "P'ing *Hung-chu*" ("On the *Red Candle*"). *Hsüeh-teng* (*Beacon of Learning*, Supplement to *New Current Affairs Daily*), November 27 and 28, 1924. (various paging).

YÜ, MING-CH'UAN. "Tao Wen I-to shih" ("Mourning My Teacher Wen I-to"). *Wen-i fu-hsing* (*Renaissance*), III, 5 (July 1, 1947), p. 539.

2. Works Mainly on Wen I-to's Life—in Chinese

CHAO, CH'EN. "I Wen I-to shih" ("Remembering My Teacher Wen I-to"). Wen I-to hsien-sheng szu-nan chou-nien chi-nien t'e-k'an (Memorial Issue on the First Anniversary of Mr. Wen I-to's Death), *THW* (1947), pp. 29–31.

CHAO, CHING-SHEN. "Wen I-to." *Wen-t'an i-chiu* (*Reminiscences About the Literary Scene*), pp. 38–42. Shanghai, 1948.

CHENG, CHEN-TO. "Tao Li Kung-p'u, Wen I-to erh hsien-sheng" ("Mourning Messrs. Li Kung-p'u and Wen I-to"). *Min-chu chou-k'an* (*Democratic Weekly*), 40 (July 1946), pp. 993–95.

CHENG, LIN-CH'UAN. "I I-to shih" ("Remembering My Teacher I-to"). *Kuo-wen yüeh-k'an* (*Chinese Literature Monthly*), 62 (December 10, 1947), pp. 27–30.

"Chi-nien Wen I-to tsai Ch'ing-hua Yüan" ("Memorial Service for Wen I-to at Tsing Hua"). *Kuan-ch'a* (*Observation*), II, 23 (August 2, 1947), p. 17.

CHI SZU. "I Wen I-to chiao-shou" ("Remembering Professor Wen I-to"). *Wen-ts'ui* (*Literary Gems*), I, 40 (July 1946), pp. 13–15.

CH'U, T'U-NAN. "Jen-min shih-jen Wen I-to" ("People's Poet—Wen I-to"). *Shih yü wen* (*Time and Literature*), I, 19 (July 18, 1947), p. 401.

CH'ÜAN, MO. "Wen I-to." *Tien-ying wen-hsüeh* (*Literature for the Movie Screen*), 2 (1959), pp. 30–58.

CORRESPONDENCE (Letters Received from the Following Persons)

BREED, ELEANOR D., friend of the Oriental Languages Department, University of California, Berkeley. January 20, 1959.

CAMPBELL, LAWRENCE, director, public relations, Art Students League of New York. June 13, 1978.

CHUANG, SHEN, faculty of Hong Kong University. August 10, 1978.

DERN, LUCILLE, of Guffey, Colorado, former schoolmate of Wen at Colorado College. January 21, 1959.

KELLER, LAMONT, of Colorado Springs, former art classmate of Wen. January 26 and March 31, 1959.

KIDDER, BRADLEY P., architect in Santa Fe, former art classmate of Wen at Colorado Springs. January 21, 1959.

KU, I-CH'IAO, schoolmate and literary friend at Tsing Hua. March 31, April 21, 1959. November 12, 1977.

LIANG, SHIH-CH'IU, classmate at Tsing Hua School, later roommate at Colorado Springs, close friend for many years. January 28, 1959. August 12 and 19, 1978.

LOFLAND, MARY M., of Kennett Square, Penn., former schoolmate of Wen at Colorado College. January 16, 1959.

SHINEW, JOAN, reference librarian, Colorado College. January 14 and 21, March 24, 1959.

WANG, CHI-CHEN, Wen's schoolmate at Tsing Hua School. April 2 and June 8, 1959. January 27 and June 21, 1978.

FANG, CHING. "Pu-hsiu-ti ling-hun" ("The Immortal Soul"). *Chi-i yü wang-ch'üeh* (*The Remembered and the Forgotten*), pp. 100–12. Shanghai, 1949.

FENG I. "Hun-che hsüeh-szu ti chi-i" ("Blood-stained Memory"). *Wen-i fu-hsing* (*Renaissance*), II, 4 (November 1946), pp. 392-96.

FENG TZU. "Hsieh tsai I-to hsien-sheng ti chou-nien chi" ("Written on the First Anniversary of Wen I-to's Death"). Wen I-to hsien-sheng szu-nan chou-nien chi-nien t'e-k'an (Memorial Issue on the First Anniversary of Wen I-to's Death), *THW* (1947), pp. 28–29.

HO, HUA. "Tsai Wen I-to i-kuan chung ch'ien" ("Before the Masoleum of Wen I-to's Personal Effects"). *Kuan-ch'a* (*Observation*), II, 23 (August 2, 1947), pp. 18–19.

HSIA, K'ANG-NUNG. "Hua shih-tai ti szu-che" ("He Died Making An Epoch"). *Ta-hsüeh* (*The Great Learning*), VI, 3–4 (August 1947), pp. 17–19.

————. "Wen I-to chiao-shou ti yü-nan yü Lu Hsün ti 'Yao'" ("Professor Wen I-to's Death and Lu Hsün's 'Medicine'"). *Wen-ts'ui* (*Literary Gems*), 45 (August 1946), pp. 10–11.

————. "Wen I-to ti ming-tzu hai chih-te tsai-t'i" ("Wen I-to's Name Is Worth Mentioning Again"). *Wen-ts'ui* (*Literary Gems*), 50 (October 1946), pp. 19, 24–25.

HSIAO HUA. "Wen I-to hsien-sheng ti hua-hsiang" ("Wen I-to's Portrait"). *Ts'ang-nan hsing* (*Journey South from Ts'ang-chou*), pp. 16–25. Hong Kong, (1947?).

HSU, WEI-CHIH. *Ts'ung Teng Yen-ta tao Wen I-to: Erh-shih-nien lai Chiang Kai-shek so sha jen-wu* (*From Teng Yen-ta to Wen*

I-to: The Personalities Killed by Chiang Kai-shek in the Last Twenty Years). Hong Kong, 1947.

Hsüeh Fang. "Chung-yü T'ai-shan" ("Weightier than Mt. T'ai"). *Ts'ang-nan hsing* (*Journey South from Ts'ang-chou*), p. 15. Hong Kong, (1947?).

"Hsüeh yü li-hsiang: Li Wen chih szu" ("Blood and Idealism: the Deaths of Li and Wen"). *Kuan-ch'a* (*Observation*), I, 1 (September 1, 1946), pp. 22–24.

Hu, Ti. "T'ung-tao wu-shih Wen I-to hsien-sheng" ("Mourning My Teacher Wen I-to"). *Wen-ts'ui* (*Literary Gems*), 40 (July 1946), pp. 10–12.

K'ang, Ch'ien. "I Wen I-to hsien-sheng" ("Remembering My Teacher Wen I-to"). *People's Daily*, July 15, 1956, p. 7.

Ku, I-Ch'iao. "Huai ku-yu Wen I-to hsien-sheng" ("Reminiscence on My Old Friend Wen I-to"). *Wen-i fu-hsing* (*Renaissance*), III, 5 (July 1947), pp. 532–35.

Kuo, Mo-Jo. "Tao Wen I-to" ("Mourning Wen I-to"). *Min-chu chou-k'an* (*Democratic Weekly*), 40 (July 1946), p. 996.

Li Wen erh lieh-shih chi-nien wei-yuan-hui (The Committee for the Memorial Service for the Two Martyrs Li Kung-p'u and Wen I-to), ed. *Jen-min ying-lieh* (*The Heroes and Martyrs of the People*). (n.p., n.d.).

Liang, Shu-Ming, and Chou, Hsin-Min. *Li Wen an tiao-ch'a pao-kao shu* (*Report on the Investigation of the Li-Wen Case*). Chinese Democratic League, September 30, 1946.

Lien-ta pa-nien (*The Eight Years of the National Southwest Associate University*). Kunming, 1946.

Liu, P'eng-Ju. "Shih-jen Wen I-to" ("The Poet Wen I-to"). *Wen-ts'ui* (*Literary Gems*), 50 (October 1946), pp. 26–27.

Liu, Wang Li-Ming. *Hsüeh chang* (*Blood Debt*). Hong Kong, 1948.

Lu, Chou. "Wen I-to ti tao-lu" ("The Path that Wen I-to Chose"). *Shih yü wen* (*Time and Literature*), I, 2 (July 25, 1947), p. 424.

Mien Chih. *Wen I-to*. Hong Kong, 1949.

Mu, Tzu-Ho. "Wu Han ho Wen I-to ti yu-i" ("The Friendship between Wu Han and Wen I-to"). *Ming Pao*, IV, 12 (December 1968), pp. 22–26.

Shih, Ching. "Shan-ch'eng ti ai-yung: Wen I-to hsün-nan chi" ("The Glory of a Mountain City: How Wen I-to Died for the Cause"). *Hung-ch'i p'iao-p'iao* (*The Fluttering Red Flag*), 1 (May 1957), pp. 106–21.

———. *Wen I-to*. Hupeh, 1958.

———. *Wen I-to ti tao-lu* (*The Path that Wen I-to Chose*). Shanghai, 1947.

SHIH, HSIU-CH'IAO. "P'ao-ch'i ko-jen pen-wei ti Wen I-to" ("Wen I-to Who Renounced His Personal Interests"). *Chin-tai Chung-kuo tso-chia lun (On Modern Chinese Writers)*, pp. 67–74. Singapore, (n.d.).

SHIH, I. "Wen I-to jen-ch'u-le pai-shou-t'ao" ("Wen I-to Tosses Out His White Glove"). *Hsin kuan-ch'a (New Observer)*, 1 (August 1977), p. 46.

SHIH-KO YIN-YÜEH KUNG-TSO-CHE HSIEH-HUI SHANGHAI FEN-HUI (The Shanghai Branch of the Association of Workers in Songs and Verses). "Ching tao Wen I-to hsien-sheng" ("With Reverence We Mourn Wen I-to"). *Wen-i fu-hsing (Renaissance)*, II, 1 (August 1, 1946), pp. 10–12.

SU, HSÜEH-LIN. "Wen I-to szu-yü chih shou" ("Wen I-to Died at the Hands of His Nephew"). *Wen-t'an hua-chiu (Reminiscences About the Literary Scene)*, pp. 143–51. Hong Kong, 1968.

TS'AI, SHANG-SZU. "Piao-chun-ti chih-shih fen-tzu: Li Ta-chao, Lu Hsün, Wen I-to, and T'ao Hsing-chih" ("Model Intellectuals"). *Chung-kuo chien-she (China's Reconstruction)*, VI, 5 (August 1948), pp. 33–36.

TU, MAI-CHIH. "Chui-i Wen I-to hsien-sheng" ("Remembering Wen I-to"). *Wen-ts'ui (Literary Gems)*, 50 (October 1946), pp. 23–25.

WANG, I. "Wen I-to shih tsen-yang tsai tang ti chiao-yü hsia ch'eng-chang" ("How Wen I-to Developed under the Party's Cultivation"). *Enlightenment Daily*, July 15, 1958, p. 3.

———. "Wen I-to ti tao-lu" ("The Path that Wen I-to Chose"). *Wen-i sheng-huo (Literary Life)*, No. 8 (September 1946), pp. 2–3.

WANG, K'ANG. *Wen I-to sung (Ode to Wen I-to)*. Hupeh, 1978.

WEN, CHIA-SZU. "Chi-nien Wen I-to T'ung-chih hsün-nan chiu chou-nien" ("Commemorating the Ninth Anniversary of the Death of Comrade Wen I-to"). *Enlightenment Daily*, July 15, 1955, p. 2.

———. "Ch'i-yüeh shih-wu—chi-nien I-to hsien-sheng szu-nan i chou-nien" ("July Fifteenth—Commemorating the First Anniversary of Wen I-to's Death"). *Ts'ang-nan hsing (Journey South from Ts'ang-chou)*, pp. 13–14. Hong Kong (1947?).

Wen I-to chiao-shou hsün-kuo chou-nien t'e-chi (Special Issue: The Anniversary of Professor Wen I-to's Death). *Ta-hsüeh (The Great Learning)*, VI, 3–4 (August 1947).

WEN, LI-HO. "Hui-i wo fu-ch'in Wen I-to" ("Reminiscing about My Father Wen I-to"). *Hsin wan pao (New Evening News)*, July 21, 1974 (Hong Kong), p. 2.

———. "Pa-pa yü tz'u chi-hsiang" ("A Detailed Account of My Father's Assassination"). *Memorial Issue, THW*, pp. 10–12.

————. "Wen I-to chia-shu tui tien-ying chü-pen 'Wen I-to' ti i-chien" ("Comments on the Movie Script 'Wen I-to' by His Family"). *Tien-ying wen-hsüeh* (*Literature for the Movie Screen*), (May 1959), p. 82

WEN, LI-TIAO AND WEN, LI-P'ENG. "Shui sha-szu-le wo-de pa-pa?" ("Who Killed My Father?"). *Wen-ts'ui* (*Literary Gems*), I, 40 (July 1946), pp. 17–18.

WEN, SHAN. "Chiao wo hsüeh-pu ti jen" ("He Who Taught Me to Walk"). *People's Daily*, July 14, 1956, p. 8.

————. "Nien Wen I-to hsien-sheng" ("Remembering Wen I-to). *Shih-k'an* (*Poetry Journal*), (July 10, 1961), pp. 71–74.

WU, HAN. "K'u I-to fu-tzu" ("Mourning I-to and His Son"). *Kuo-wen yüeh-k'an* (*Chinese Literature Monthly*), 46 (August 20, 1946), pp. 31–32.

————. "K'u wang-yu Wen I-to" ("Mourning My Late Friend Wen I-to"). *Min-chu chou-k'an* (*Democratic Weekly*), 40 (July 1946), pp. 1000–1002.

————. "P'ai-an erh-ch'i ti Wen I-to" ("Wen I-to Pounded on the Desk and Stood Up"). *People's Daily*, January 12, 1960, p. 8.

————. "Wen I-to ti i-sheng' ("The Life of Wen I-to"). *Shih yü wen* (*Time and Literature*), I, 6 (April 15, 1947), pp. 112–13.

————. "Wen I-to ti shou-kung-yeh" ("Wen I-to's Handcraft Industry"). *Shih-shih yü jen-wu* (*Historical Facts and Personages*), pp. 63–68. Shanghai, 1948.

YIN, CH'UNG-CHING AND CHIANG, HSIEN-FAN. "Fang pei wu-sheng shou-ch'iang shang-hai-kuo ti jen" ("Interviewing One Who Has Been Wounded by a Noiseless Pistol"). *Enlightenment Daily*, June 29, 1957, p. 2.

YEH, SHENG-T'AO. "To shuo mei-yu yung, chih shuo chi-chü" ("It's Useless to Talk Too Much; Let's Just Say a Few Words"). *Min-chu chou-k'an* (*Democratic Weekly*), 40 (July 1946). p. 997.

3. Works in English

HSU, KAI-YU. "The Intellectual Biography of A Modern Chinese Poet: Wen I-to (1899–1946)." Unpublished doctoral dissertation, Stanford University, 1959.

————. "The Life and Poetry of Wen I-to." *Harvard Journal of Asiatic Studies*, XXI (1958), pp. 135–79.

————. *Twentieth Century Chinese Poetry*. Cornell University Press, 1970.

LIN, JULIA. *Modern Chinese Poetry*. University of Washington, 1972.

SHAW, YÜ-MING. "Wen I-to: The Early Life and Writings of a Modern

Chinese Intellectual, from 1899 to 1933." Unpublished paper, University of Notre Dame, 1974.

TUNG, CONSTANTINE. "The Search for Order and Form: The Crescent Moon Society and the Literary Movement of Modern China, 1928–1933." Unpublished doctoral dissertation, Claremont Graduate School, 1971.

UBEROI, PATRICIA. "Rhythmic Techniques in the Poetry of Wen I-to." *United College Journal* (Hong Kong), VI (1967–1968), pp. 1–25.

4. Works in Japanese

AKIYOSHI, KUKIO. "Mon Itta ni tsuite" ("About Wen I-to"). *Gendai Chugoku shijin ron (On Modern Chinese Poets)*, pp. 23–36. Tokyo, 1964.

HORITA, NATSU. "Mon Itta no kakuritsushi to sono genkai" ("Wen I-to's Formalist Poetry and Its Limitations"). *Proceedings of the Chinese Literature Forum*, pp. 1–14. Kyushu daigaku Chugoku bungaku kenkukai, 1962.

IMAMURA, YOSHIO. "Mon Itta—aru shijin, gakusha no shogai" ("Wen I-to—Life of a Poet and Scholar"). *Chugoku jindai chishikijin no kaishu, lichi to jokan (The Rational and Emotional Development of Modern Chinese Intellectuals)*, pp. 204–43. Tokyo, 1976.

KUSAMORI, SINICHI. "Mon Itta, Chugoku" ("China's Wen I-to"). *Nijuseiki no shijintachi (Twentieth Century Poets)*, pp. 187–208. Tokyo, 1972.

MEKATA, MAKOTO. 'Wen I-to hyoden" ("An Evaluative Biography of Wen I-to"). *Rakushin no fu (The Fu of the Goddess of River Lo)*, pp. 183–224. Tokyo, 1966.

MITSUO, KONDO. *Mon Itta: Uta to shi (Wen I-to: Song and Poetry)*. Tokyo, 1956.

NAGANO, SHIGEJI AND IMAMURA, YOSHIO. "Chugoku no kakumei to bungaku" ("Literature of Chinese Revolution"). *Yakushi to ryakuten (Poetry in Translation with Biographical Sketches of Poets)*, pp. 74–89. Tokyo, 1972.

OGAWA, TAMAKI. "Mon Itta—shijin no shogai" ("The Life of Poet Wen I-to"). *Bungaku (Literature)*, Vol. 22 (Feb. 10, 1954), pp. 87–96.

ONO, SHINOBU. "Mon Itta zenshu" ("The Complete Works of Wen I-to"). *Chugoku bungaku zakko (Miscellaneous Studies on Chinese Literature)*, pp. 309–13. Tokyo, 1967.

SAITO, AKIO. "Chugoku sinshijin no iki to shi—Mon Itta, Chujisei no sobyo" ("The Lives of Modern Chinese Poets—Sketches of Wen I-to and Chu Tzu-ch'ing"). *Chugokugo zashi (Chinese Language Magazine)*, VI, 4, 5, 6 (1951), pp. 25–29.

SATO, TAMOTSU. "Wen I-to to Toshi" ("Wen I-to and T'ang Poetry").
Kindai Chugoku no shiso to bungaku (Literature and Thought in
Contemporary China), pp. 585–602. Tokyo, 1967.

SAWADA, MIZUHO. "Hakuwashi kakinoto–shiryoshokai" ("Notes on
Pai-hua Poetry–Introduction to Source Material"). Tenri daiga-
kugakuho (Journal of the Heavenly Principle University) (June
1967), pp. 71–73.

TAKEUCHI, MINOTU. Chugoku no shiso–dento to gendai (Chinese
Thought–from Traditional to Modern), pp. 73–79. Tokyo, 1967.

YOKOYAMA, EIZO. " 'Mon Itta sono shi' no ichikosatsu" ("A Study of
'Wen I-to and His Poetry' ") Yamaguchi daigaku bungaku kaishi
(Proceedings of the Literary Society, Yamaguchi University),
pp. 1–21. Yamaguchi, 1961.

5.   Works in Russian

SUKHORUKOV, V. T. "Wen I-to." Dumy o Khrizanteme (Thoughts on
the Chrysanthemum). Perevod s Kitaiskogo Gennadiia Jaroslavtseva (Translated from Chinese by Gennadii Jaroslavstsev),
pp. 5–21. Moscow, 1973.

6.   Miscellaneous

FEDORENKO, N. T. Kitaiskaia Literatura (Chinese Literature). Moscow,
1956.

FUNG, MARY M. Y., and others. Hsien-tai Chung-kuo shih-hsüan
(Modern Chinese Poetry: An Anthology, 1917–1949). Hong
Kong, 1974.

HOM, MARLON KAU. "Poetry and Nationalism: Wen I-to as a Modern
Chinese Poet." Unpublished M. A. thesis, Indiana University,
1971.

JAO, MENG-K'AN. "Hsin-shih ti yin-chieh" ("The Meter in New
Poetry"). Poetry Journal (Supplement to Peking Morning News)
(April 22, 1926), pp. 49–50.

———. "Tsai lun hsin-shih ti yin-chieh" ("Further Discussion on the
Meter in New Poetry"). Poetry Journal (Supplement to Peking
Morning News), (May 6, 1926), pp. 13–14.

OLNEY, CHARLES V. "The Chinese Poet Wen I-to." Journal of Oriental
Literature (University of Hawaii), 7 (1966), pp. 8–17; 8 (1967),
pp. 38–42.

PAYNE, ROBERT. Contemporary Chinese Poetry. London, 1947.

SANDERS, TAO TAO, trans. Red Candles. London, 1972.

TSANG, K'O-CHIA. "The Poetry of Wen I-to." Chinese Literature, No. 2
(1960), pp. 3–17.

WHITACRE, MARC MICHEL. "The English Influence in the Poetry of Wen I-to (1899–1946)." Unpublished M. A. thesis, University of Arizona, 1974.

WU, HAN. "Wen Yi-tuo Rises to His Full Height." *China Reconstructs*, X, 6 (June 1961), pp. 27–29.

Index

238